THE RUSSIAN PEOPLE AND FOREIGN POLICY

THE RUSSIAN PEOPLE
AND FOREIGN POLICY

RUSSIAN ELITE AND
MASS PERSPECTIVES, 1993–2000

William Zimmerman

PRINCETON UNIVERSITY PRESS   PRINCETON AND OXFORD

Library of Congress Cataloging-in-Publication Data

Zimmerman, William, 1936–
The Russian people and foreign policy : Russian elite and mass
perspectives, 1993–2000 / William Zimmerman
p. cm.

Includes bibliographical references and index

ISBN 0-691-09167-6 (cloth : alk. paper)—ISBN 0-691-09168-4
(pbk. : alk. paper)

1. Elite (Social sciences)—Russian (Federation) 2. Russian
(Federation)—Politics and government—1991– 3. Political
participation—Russia (Federation) 4. Russia (Federation)—Foreign
relations. I. Title.

HN530.2.Z9 E496 2002
305.5'2'0947—dc21   2001043158

British Library Cataloging-in-Production Data is available

This book has been composed in Galliard

Printed on acid-free paper.∞

www.pup.princeton.edu

Printed in the United States of America

10 9 8 7 6 5 4 3 2 1

Contents

Acknowledgments

"I get by with a little help from my friends" is the subtitle to all prefaces. In this instance, my indebtedness to many American and Russian friends and colleagues, as well as to American institutions, is immense. My Michigan colleagues, Christopher Achen, Zvi Gitelman, and the late Harold Jacobson, have helped me sharpen my thoughts in many ways. Chris helped me in the most tangible way possible my serving as Acting Director of the Center for Political Studies during my sabbatical. Judith Kullberg and I coauthored an article in *World Politics* and a paper for the 1999 Midwest Political Science Association annual meeting on which I draw in chapter 2. I have benefited enormously from our research collaboration over the years. I similarly benefited from many conversations with Allan Stam. A paper he and I coauthored too many years ago served as the starting point for what became chapter 3. George Breslauer, Ole Holsti, and Michael McFaul read the manuscript carefully and provided many useful suggestions, both substantive and stylistic. An anonymous reviewer also made valuable suggestions.

My former research assistant Bear Broemoeller and my current research assistants, Aman McLeod and Clint Peinhardt, have helped me in ways ranging from chasing down fugitive citations to offering pointed and telling comments about drafts of my manuscript. Barbara Opal and Carol Milstein maintained their good cheer even while typing and retyping most of the tables. Elizabeth Gilbert skillfully edited the final draft and Chuck Myers provided valuable encouragement along the way.

I owe a special debt to Timothy Colton for his multiple roles as principal investigator in the mass survey he and I executed in 1995–96 and to him and Michael McFaul for including several of my survey questions in their 1999–2000 mass survey. The surveys that provide the data on which this book is based were carried out by two Russian survey research firms, Demoscope, headed by Polina Kozyreva of the Institute of Sociology of the Russian Academy of Sciences, and ROMIR (Rossiiskoye Obshchestvennoe Mnenie i Rynok), headed by Elena Bashkirova. I cannot say enough about how helpful Kozyreva and Bashkirova and their colleagues have been nor about their professionalism.

My wife, Susan McClanahan, has been an enormous support throughout; more than anything she has helped me stay focused on the task of completing this project.

In addition to thanking people, I am delighted to express my appreciation to several institutions for their important contributions. Grants from the National Council for Eurasian and East European Research and from the Davidson Institute of the University of Michigan Business School to me and grants to Colton (Principal Investigator) and me from the MacArthur Foundation and the Carnegie Corporation made the gathering of the data for the core mass and elite surveys possible. The North Atlantic Treaty Organization provided funds to Bashkirova that allowed ROMIR to include questions about NATO expansion in ROMIR's 1996 and 1997 omnibus surveys. The actual writing of a draft of the manuscript was greatly aided by a sabbatical funded by the University of Michigan's College of Literature, Science, and the Arts and the Center for Political Studies of the Institute of Social Research. The usual caveat applies: the views and the errors in what follows are mine and mine alone.

Some parts of chapter 2 appeared as "Synoptic Thinking in Post-Soviet Russia" in the fall 1995 issue of *Slavic Review* and are reprinted with permission of the American Association for the Advancement of Slavic Studies. Other parts of that chapter appeared in *World Politics* and much of chapter 6 was published first in *Post-Soviet Affairs*; they too are reprinted with permission.

THE RUSSIAN PEOPLE AND FOREIGN POLICY

Introduction _____

WITH THE collapse of the Soviet Union in December 1991, the era of Soviet power in Russia came to a definitive end. Among its many features, the Soviet system was one in which political participation was minimal—Philip Roeder speaks of "forced departicipation"[1]—and information was at a premium. The regime was insulated from society. The Soviet system was characterized by low trust in its citizenry by its leaders. The sorts and sources of influence to which mass publics were exposed were controlled by the regime's near monopoly on the socialization process and the political system's extensive penetration of the society. Though no longer totalitarian[2] and demonstrating a decreasing capacity to mobilize its citizens effectively,[3] the Soviet Union remained until the last years of *perestroika* an effectively closed political system.

The Russian Federation that supplanted the Soviet system, by contrast, is considerably more open. Elite involvement in the policy process has been far greater than it was under Soviet power and is no longer restricted to persons on the *nomenklatura* lists of "the Party" (by which in the Soviet period one always meant the Communist Party of the Soviet Union, or CPSU). Likewise, mass publics have been more involved in the policy process. A widely diverse and lively press has developed. Information about the workings of the political system and the attitudes and beliefs of the participants in that process is far more available than it was in the Soviet Union.

It is the greatly enhanced role of a broader circle of elites, the empowerment of mass publics, and the radically new opportunities for access to elites and mass publics that explain this book. This is a book about the foreign policy orientations of Russian elites and mass publics in the first decade after the December 1991 collapse of the Soviet Union—about *The Russian People and Foreign Policy*, to paraphrase the title of Gabriel Almond's classic study of American foreign policy.[4]

[1] Philip G. Roeder, *Red Sunset: The Failure of Soviet Politics* (Princeton: Princeton University Press, 1993), p. 7.

[2] For an argument that the Soviet Union remained totalitarian virtually to the end, see William Odom, "Soviet Politics and After: Old and New Concepts," *World Politics* 45, no. 1 (October 1992): 66–98.

[3] Donna Bahry, "Politics, Generations, and Change in the USSR," in James R. Millar, ed., *Politics, Work, and Daily Life in the USSR*, (Cambridge, UK: Cambridge University Press, 1987), pp. 61–99; William Zimmerman, "Mobilized Participation and the Nature of the Soviet Dictatorship," in Millar, *Politics, Work, and Daily Life*, pp. 332–53.

[4] Gabriel Almond, *The American People and Foreign Policy* (New York: Praeger, 1960). First published in 1950.

The importance of these orientations to the study of Russian foreign policy flows directly from the increased openness of the political system. Along with the severe restrictions on political participation, another major feature of the old Soviet system was that it had many of the superficial facades of conventional democratic institutions. The USSR had a constitution, voting, federalism, a bicameral legislature, organized interest groups (Stalin's famous transmission belts), and the like. For the bulk of the Soviet period, all were essentially contentless and ineffectual mechanisms which, unlike their counterparts in "bourgeois democracies," did not perform the function of limiting executive power, in this instance the dictatorship of the CPSU. Ironically, much of the story of the collapse of the Soviet Union centers on the efforts, largely successful, to imbue these bogus institutions with genuine content.

New, or newly authentic, institutions have made for new politics. In the new circumstances brought on by the introduction of democratic institutions, elite and mass attitudes bear directly on the choices policy makers make about foreign policy. Moreover, the research for this book simply could not have been carried out in the absence of the changes that occurred in the Soviet Union in the Gorbachev era and then in Russia in the 1990s. As readers will quickly see, the book is based primarily on elite and mass surveys conducted in Russia during 1991–2000. (The major surveys are described in detail in chapter 1). At the dawn of the twenty-first century there are still Russians who regard such activities with suspicion— witness the Federal Security Service's arrest of Igor Sutiagin of the Institute for the Study of the US and Canada of the Russian Academy of Sciences in October 1999 in part, evidently, for collaborating with Canadian students of civil-military relations. Such acts, however, were infrequent in the first ten years of the Russian Federation. In the early 1980s, my behavior in commissioning elite and mass surveys dealing primarily with Russian foreign policy topics would have been regarded as espionage, and the active collaboration of my Russian colleagues, treasonous. Even in the late 1980s with *glasnost'* in full swing, my efforts, based on data acquired through interviewing former Soviet citizens, to assess the changing ability of the Soviet regime over time to mobilize its citizenry were dismissed by scholars from the Institute of State and Law of the Soviet Academy of Sciences at a conference in Tallin (in what was then the Estonian SSR) as being "of interest only to Western intelligence sources." (It is an indication of the pace of change in the erstwhile Soviet Union in the late 1980s that a year later, others from the same institute would assert that they would never again come to an international meeting "without data.")

In the heyday of Soviet power, it would have been impossible for anyone—Russian or Westerner—to acquire data concerning elite and mass foreign policy attitudes through direct face-to-face interviews. Those of us who were concerned with the systematic assessment of Soviet perspectives on international relations were forced to wade through a precensored press in a search for evidence.[5] The idea of American and Russian social scientists collaborating in a study that systematically interviewed both foreign policy elites and mass publics about their basic dispositions to the international system would have been risible. By the mid-1990s all that had changed, with the consequence that the data from six surveys, three of foreign policy elites and three of mass samples, constitute the evidentiary basis for this book. The surveys of Moscow-based foreign policy elites were conducted in 1992/1993 (usually referred to as the 1993 survey), 1995, and 1999. The mass surveys were conducted at the same times: 1993, 1995/1996 (or, referred to more economically, 1995), and 1999/2000 (or 1999).

The 1993 survey was based on a sample of mass publics in European Russia, while the 1995/1996 and 1999/2000 panel studies were based on national samples consisting of three waves each—before and after the 1995 and 1999 Duma elections and after the final balloting for the president in 1996 and 2000. (Readers will recall that there were two rounds to the presidential election in 1996.) With respect to NATO expansion, in addition, I further benefited considerably from items included in ROMIR's (Rossiiskoye Obshchestvennoe Mnenie i Rynok) omnibus surveys conducted in 1996 and 1997.

This book contains a great deal of descriptive material. I do not intend to engage in what Stalin termed "vulgar factology." Rather, the purpose is to convey to readers how Russian foreign policy is likely to vary in response to changes in the configuration of domestic political coalitions or in the nature of the political system. My theoretical take on this is that providing answers to three sets of questions about elite and mass orientations is crucial in this respect.

The first set concerns "democratization" and Russian foreign policy. I find myself in something of a quandary with respect to terminology in this context. Generally I follow the practice of Freedom House, a nonprofit organization that has published annual assessments of the level of freedom in various countries since 1972, and refer to Russia as being "partly free."

[5] William Zimmerman, *Soviet Perspectives on International Relations* (Princeton: Princeton University Press, 1969); William Zimmerman and Robert Axelrod, "The 'Lessons' of Vietnam and Soviet Foreign Policy," *World Politics* 34, no. 1 (October 1981): 1–24; Allen Lynch, *The Soviet Study of International Relations* (Cambridge, UK: Cambridge University Press, 1987); Frank Griffiths, "Ideological Developments and Foreign Policy," in Seweryn Bialer, ed., *The Domestic Context of Soviet Foreign Policy* (Boulder: Westview Press, 1981), pp. 19–48; William Wohlforth, *The Elusive Balance* (Ithaca, N.Y.: Cornell University Press, 1993).

But I follow the practice of comparativists studying the transitions from authoritarian systems in referring to "democratizing states," despite my reservations about the use of this term. I am guardedly optimistic about the long-term prospects for Russian democracy. But by my use of the term "democratizing" in no way do I mean to connote any kind of teleological quality to what is most assuredly an open-ended process. Moreover, I do not use the term to imply that my data with respect to Russian elite and mass attitudes bear out the propensity for assertive behavior Edward Mansfield and Jack Snyder associate with democratizing rather than fully democratic states.[6] Indeed, I present evidence that calls into question how transferable some of their findings are to the Russia of 1991–2000. Russian elites were more disposed to use force internationally than were mass publics, and that disposition to use force increased between 1993 and 1995. Mass publics were a drag on such inclinations. They were no more inclined to use force abroad in 1995 than they had been in 1993—they did not respond to elite attitude shifts—and their response to NATO expansion was restrained.[7]

What are the consequences for Russia's foreign policy of the transformation of the political and economic system with its concomitant increase in political participation by a more diverse elite and by mass publics? How, for instance, did Russian foreign policy differ from Soviet foreign policy as a result of the change in domestic political and economic institutions?[8] What is the impact of institutional changes on the participants in the policy process and how does that in turn shape foreign policy outcomes?

The second set of questions relates to those Russians, both in the leadership and in the public, whose views about the domestic political economy may be properly classified as liberal democratic in a sense recognizable to Western scholarly literature.[9] How do elite and mass orientations to for-

---

[6] Edward Mansfield and Jack Snyder, "Democratization and the Danger of War," *International Security* 20, no.1 (Summer 1995): 5–38; Snyder, "Democratization, War, and Nationalism in the Post-Communist States," in Celeste Wallander, ed., *The Sources of Russian Foreign Policy after the Cold War* (Boulder: Westview Press, 1996), pp. 21–40; Snyder, *From Voting to Violence: Democracy and National Conflict* (New York: Norton, 2000).

[7] See chapter 6.

[8] For comparisons, both drawn from the study of environmental policies, of the impact on Moscow's policies of the changes in institutions brought on by the collapse of the Soviet Union, see Jane I. Dawson, *Eco-nationalism: Anti-nuclear Activism and National Identity in Russia, Lithuania, and Ukraine* (Durham: Duke University Press, 1996); William Zimmerman, Elena Nikitina, and James Clem, "The Soviet Union and the Russian Federation: A Natural Experiment in Environmental Compliance," in Edith Brown Weiss and Harold K. Jacobson, eds., *Engaging Countries: Strengthening Compliance with International Accords* (Cambridge: MIT Press, 1998), pp. 291–326.

[9] J. Roland Pennock, *Democratic Political Theory* (Princeton: Princeton University Press, 1979); John L. Sullivan et al., "Why Politicians Are More Tolerant: Selective Recruitment

eign policy correlate with orientations to democracy and the market? In what ways did it matter that it was those who overtly favored democracy and the market who dominated foreign policy decisions? How would Russia's foreign policy differ if, for instance, an ideological communist or others of a strongly statist or authoritarian bent were to win the presidency, even if such a victory were not accompanied by a return to conventionally Soviet political institutions?

The third set involves the relevance of the literature on American foreign policy, principally that on the role of elites and mass publics in Western democracies, to the understanding of Russian foreign policy. A radical change in thinking about the role of mass publics in the American foreign policy process took place beginning roughly 1985. (Ole Holsti dates the change from the end of the Vietnam War. He may be right in ascribing the change in thinking to that war but the publication dates of most of the relevant scholarship are largely post-1985.)[10] Prior to 1985, what Holsti has termed the Almond-Lippmann consensus dominated scholarly thinking about American foreign policy. In that consensus, foreign policy was of limited relevance to the daily lives of plain folks. Public opinion, especially about foreign policy, lacked "structure and coherence,"[11] so much so that in a classic paper Philip Converse questioned whether it was even appropriate to speak of mass "attitudes" toward foreign policy.[12] Survey after survey demonstrated that sizable fractions of the public knew virtually nothing about the subject.[13] From the point of view of effective foreign policy making in a democracy, the only good news was that mass opinion played little role.[14]

Beginning roughly in the late 1980s, however, the overall consensus about the role of the public in American foreign policy changed dramatically. To be sure, no challenge has occurred concerning the ignorance of large segments of the American public. Most of the remaining consensus, though, has been sharply challenged. Benjamin Page and Robert Shapiro have argued that in the aggregate, the American public judges foreign

---

and Socialization among Political Elites in Britain, Israel, New Zealand, and the United States," *British Journal of Political Science* 23 (1993): 53–76; Robert Dahl, *On Democracy* (New Haven: Yale University Press, 1998).

[10] Ole Holsti, "Public Opinion and Foreign Policy: Challenges to the Almond-Lippmann Consensus," *International Studies Quarterly* 36, no. 4 (December 1992): 439–66; Ole Holsti, *Public Opinion and American Foreign Policy* (Ann Arbor: University of Michigan Press, 1996).

[11] Holsti, "Public Opinion," p. 443.

[12] Philip Converse, "The Nature of Belief Systems in Mass Publics," in David Apter, ed., *Ideology and Discontent* (New York: Free Press, 1964), pp. 206–261.

[13] Holsti, "Public Opinion," p. 443.

[14] Bernard C. Cohen, *The Public's Impact on Foreign Policy* (Boston: Little, Brown, 1973).

policy issues rationally. Miroslav Nincic speaks of a "sensible public" and Bruce Jentleson found the American public "pretty prudent" in 1992 and "still pretty prudent" in 1998.[15] Moreover, there has been a shift in the direction of emphasizing the impact of mass opinion on foreign policy[16] and in assessments of the role of foreign policy in explaining the outcomes of presidential [17] and congressional[18] elections.

How "portable" are these relatively recent findings about the role of mass and elite public opinion in American foreign policy? There is a vast discrepancy between the consensus about American foreign policy in the first quarter century after World War II and the consensus as the twentieth century drew to a close. Which, if either, of these alternative perspectives better contributes to an understanding of Russian foreign policy at century's end?

In short, this is a book intended for relatively diverse audiences. It is targeted first at those interested specifically in Moscow's foreign policy after the end of the cold war and the collapse of the Soviet Union. But I have other audiences in mind as well. My intention is to explore the extent to which support for democracy and markets in Russia is a mile wide and an inch deep—the subject of a long-running discussion between James Gibson and me[19]—and the implications for the workings of Russian de-

---

[15] Benjamin Page and Robert Shapiro, *The Rational Public* (Chicago: University of Chicago Press, 1992); Miroslav Nincic, "A Sensible Public: New Perspectives on Popular Opinion and Foreign Policy," *Journal of Conflict Resolution* 36, no. 4 (December 1992): 772–89; Bruce Jentleson, "The Pretty Prudent Public: Post-Vietnam American Opinion on the Use of Military Force," *International Studies Quarterly* 36, no. 1 (January 1992): 49–74; Bruce Jentleson and Rebecca L. Britton, "Still Pretty Prudent: Post–Cold War American Opinion on the Use of Military Force," *Journal of Conflict Resolution* 42, no. 4 (August 1998): 395–417. For empirical support that public reaction is of an appropriate magnitude and timeliness, coupled with a cautionary note, see Jeffrey W. Knopf, "How Rational Is 'The Rational Public'?" *Journal of Conflict Resolution* 42, no. 5 (October 1998): 544–71.

[16] Thomas W. Graham, "The Politics of Failure: Strategic Nuclear Arms Control, Public Opinion, and Domestic Politics in the United States, 1945–1980" (Ph.D. dissertation, MIT, 1989).

[17] John H. Aldrich, John L. Sullivan, and Eugene Borgida, "Foreign Affairs and Issue Voting: Do Presidential Candidates 'Waltz before a Blind Audience'?" *American Political Science Review* 83, no. 1 (January 1989): 123–42; Jon Hurwitz and Mark Peffley, "How Are Foreign Policy Attitudes Structured?" *American Political Science Review* 81, no. 4 (December 1987): 1099–1120.

[18] R. Michael Alvarez and Paul Gronke, "Constituents and Legislators: Learning about the Persian Gulf War Resolution," *Legislative Studies Quarterly* 22, no.1 (February 1996): 105–127.

[19] James Gibson, "A Mile Wide but an Inch Deep (?): The Structure of Democratic Commitments in the Former USSR," *American Journal of Political Science* 40, no. 2 (May 1996): 396–420; William Zimmerman, "Synoptic Thinking and Political Culture in Post-Soviet Russia," *Slavic Review* 54, no.3 (Fall 1995): 630–42.

mocracy of foreign policy–relevant behavior by Russian elites and mass publics. In this respect, my aim is to reach the much larger community of scholars, policy makers, and the general public with interests in the prospects for democracy and a market economy in Russia. I use foreign policy, rather than, say, social welfare or economic reform, as my policy entry wedge.[20]

At the same time, I intend this book for those whose interest is primarily in the role of mass and elite opinion in democratic policy processes generally. Overwhelmingly, this literature has taken the American experience as its reference point. By focusing on post-Soviet Russia I hope to move the study of comparative foreign policy some distance in discriminating between those propositions about elite and mass opinion and foreign policy that are American-specific, or specific to Western democracies, and those that are of relevance to a broader class of open political systems.[21]

The evidence of this book reinforces the position of those who would characterize Russia in the first decade after the collapse of the USSR as having many democratic aspects. Nevertheless, the historically brief hiatus between the present and Russia's authoritarian past and the persistent nostalgia for the Soviet Union and the Soviet political system among a sizable proportion of the Russian citizenry[22] are among the unpleasant realities that serve to explain why knowledgeable scholars characterize Russia at the dawn of the new century as "proto-democratic," as a "consolidating" rather than a "consolidated" democracy, or as "partly free."[23] If one views democratic and authoritarian systems as being located at the low and high

[20] On economic reform, see Anders Aslund, *How Russia Became a Market Economy* (Washington, D.C.: Brookings Institution, 1994); Thane Gustafson, *Capitalism Russian-Style* (Cambridge, UK: Cambridge University Press, 1999).

[21] James Rosenau deserves much of the credit for advocating the comparative study of foreign policy. See, for instance, *The Scientific Study of Foreign Policy* (New York: Free Press, 1971). See also Harold K. Jacobson and William Zimmerman, eds., *The Shaping of Foreign Policy* (New York: Atheron, 1969), and Charles Hermann, Charles Kegley, and James Rosenau, *New Directions in the Study of Foreign Policy* (Boston: Allen and Unwin, 1987). Although there has been a proliferation of studies based on aggregate data in the generation since Rosenau's seminal papers in the 1960s, many areas relevant to the comparative study of foreign policy—elite-mass interactions and their links to foreign policy, public opinion, and foreign policy, for instance—retain a primary focus on the United States and are rarely comparative.

[22] For greater detail, see chapter 2. See also Judith Kullberg and William Zimmerman, "Liberal Elites, Socialist Masses, and Problems of Russian Democracy," *World Politics* 51, no. 3 (April 1999): 323–59, and Judith Kullberg and William Zimmerman " 'Perezhitki proshlogo' and the Impact of the Post-Soviet Transition" (paper presented at the annual meeting of the Midwest Political Science Association, April 1999).

[23] The term "proto-democratic" is Timothy Colton's. See Timothy J. Colton and Jerry F. Hough, eds., *Growing Pains: Russian Democracy and the Election of 1993* (Washington, D.C.: Brookings Institution Press, 1998), pp. 75–114.

ends, respectively, of a seven-point scale, rather than as constituting dichotomous choices,[24] then it is difficult to quarrel with Freedom House's rankings of Russia in the decade after the collapse of Soviet power. For those years, Freedom House categorized Russia as either a 3 or a 4 or a 5 with respect to both civil liberties and political freedom. These rankings, which are made using explicit criteria, constitute recognition of both how much Russia in the 1991–2000 decade differed from the Soviet Union of the mid-1970s and how it has fared in comparison with other European and Eurasian post-communist systems in that time period.[25] In the 1970s and through the mid-1980s, the Soviet Union was literally at sixes and, largely, sevens by Freedom House criteria. By that standard the Russian Federation has been a far more open political system. Viewed in comparison with almost all the formerly communist states of Europe, Russia does not fare as well, however. Table I.1 presents the average of Freedom House's civil liberties and political freedom scores for many of the formerly communist states of Europe and Central Asia. The Freedom House rankings reflect not only the changes since the years before *perestroika* but also an awareness of Russia's obvious warts—the grossly inadequate judicial system, the enormous asymmetry in the powers of the president and the Parliament, the role of the mafia. They also distinguish the Russian Federation in the first decade after the collapse of the USSR from the Baltic states or most of the members of the former Warsaw Treaty Organization, on the one hand, and a Central Asian country like Tadjikistan, on the other. Most of the former were consistently being accorded 1's and 2's on both the civil liberties and the political freedom scales that Freedom House requires to label a country "free" rather than "partly free" or "not free," whereas at the beginning of the twenty-first century the Central Asian countries were all coded as "not free."

In short, on the basis of Freedom House's evaluation of behavioral indicators, the long-term prospects for democracy in Russia are problematic. The survey data reinforce this observation. To take but one case in point—discussed in more detail below—immediately after the July 1996 presidential election, the Russian citizenry was almost equally divided between those who said the old Soviet system was more suitable for Russia and those who preferred the current situation or Western-style democracy; re-

---

[24] A strong argument for dichotomizing the concepts is Raymond Aron, *Democracy and Totalitarianism: A Theory of Political Systems* (Ann Arbor: Ann Arbor Paperbacks, 1990).

[25] It has been objected that Freedom House evaluates former Soviet republics with close ties to the United States uncritically. There is some merit to this charge with respect to individual scores for particular countries in particular years. In my judgment, though, Freedom House scores nevertheless serve reasonably well as an indication of cross-national progress or lack thereof by former Soviet republics and formerly communist East European states. I think the trajectory for Russia in the 1990s is exactly right.

Table I.1.
Democratic Evolution of Selected Former Soviet Republics and Members of the
Warsaw Treaty Organization, 1991–2001

	Year								
Country	91–92[a]	92–93	93–94	94–95	95–96	96–97	97–98	98–99	99–00
Russia	3	3.5	3.5	3.5	3.5	3.5	3.5	4	4.5
Estonia	2.5	3	2.5	2.5	2	1.5	1.5	1.5	1.5
Ukraine	3	3	4	3.5	3.5	3.5	3.5	3.5	3.5
Armenia	5	3.5	3.5	3.5	4	4.5	4.5	4	4
Tadjikistan	5	6	7	7	7	7	6	6	6
Poland	2	2	2	2	1.5	1.5	1.5	1.5	1.5
Hungary	2	2	2	1.5	1.5	1.5	1.5	1.5	1.5
Bulgaria	2.5	2.5	2	2	2	2.5	2.5	2.5	2.5

Sources: For 1991–2000, Freedom House [*http://www.freedomhouse.org/rankings*] for 2000–
2001, Aili Piano and Arch Puddington, "Gains Offset Losses," *Journal of Democracy* 12, no. 1
(January 2001): 87–92.
    Note: These scores represent the average of Freedom House's civil liberties and political free-
dom scores for each country in each year.
    Free: 2.5 and below.
    Partly free: 3 to 5.5.
    Unfree: greater than 5.5.
    [a]For 1990–91, the USSR was scored 4.5 overall.

spondents were even more prone to say the Soviet system before *perestroika* was most suitable for Russia in December 1999 (below, chapter 2).
    Evaluations such as those done by Freedom House should not, however,
encourage us to accept uncritically some of the more disparaging characterizations of the Russian political system and the rather widespread view
expressed in Western public commentary that Russia is inherently authoritarian. Assertions, for instance, in the popular press that the West and the
Russians do not have anything even approximating a common understanding of the key concepts associated with democracy or that the Russian attachment to order dominates any desire for freedom are not sub-
stantiated by the data at hand. (See chapter 2.) There are those in Russia
whose dispositions are overwhelmingly authoritarian and those whose
concepts of democracy are far afield from perpectives conventional in the
West. These orientations, however, are not the only views one encounters
among Russian elites or mass publics but rather illustrate one strand in
the overall distribution of views in the Russian Federation. Support for

democracy in Russia is substantial; especially among the beneficiaries of the present system, there are those for whom support for democracy is a constituent part of an overall way of thinking about people and politics (chapter 2).

But there are also many who have not benefited from the post-Soviet political economy. One scarcely needs to be a vulgar Marxist to recognize that benefiting materially and having favorable opportunities contributes mightily to support for democracy. The introduction—indeed, the imposition—of democracy in Japan and erstwhile West Germany after World War II was enormously facilitated by the economic success that attended it.

Nothing like the German or Japanese miracles occurred in Russia in the 1990s. Although at the dawn of a new century there were glimmers of hope for the economy, the preceding decade had been one in which the material position of sizable numbers of Russians declined, often precipitously. Timothy Colton has provided a balanced summary of the good and bad features of that decade for Russia. "True," he observes, "the reforms pursued under Boris Yeltsin's aegis did bear some fruit: a price liberalization which eliminated most queues in retail trade; stabilization and internal convertibility of the ruble from 1994 to 1998; membership in the International Monetary Fund; a spike in foreign investment; the gutting of the USSR's planning bureaucracy and the extrusion of many facilities from state control; and the startup of thousands of businesses, banks, a stock exchange, and a bond market. That said, the reform ledger also overflows with mishap and mismanagement. The bankers and industrialists at the heart of Russia's 'crony capitalism' excelled at asset stripping and currency speculation, not at investment and growth. National output fell every year in the decade but 1997 and 1999, and the ruble devaluation and stock-market crash that hit in 1998 were . . . a devastating reminder of the fine line between an emerging and submerging market."[26]

Moreover, the benefits and costs of the decade were borne quite asymmetrically. Elites benefited, sometimes enormously, from the turn to the market and to democracy; huge sectors of the ordinary Russian population did not.[27] Not surprisingly, Russian elites in the 1990s were far more supportive of democracy and particularly the market than were average citizens.

In asserting that recognizably democratic features existed in Russia in the 1991–2000 decade, I intend several points about the nature of elites,

[26] Timothy J. Colton, *Transitional Citizens: Voters and What Influences Them in the New Russia* (Cambridge Mass.: Harvard University Press, 2000), p. 90. It should be added that the devaluation of the currency in 1998 has clearly benefited the economy by making Russian products relatively more attractive than foreign goods to Russian consumers.

[27] Kullberg and Zimmerman, "Liberal Elites."

attentive publics, and other mass publics in contemporary Russian politics. As discussed further in chapter 1, post-Soviet Russian elites were as much like the characterization of American elites in Almond's classic work as they were like Soviet elites in the heyday of Soviet power.[28] Gone were the days in which there was a "single point in the policy-making process where the strings of influence . . . are held in a single hand."[29] The functional coordination of which Almond spoke in respect to Soviet decision making was gone. Elite controls over the rank and file were a contingent rather than a command relationship. Elite selection was by no means exclusively top down.[30] Russian elites, like American elites,[31] were on many dimensions ideologically heterogeneous. These elites presented mass publics with meaningful—and in the case of the 1996 presidential election, stark—choices.

Moreover, while Russian mass publics were less constrained in their beliefs than were Russian elites, the former turned out, in the aggregate, to have belief systems that were sufficiently patterned and stable to warrant their being depicted as attitudes or preferences (chapter 3). Mass publics have been able to link their preferences and the preferences of leaders. In the 1996 presidential election, though less clearly in the 2000 election, the country's voters played the role they should in a democracy. They constituted an audience that could be reached by Russian elites. In response to elite assertions—and an enormous media campaign—the citizenry knew what they liked and made their choice (chapter 4).

At the same time, it bears emphasizing that sizable sections of the Russian mass public turn out to be every bit as ignorant of the world outside as their American counterparts, and foreign policy, narrowly construed, plays a small role in their lives. (For an elaboration, see throughout, especially chapters 1 and 4.) As in the United States, the role of the attentive public—those who are knowledgeable and interested in politics—proves to be crucial in connecting the views of other parts of the mass public and foreign policy elites. More problematic, though, is when elites successfully mobilize mass opinion and when mass dispositions (which may be carryovers of prior elite socialization) are so intensely held or widespread as to be accepted by those most exposed to elite cues and are ultimately reflected in elite dispositions as well. In chapter 3 I develop an argument about the links between resistance to, and acceptance of, elite cues by those who are least connected to the realm of national and international

---

[28] Almond, *The American People*, pp. 143–45.

[29] Ibid., p. 144.

[30] David Lane and A. Cameron Ross, *The Transition from Communism to Capitalism* (New York: St. Martin's Press, 1999); Sharon Werning Rivera, "Elites in Post-Communist Russia: A Changing of the Guard," *Europe-Asia Studies* 52 (2000): 413–32.

[31] Aldrich, Sullivan, and Borgida, "Foreign Affairs and Issue Voting."

politics and attitudes among various sectors of the Russian public. That argument implies that on some dimensions mass resistance has contributed to the reorientation of elite dispositions even in conditions where elite consensus had been high previously. This is good news for the proposition that masses matter in relatively open systems. But it suggests a cautionary note about extending a reception-acceptance model—which implies a central role for elites in the determination of mass responses to survey items about policy—across a wider spectrum of responses than the policy issues John Zaller brilliantly explored, at least for Russia.[32]

By terming Russia as partly free, proto-democratic, or democratizing I also mean that the distribution of politically relevant attitudes differs in the Russian Federation from what would have obtained under Soviet power and that these differences flow from the transformation of the political and economic system with its concomitant increase in political participation. Notably, the changes in the Russian political economy in the 1990s altered the structure of elite composition. Operationalizing the notion of eliteness is always a difficult matter, even in stable systems. Determining eliteness is an especially problematic matter for a country undergoing radical sociopolitical transformation; one usual consequence of such transformations is that power relations are fundamentally reconfigured in the process. So it has been in Russia. New terms reflect new realities. The former Soviet Union was, after all, a place where capitalism, the capital market, and capitalists—foreign and domestic—had been eliminated. Certainly there was no role for powerful entrepreneurs in the USSR, whereas in contemporary Russia the emergence of a "*biznes-elita*"[33] is a phenomenon that must be reckoned with in thinking about decision making. That elite represents players who, as role occupants, would not have participated in decision making under Soviet power.[34] The transformation of the political and economic system with the collapse of the Soviet Union resulted in elite roles that had not existed under Soviet power.

Moreover, persons who would have played no part in the Soviet system have occupied key foreign policy roles in the Russian Federation, even in

---

[32] John Zaller, *The Nature and Origins of Mass Opinion* (Cambridge, UK: Cambridge University Press, 1992). But see also Zaller's more recent and somewhat self-critical "The Impact of Monica Lewinsky on Political Science," *PS* 31, no. 2 (June 1998): 182–89.

[33] Olga Kryshtanovskaia, "The Russian *biznes-elita*," manuscript, Ann Arbor, Mich., 1992.

[34] In so saying, I grant immediately that many of the people who constituted the business elite in Russia in the 1990s were persons who had been in the CPSU *apparat* and especially among the Komsomol leadership. See Steven Solnick, *Stealing the State* (Cambridge, Mass.: Harvard University Press, 1997). Nevertheless, these people have to be seen as the occupants of roles that did not exist in the Soviet system. I have no way of assessing the counterfactual question of what their views might have been had they become ministers in the USSR or regional secretaries of the CPSU.

roles that existed in both Soviet and post-Soviet Moscow—editors of major newspapers that existed under and after Soviet power, military officers, senior officials in the Ministry of Foreign Affairs, and the like. Most obviously, about a quarter of the foreign policy elites interviewed had never been members of the CPSU. Prior to the collapse of the Soviet Union, CPSU membership and indeed being a member of the *nomenklatura* of the Central Committee had been sine qua non for effective participation in the policy process. Chapter 5 explores, among other things, whether CPSU membership is an important predictor of foreign policy attitudes. It concludes that CPSU membership or absence thereof played a modest role in the early 1990s but finds that role had increased by 1999. A larger determinant in the 1990s of foreign policy attitudes than formal membership in the CPSU, it turns out, was how those with orientations to the political economic system that were congruent with core strands of Leninist thought differed from other elites, especially those whose orientations were characteristically liberal democratic in ways recognizable to Westerners. A describably Leninist ideological orientation with socialist, authoritarian, and autarkic ("national bolshevik") tendencies implied systematic differences in orientation to many, but scarcely all, foreign policy–related themes when compared with the responses of other elite members.

Along with the change in the composition and orientation of elites, an additional important consideration in assessing the consequences of the transformation of the political and economic system for Russia's foreign policy was the emergence of the public. I don't wish to over-claim in regard to the public's role. Chapter 2 provides ample evidence of the perceived domination of elites in the policy process. At the same time, domination does not mean "exclusive role." It is instructive to recall Almond's *American People and Foreign Policy.* In 1950, when it was first published, Almond was at pains to compare and distinguish between the nature of elites in the Soviet Union and in the United States in order to make a normative case for American democracy, while at the same time coming to grips with a fundamental reality. That reality is that there is a nontautological sense in which elites everywhere dominate the foreign policy process. (There is clearly a tautological sense: it is an easy trap to define elites as those who make crucial decisions and then to declare that elites play a crucial role in decision making.) In Almond's treatment of mass opinion, by contrast, he makes no mention at all of the role of mass publics in Soviet foreign policy. I assume that he did this for a good reason. It likely never even occurred to him to imagine that they played any role in Soviet foreign policy making. There are grounds for serious dispute over the impact of mass publics in Russian foreign policy, 1991–2000. What is not at issue, though, is that Russian publics did play some role. As discussed in chapter 4, broad-gauged concerns about Russia's relation to the outside world had a demonstrable impact on the outcome of the 1996 presidential election. In addition, I provide evidence to suggest that mass publics were sometimes nicely situated to serve as arbiters of the discrepant preferences of discordant elites. In some instances, furthermore, the movement of opinion over time has been in the direction of the responses of Russian citizens, rather than the other way around. And even the somewhat truculent and skeptical comments of Russian policy makers about the role of mass publics have revealed the impression that the latter must be mobilized in order for Russia to engage in an effective foreign policy.

In short, change in Moscow's political and economic institutions changed the mix of relevant players in the policy process. This is an obvious point, though one sometimes ignored by enthusiasts for the new institutionalism in political science, but nevertheless an important one to keep in mind. The distribution of attitudinal "considerations"[35] was altered by broadening the selectorate beyond the confines of the *nomenklatura* of the CPSU and by moving in the direction of a market economy. Likewise, it also mattered in important ways that those who were largely disposed to market democracy have dominated the political system. Chapter 5 argues that with respect to East-West relations the pattern at the elite level was quite clear: despite a sharp increase in negative views of the United States, in support for military spending, and in support of balancing against the West's military power across the board in the 1990s, those who favored market or liberal democracy in the Western sense were noticeably less inclined to regard the United States as a threat, less concerned about NATO expansion, less prone to increase military spending, and less disposed to assert that Russia could solve its economic problems without the aid of the West. Those I have termed socialist authoritarians—those whose statist and authoritarian responses are characteristically Leninist— by comparison were far more likely to desire increased military spending, to assert that Russia can solve its economic problems without the aid of the West, to express concern about NATO expansion, and to be much more disposed to regard the United States as a threat. Similar results hold for mass publics as well. As we shall see, though, orientation to the domestic political economy was far less clearly associated with orientation to foreign policy matters involving Russia's relations with the states on its periphery, for both elites and mass publics.

That qualification notwithstanding, on many important matters relating to Russia's relationship to East-West political relations, to the reunification of Russia with Ukraine and Belarus, and to the global economy as well, those (both among elites and mass publics) whose orientations to Russia's domestic political economy were congruent with traditional Le-

---

[35] Zaller, *The Nature and Origins*, p. 59.

ninist norms viewed the world differently from other Russians. The old joke during the period of stagnation, what the Russians termed *zastoi*, concerning Brezhnev's mother, who, on seeing all the expensive cars accumulated by her son over the years, ostensibly asked him, "But what will happen if the Bolsheviks return?" is relevant here. Assume for the moment—*arguendo*, as the lawyers say—what would probably be a counterfactual: that the election of an attitudinally communist President in Russia would not result in shifts in the political and economic institutional makeup that had begun to take shape in Russia by the mid-1990s.[36] Even so, were those who think like conventional Bolsheviks, though not necessarily some specific member of the Communist Party of the Russian Federation (KPRF), to come to power, it would have profound implications for East-West relations, unless one assumes utterly no relation between what politicians say out of power and what they do in power. Moreover, chapters 5 and 6 muster evidence that suggests that with respect to East-West relations and Russian reunification with Ukraine and Belarus, having been a member of the CPSU had in 1999 become an important discriminator among elite responses, something that had not been the case in 1993 or 1995.

The argument I develop with regard to the first two sets of questions—those concerning democratization and foreign policy and those pertaining to Russian liberal democrats and foreign policy—has implications for my answers to the third set of questions. All things considered, the current consensus about the role of the public in American foreign policy in 1999 bears some resemblance to the role of mass publics in Russian foreign policy. It is certainly more appropriate than extrapolations drawn from Soviet experience. Like my Americanist counterparts, I issue no challenge either to the view that sizable fractions of the mass public are enormously ill informed or to the proposition that, narrowly construed, foreign policy issues were way down the list of those matters that seized the attention of Russian mass publics; indeed, I document them in chapters 3 and 6. Nor do I claim to have undertaken in this book an effort that parallels Thomas Graham's 1989 dissertation which directly links public opinion about arms control issues to American foreign policy behavior.[37] That is another volume. I do, though, present strong evidence to bear out the portability to Russians' partial democracy of John Aldrich's proposition, based on American data, that leaders in a democracy do not waltz before a blind

---

[36] Note that this statement refers to someone who is attitudinally communist—that is, endorses the kind of socialist authoritarianism we associate with traditional Leninism—not to someone who was a member of the CPSU or is currently a member of the Communist Party of the Russian Federation. Among elites in particular, these are not necessarily the same.

[37] Graham, "The Politics of Failure."

audience. Russian respondents turn out to be able to make grossly accurate characterizations of their leaders. They were, moreover, able to link their preferences about foreign policy to the intensity of their feelings pro and con for Russian presidential candidates in 1966 and, less clearly, in 2000 (chapter 4). I also argue that for mass publics their orientations to Russia's place in the world broadly conceived—though much less to specific foreign policy issues—hang together in a way that justifies these utterances' being described as making up alternative belief systems and that these orientations bear substantially on their electoral behavior.

Moreover, when the gravamen of mass views differed from the consensus of elites, it is easy to tell a story about the consequences of policies that touch directly on such matters for mass publics that is different from the story about the consequences of policies for elites. In this story, we witness a kind of rationality to the mass publics' collective judgment akin to that observed of American mass publics in Page and Shapiro's *Rational Public*. Indeed, this produces some instances where mass views preceded rather than followed elite assessments.

The differences reported between elite and mass orientations to foreign policy may have impeded Russia's integration into the international economy, but they also served as a constraint on foreign policy activism. Moreover, as the response to NATO expansion vividly illustrates (chapter 6), there is little evidence for the kind of impetuous and overreactive behavior among Russian mass publics of which George Kennan and other realists were so fearful concerning the role of mass publics in *American* foreign policy in the early years of the cold war.[38]

In short, the argument of this book is that the opening up of the Russian political system has identifiable consequences for Moscow's foreign policy. A more heterogeneous elite enlarges the range of possible policies the country might adopt, and the orientation to the political economy of those who dominate policy decisions has huge implications for Russia's relations with the West, though considerably less for its behavior on its periphery. Mass publics in the 1990s played the minimal role one would expect them to play in a democracy; on the average and in general they were able to sort out the policy preferences of elites and to link those preferences to their own. By and large, they were more isolationist and noticeably less activist than were Russian elites (chapter 3).[39] At the same

---

[38] George Kennan, *American Diplomacy, 1900–1950* (Chicago: University of Chicago Press, 1951).

[39] On isolationist and internationalist attitudes in American foreign policy, see Eugene Wittkopf, "On the Foreign Policy Beliefs of the American People: A Critique and Some Evidence," *International Studies Quarterly* 30, no. 4 (1986): 423–45. For fresh and innovative thinking about isolationism in general, see Bear Braumoeller, "Isolationism in International Relations" (Ph.D. dissertation, University of Michigan, 1998).

time, their policy preferences in response to actions taken abroad appear proportionate. What this suggests in policy terms is that, both because of the policy orientations of the predominant elites and because mass publics played a modest but real role in foreign policy decision making, the outcome of the two great choices facing Russia concerning its political economy—democracy versus dictatorship and market versus the state—matter fundamentally for Russia's relations with the West. For students of foreign policy, the evidence of the book is to strengthen the view that conclusions about mass-elite interactions and foreign policy drawn largely from data generated in the United States are transferable to other, less stabilized, partly free political environments.

1

Elites, Attentive Publics, and Masses in Post-Soviet Russia

Elites

Elites everywhere dominate most foreign policy processes. But how do we identify the elites in post-Soviet Russia? In the bad old days of the Soviet Union, it was relatively easy to identify them. Elite status was defined by inclusion in the *nomenklatura* lists at various levels of the Communist Party of the Soviet Union. The focal point of Soviet elite studies was "the Party."[1] Determining elite status is more problematic in post-Soviet Russia, as it is in any country undergoing rapid sociopolitical transformation. Most obviously, the emergence of a *biznes-elita*,[2] including the much remarked-upon "oligarchs," was one of the empirical realities of which account had to be taken in determining whom we would consider members of the post-Soviet Russian foreign policy elite.

To account for these realities, I defined the foreign policy elites sectorally and positionally. The goal was to identify and interview a sample of those with resources that matter in foreign policy decision making. Because the selection criterion was the respondents' position and influence in the foreign policy decision process, it should be stressed that, even assuming—properly, I believe—that I have succeeded in identifying a reasonable sample of the foreign policy elite population, it is not proper to draw inferences from the data reported in this book to the views of the elite in general about foreign policy or to infer the foreign policy beliefs of the media in general, the military overall, or some other key sector in Russian society. The surveys of elites to which reference is made in this study focus almost exclusively on persons who are occupied in a major way with foreign policy and national security questions on a daily basis. As a result, their responses on these topics may not be representative of the way other journalists or scholars or officers think about foreign policy. At the

---

[1] Among a vast literature, see, for instance, Jerry Hough, *The Soviet Prefects* (Cambridge, Mass.: Harvard University Press, 1969); Merle Fainsod, *How Russia is Ruled* (Cambridge, Mass.: Harvard University Press, 1953); T. Harry Rigby, *Communist Party Membership in the USSR, 1917–1967* (Princeton: Princeton University Press, 1968); Roeder, *Red Sunset*; and Michael Voslensky, *Nomenklatura* (Garden City, N.Y.: Doubleday, 1984).

[2] Kryshtanovskaia, "The Russian *biznes-elita*."

same time, the composition of the elite sample was sufficiently representative of the Russian foreign policy elite that one can reasonably draw inferences about the pattern of attitudes among the foreign policy elite overall on the basis of the answers given by our respondents. What could not be done was to infer from this sample of foreign policy elites to what elites in general think about foreign policy, the criterion on which the sample was selected.

On the other hand, since these persons were not selected for their attitudes to other key questions about Russian society, on matters where the between-group differences are quite sharp we may reasonably, for instance, utilize these interviews to make gross distinctions between elite dispositions and those of mass publics. There is a statistical basis for believing that, as a result of the *size* of the elite sample, the elite respondents interviewed in 1993, 1995, and 1999 may be regarded as samples of the Russian national elite in general with respect to issues for which the sample was *not* constructed—for instance with regard to elite attitudes toward markets and democracy.

Moreover, there is some empirical basis as well. I have been able to compare my findings with a Moscow elite sample drawn from an entirely different study that asked many of the same questions as in the surveys reported in this study.[3] I compared the distribution of ideological preferences of that study's respondents, subelite samples of high-level managers and those employed in government administration extracted from our 1993 mass survey of European Russia, and the 1993 elite survey and got similar results. The substantive implications of these preferences are discussed in chapter 2. What warrants emphasis here is that when the same indicators to identify orientations to the economy and the political system are used for different data sets, the distribution of orientations favorable to the market and democracy and the distribution of those favoring statist or authoritarian alternatives in the data sets are similar. Our findings thus have an immediate bearing on Russian foreign policy, on the links between orientations to the market and democracy and orientations to foreign policy among elites, and on elite orientations to the Russian political economy.[4]

In identifying those who turn out empirically to have disproportionate influence on the foreign policy process, I followed Lasswell and his colleagues[5] and took Russian foreign policy elites to be those who controlled the instruments of coercion or persuasion, dominated key parts of the

[3] Judith Kullberg, "The Ideological Roots of Elite Political Conflict in Post-Soviet Russia," *Europe-Asia Studies* 46 (1994): 929–53.

[4] With the exception of civil-military differences, little emphasis is given in this book to efforts to distinguish among the dispositions of elite subgroups.

[5] Harold Lasswell, Daniel Lerner, and C. Easton Rothwell, *The Comparative Study of Elites* (Stanford: Stanford University Press, 1952).

economy, had specialized knowledge, or occupied key formal political positions in Moscow.[6] Expressed less ponderously, persons from each of five
key sectors of Russian society relevant to the foreign policy process were
interviewed: the media, foreign policy–relevant research institutes, the
economy, the government (including persons from both executive and
legislative branches), and the armed forces.

There were three elite surveys. The first was undertaken in Moscow
between December 1992 and February 1993, the second in October–
November 1995 just prior to the December Duma election, and the third
in November 1999 just prior to that December's Duma election. All three
surveys were conducted by ROMIR, directed by Elena Bashkirova. In the
first survey, 40 persons from each of the five sectors—the media, the economy, the foreign policy institutes, the government, and the armed forces—
were interviewed. In the 1995 elite survey, a total of 180 persons were
interviewed, 30 each from the media, the foreign policy research institutes, the government, and the armed forces plus 30 from persons with
major management responsibilities in the more or less private sector and
30 from the economic ministries. The same selection process occurred in
the November 1999 survey with a couple of exceptions. This time 30 were
interviewed from the foreign policy–relevant committees of the legislative
branches and 30 from the executive.[7] Moreover, the staff at ROMIR decided to include the entire range of institutes subsumed under the umbrella of the Russian Academy of Sciences (and several comparable univer-
sities) rather than limiting their coverage to social science institutes. They
did this, they explained, because directors and their deputies of institutes
across the board "actively participate in international meetings . . . [which
are] not only purely scientific, but political . . . as well," "are frequently
members or participants [in various] international organizations or associations," and have "contacts with various international funds [founda-
tions]." To the extent possible, ROMIR constructed what amounted to a

[6] Foreign policy elites were defined as residing in Moscow. This omitted regional elites.
The decision to exclude regional elites was made partly on financial grounds, though in 1993
and 1995 there was little to suggest that they played a key foreign policy role. In 1999,
however, the perception of other elites was that the relative role of regional elites had increased modestly. In writing the NATO chapter (chapter 6) I did benefit from having access
to a State Department–sponsored survey of regional elites.

[7] ROMIR also interviewed thirty persons selected from among those national legislators
who were not involved with foreign policy matters—that is, they were *not* selected randomly
from the overall population of the two legislative branches. Because these elites were not
selected for their foreign policy roles, I decided not to include them in the analysis that
follows. If one were writing a study of the attitudes of the Russian legislators before the
December 1999 elections, combining those drawn from the foreign policy committees and
those who were not on those committees would, I think, constitute a reasonable sample of
legislators. That, however, is not the task of this book.

population, for instance, of persons in the print and voice media directly concerned with foreign policy and then contacted persons randomly from that list. By 1995 source books that facilitated the construction of such lists had become relatively available, and by 1999 they were widespread. The era in Russia when one's chief and nearly sole resource was the Spravochnoe Biuro (Information Bureau), where one was regularly asked "When was he born?" when asking the telephone number of someone even after you had provided the person's first name, patronymic, last name, and address, has passed. It is possible to construct something approximating populations of the various sectors from which the elite respondents were drawn, especially given the increased availability of inventories of governmental position holders in text and on the Internet,[8] business directories for the two houses of the Duma, and advertising and informational directories for persons in the business sector. It was roughly as easy to identify elites by name in the Russian context at century's end as for years it has been for Ole Holsti and James Rosenau in the United States.[9]

As a criterion for selection, those classified as elites had to have occupations that suggested a prima facie expectation that they would have substantial potential to affect policy. They had what would in any contemporary society be considered elite status. In each subarea, those interviewed were people of substance. Thus among the media respondents were political observers, editors, and first deputy editors of major mass media sources, ranging in orientation from the *Moscow News* (*Moskovskie novosti*), *Izvestiia*, *Kommersant*, and *Komsomol'skaia Pravda* to *Pravda*, *Rossiiskaia Gazeta*, and *Trud*, and foreign policy commentators for major television channels.

In the 1995 survey, persons from the government included eleven people in the President's Office and the Ministry of Foreign Affairs and nineteen in the Russian parliament. The latter were almost evenly divided between chairs or deputy chairs and ordinary members of foreign policy committees of one or the other branch of the parliament. The Duma committees represented included, for example, the Committee on Defense, the Committee for Relations with the Commonwealth of Independent

---

[8] *Federal'noe Sobranie—Sovet Federatsii: Gosudarstvennaia Duma* (Moscow: IEG Panorama, 1996); G. V. Belonychkin, comp., *Pravitel'stvo Rossii i federal'nye organy ispolnitel'noi vlasti* (Moscow: IEG Panorama, 1997–98). An especially useful website is <www.ku.edu/~herron>.

[9] Among the many publications drawing on elite data in the United States, see, especially Holsti, *Public Opinion*; see also Ole Holsti and James Rosenau, "The Post–Cold War Foreign Policy Beliefs of American Leaders: Persistence or Abatement of Partisan Cleavages?" in Eugene R. Wittkopf, ed., *The Future of American Foreign Policy* (New York: St. Martin's Press, 1994), pp. 127–47; Holsti and Rosenau, "Vietnam, Consensus, and the Belief Systems of American Leaders," *World Politics* 32 (1979): 1–56; as well as the numerous publications of the Chicago Council on Foreign Relations.

States and Ties with Russians Abroad, the Security Committee, and the Committee on International Relations. Council of the Federation committees included, among others, the Committee on International Relations, the Committee on Security and Defense, and the Committee on "Budget, Finance, Hard Currency [*valuta*] and Credit Regulation, Monetary Emission, Tax Policy, and Tariff Regulation." In the 1999 survey, ten of the thirty respondents came from the presidential administration or the federal government and twenty were top-level executives—ministers, their deputies, heads of directorates, or mid-level departmental heads and their deputies. The group of *biznesmeni* in all three surveys similarly came from high-profile occupations, including presidents, general directors, and key administrators of stock companies, banks, and stock exchanges along with leaders, key administrators, and commercial directors of private firms, joint enterprises, and small business enterprises with major foreign dealings.

Even the persons drawn from the military were leading specialists and experts on foreign policy and security matters, though unlike their counterparts in the civilian sectors, they were often not the leading figures in the institutions sampled, but rather a notch down. (Although a handful of the officers were in the security forces, virtually all were in the military and I refer to them as the military and the armed forces interchangeably.) As the unpublished methodological note prepared by the staff of ROMIR observed rather drily in 1993, "The uniqueness of this particular elite group (the closed and secret nature of activities in this domain) resulted in it not being the case that the leading figures in the selected organizations were always those interviewed."[10] Nevertheless, those interviewed ranged from "a Deputy Minister of Defense to leading specialists and experts in security problems and foreign policy." As a rule, the latter in 1995 were people with ranks not lower than colonel who were drawn from among chairs of faculties of military research institutes and section heads of military institutes and in 1999 were colonels or above drawn from the various general staffs, along with military institutes.[11]

Those interviewed turned out to be elites by multiple criteria aside from their role incumbency. For them, politics consequently was much more a part of their daily lives than was true for other Russians. Table 1.1 illus-

---

[10] "Metodologicheskii otchet po issledovaniu 'Vneshniaia politika Rossii' " manuscript, 1993. Available from the author.

[11] Forty-three of those interviewed (28 of whom were in the media or in the academy) in 1995 had been interviewed in the 1992/93 survey. To ensure respondents' confidentiality, links between the respondent's names and their survey responses were not preserved after 1993. As a result, it was not possible to compare an individual's responses in 1992–93 and in 1995, even though it was possible to distinguish between those in the 1995 elite survey who had been previously surveyed and those who had not. Only 11 of those interviewed in 1995 were among the 210 persons included in the 1999 elite sample.

Table 1.1.
Revealed Interest in Politics: 1995–1999

Activity in Past Week	Elite 1995	Elite 1999	Attentive Public 1995	University Attendees 1995	University Attendees 1999	Mass Public Overall 1995	Mass Public Overall 1999
I. Had conversations about politics with friends or family almost or every day (two formulations)	74% (132) —	60% (125) —	43% (129) 56% (170)	34% (199) 49% (298)	— 51% (203)	29% (796) 40% (1119)	— 41% (780)
II. Watched television almost or every day	91% (163)	95% (199)	86% (259)	79% (463)	81% (312)	73% (2007)	76% (1367)
III. Listened to domestic radio almost or every day	54% (96)	62% (130)	54% (164)	46% (268)	42% (169)	46% (1238)	42% (763)
IV. Read domestic newspapers almost or every day	80% (144)	83% (174)	41% (124)	38% (223)	37% (148)	26% (687)	28% (530)
V. Listened to foreign radio once or more times a week	49% (87)	40% (83)	13% (39)	10% (56)	—	6% (160)	—

Sources: The two elite surveys were conducted by ROMIR. Both the 1995 and the 1999 mass surveys were based on national samples and conducted by Demoscope.

Note: Actual number of respondents for particular cells shown in parentheses. Dashes indicate question not asked.

Questions asked in the 1995 and 1999 elite surveys and the 1993 and 1995 mass surveys:

People learn about events in the world and within the country from many sources, by radio, television, and from newspapers. Speaking of the past week, how often did you learn about events in the world and within the country from each source?
    TV
    Foreign radio
    Domestic radio
    Newspapers

In the course of the last week how often did you speak with friends or members of your family about events in the world or within the country?

Asked in the 1999 mass survey:
In the past week did you talk about politics with members of your family or with friends?
    [If yes] How often in the past seven days did you talk about politics?

Do you watch any daily news programs?
    [If yes] How often *in the past seven days* have you watched daily news programs?

When you watch news programs, how much attention do you usually pay to the political news?

Please tell me, do you read newspapers?
    [If yes] When you read newspapers, how much attention do you usually pay to articles about politics?

How often *in the past seven days* have you listened to the news on the radio?

trates this point. Respondents in both the 1995 and the 1999 samples of elites and in the 1995 mass survey were asked, "Speaking about the past week, how often did you learn about events in the world and within the country [through television, by foreign radio, by domestic radio, from newspapers]?" and "How often in the course of the past week did you speak with friends or members of the family. . . .?" about such events. The 1995 mass survey also asked respondents whether they talked "about politics with family members or friends," and this question was also asked in the 1999 mass survey.

This provides something of a bridge between the 1995 and 1999 mass surveys, as row I in table 1.1 reveals. That row contains the distribution of responses in the 1995 survey for the attentive public (defined in the next section), the university educated, and the mass public overall for both versions of the question, the elite responses to the first variant, and the responses in 1999 by the mass public overall as well by those with university education to the second formulation.

The other relevant questions in the 1999 survey also differed somewhat from those asked of elites in 1995 or 1999 or of mass publics in 1995. Thus the 1999 mass survey asked respondents whether they watched "any daily news programs" on television and whether they listened to the news on the radio; it is the responses to these questions that are included in categories II and III in table 1.1. Likewise, the 1999 mass survey asked respondents if they read the paper every day; if yes, how often they read national newspapers and how often they read local newspapers. It did not ask whether they read about politics or about "events in the world or within the country." Category IV, consequently, shows those in the 1999 mass sample who answered "very attentively" or "quite attentively" to an item asking "how much attention [they devoted to questions] about politics." The 1999 survey did not ask about foreign radio listenership (row V).

Foreign policy elites were much more likely to employ foreign radio and domestic newspapers to obtain information about international or domestic events or to talk with friends about such events than were others in Russia, even in comparison with those who were university educated or with those in mass surveys who were most knowledgeable about the outside world.

Half of the 1995 and two-fifths of the 1999 elite sample reported having gotten information about domestic and international events from foreign radio during the past week (table 1.1). By way of comparison, a likely consequence of the opening of Russia in the mid-1980s and in the 1990s is that mass publics simply did not use foreign radio as a source of domestic and international events. (Of course, they may never have.) In the Russia-wide mass survey conducted on the occasion of the 1995 Duma elections, only 6 percent stated that they had "found out about domestic and international events" in the past week by listening to foreign radio. Even among those with university education, only 10 percent in the same survey said they had gotten information about domestic and international events in the past week via foreign radio. The same results were also obtained in a survey conducted in 1996. ROMIR, in its omnibus quarterly survey, asked a national sample of 1047 respondents in October 1996 how often they had listened to foreign radio in the past week. Seven percent overall and 11 percent of those with higher education reported listening on some occasion.

Likewise, foreign policy elites were far more likely to read newspapers to be informed about domestic and international events than were others. As table 1.1 again illustrates, four out of five of the foreign policy elites interviewed in 1995 and 1999 (80 and 83 percent, respectively) reported reading the paper every or almost every day to learn about domestic and international events. By way of comparison, roughly two out of five from among the internationally attentive public and respondents with university education in both the 1995 and the 1999 Russia-wide mass surveys, and a quarter overall in both mass surveys reported doing so.[12] (The questions used in the 1993 and 1995 mass surveys to identify the internationally attentive public were not asked in 1999.)

Similarly, three out of four in 1995 and three out of five in 1999 (table 1.1) from among the foreign policy elites said that in the past week they had talked with friends or family members about foreign and domestic events every or almost every day. Those in the attentive public in 1995 were more likely to talk politics than those who had attended university, who were in turn more likely to engage in such conversations than mass publics overall. Nevertheless, even among the attentive public, only slightly more than two out of five asserted that they had talked about foreign and domestic events and less than a third of the mass public respondents overall indicated that they had talked with friends or members of their family about domestic and international events. The numbers for the mass public responses in 1999 were higher than in 1995, in part because of the context in which and the way the question was asked. It still remains the case that foreign policy elites talked more about politics than the university educated, who in turn talked more than mass publics overall.

---

[12] In the October 1996 survey by ROMIR referred to in the previous paragraph, respondents were asked how frequently they had read democratically oriented and communist-oriented newspapers in the past week. With the parliamentary and presidential election behind them, only 5 percent overall said they read the democratic press every day or practically every day and a mere 2 percent of the overall sample reported reading the communist press every day or practically every day. Of those with higher education, 18 percent asserted they

By contrast, listening to domestic radio and watching television to learn about domestic and international events had become typically quotidian events for all Russians in the 1990s. Thus the attentive public tuned into television and domestic radio to learn about domestic or international events as often as those in the elite samples, and large numbers of other respondents in the mass samples reported the use of television for such purposes as well. Only relatively small differences were detected in the proportions among foreign policy elites and others reporting that during the past week they had learned about domestic or international events by listening to domestic radio "almost every day" or "every day." Indeed, those classified here as the attentive public reported listening to domestic radio as a source of information as frequently as did the foreign policy elites sampled in 1995.

The persons interviewed whom we classified as elites positionally were not only more attuned to political events. They were also markedly more likely to say that people like themselves were politically efficacious than were ordinary Russians and much more likely to state that they personally had affected foreign policy decision making. Those whom we defined as elites were, needless to say, much more likely to say that people like themselves had some impact on foreign policy decisions. Well over half of those interviewed both in 1993 and in 1995 indicated that people like themselves played a part in the foreign policy decisional process, though this proportion had decreased substantially by century's end. In 1993, 51 percent, in 1995, 46 percent, and in 1999, 30 percent, said people like themselves had "some" influence over foreign policy decision making. An additional six (1995) or seven (1993, 1999) persons answered that people like themselves had a "significant" or "decisive" impact on foreign policy making.

The latter were of course a small proportion of the elite respondents. The proportion of persons in the 1993 mass survey of European Russia answering in this way was, however, much smaller. (This question was not asked in either the 1995 or the 1999 mass survey.) Consequently, almost three times as many (40) members of the three elite samples, which, excluding duplication of those interviewed twice, totaled 501 respondents, answered that such people had a significant or decisive impact on foreign policy decision making as did the participants (14) in a mass sample of 1243 respondents. When we asked a sample of persons in European Russia in 1993 whether they thought "persons like [themselves]" could "influence decision making in the area of foreign policy," almost nine out of ten respondents (89 percent) of those who responded answered negatively. Ten percent said that people such as they had "some" impact. Only one

---

read a democratic paper every, or nearly every, day and 4 percent acknowledged that they read the communist press on a similar basis.

percent indicated that people like themselves had either a "significant" or "decisive" impact on foreign policy.

Moreover, when we asked the respondents in the 1993 mass survey who had responded affirmatively to the question whether people like themselves influenced foreign policy decision making how they personally had influenced foreign policy, the answers were quite telling. Only 39 percent of the respondents who had indicated that people like themselves—a tenth of the sample—could influence foreign policy decision making said that they themselves had actually done so. But virtually all the elite respondents who answered that people like themselves had an impact on foreign policy decisions then gave examples of how they themselves had personally influenced foreign policy decisions.[13]

Typically, the few respondents in the mass sample who said they had influenced foreign policy gave voting or participating in a referendum as the ways they had influenced decision making. By contrast, the elite respondents mentioned quite direct and specific ways that their actions had had a bearing on the foreign policy decision-making process. Among the open-ended responses given by persons in the elite surveys were "influencing the media," "parliamentary activity," "compiling analytic papers," "negotiating with foreign oil companies," "negotiating contracts with Western businessmen," and the like. In answers illustrating the way the world has changed with the collapse of the Soviet Union, three respondents in the 1995 survey even gave as examples of their personal impact on foreign policy "participating in the activities of NATO."

Demographically, the elites differed most sharply from those in the surveys of mass publics in five ways characteristic of elite status. They were on the whole much better off than persons in the mass public. The age structure of the elites was more truncated. Almost uniformly they reported having university education, and their parents were far more likely to have been university-educated professionals or administrators. To a man, so to speak, they were male. And they were far more likely to have been members of the Communist Party of the Soviet Union than those in the mass surveys, even among those who had attended university.

Like other elites, foreign policy elites are material beneficiaries of the present Russian political economy. The mean income of the elites was almost three times that of those with university education in the mass sample. Among those with university education who answered a question about their monthly earnings in rubles, four (less than 1 percent) in the national sample of Russians surveyed at the time of the 1995 Duma election reported their family income as being more than R10,000,000 in earnings in the previous month (In late 1995, the exchange rate between

---

[13] Here "Virtually all" = 95 percent, 1993; 93 percent, 1995; 99 percent, 1999.

the ruble and the dollar was approximately 4650 to one.)[14] Six (4 percent) of the foreign policy elites reported similar earning levels. Almost five-sixths (82 percent) of the foreign policy elites reported incomes of R1,000,000 or more. Only 37 percent of the respondents in the national sample with university education reported receiving similar earnings. Less than a quarter (23 percent) overall of the 1995 national sample said that their family income had been that much or more.

In 1999, after the ruble had been devalued (in 1998) so that the exchange rate in November 1999 was about R25 to the dollar, the mean family income reported in the mass survey was 1977 rubles (after the March 2000 presidential election, R1969). The mean for those with university education was R2882. The mean family income of the foreign policy elites was R9415. Two percent (eleven respondents) with university education in the 1999 mass survey reported family incomes in excess of R10,000 and 17 percent in the 1999 foreign policy elite survey. None (zero) of the elite respondents reported family income less than R2000, and only four indicated that their family income was less than R3000. If the old Marxist dictum that being determines consciousness has any merit, it is scarcely surprising that elites view the post-Soviet Russian political economy more favorably than do others. Elites have largely not experienced the hardships sizable parts of the mass publics have undergone as a result of the turn to the market.

In all six core surveys, the mean ages of the respondents were typically in their late forties. The spread among elites was, however, considerably narrower than in the mass surveys. Proportionately fewer were less than forty or over sixty. Slightly less than two-thirds of the 1995 (64 percent) and exactly three-fourths of the 1999 elite samples were between forty and sixty when they were interviewed. Only three out of eight in the mass sample (38 percent, 1995 mass sample; 37 percent in 1999) were that age when interviewed. Both those younger and older are substantially underrepresented in the elite sample; put differently, a standard deviation for the elite surveys was less than ten years and for the 1995 and 1999 national mass samples, almost seventeen years. The days of stagnation (*zastoi*), when key levers of power were controlled by persons in their dotage, were no longer. At the same time, the phenomenon of the replacement of the previous leadership by very young elites often observed in genuinely revolutionary transformations had not occurred in Russia in the 1990s either.

Virtually all the elite respondents, or all but 1 percent of the 1995 and 1999 foreign policy elite samples (2 percent in the 1993 sample), said they

---

[14] Thomas Remington provides a useful table of the ruble/dollar exchange rate at the end of the years 1990 through 1997 in his *Politics in Russia* (New York: Longman, 1999), p. 203.

had had university education. By comparison, slightly more than a fifth in the 1993, 1995, and 1999 mass samples said they had had university education. Moreover, the elite respondents were far more likely to have had parents who were university-educated professionals or administrators. In the 1993 survey of European Russia, one in six (16 percent) of those who reported their father's occupation said his or her father had been an administrator or a professional. Eleven percent asserted their father had attended or completed university. By contrast, about half of the 1995 (51 percent) and 1999 (48 percent) elite respondents and slightly less than half in 1993 (44 percent) asserted their father had been an administrator or professional and more than half said he had attended or completed university (57 percent, 1993; 58 percent 1995; 54 percent 1999).

In post-Soviet Russia, elites are male. In all three elite surveys—1993, 1995, and 1999—over 90 percent of those interviewed were males in a country where women easily outnumber men. This situation is part of a larger trend extending back to the Gorbachev era. The empowerment of institutions first in the Soviet Union and then in the Russian Federation has been accompanied by the greatly diminished involvement of women in such institutions. In the Soviet Union, women had been systematically underrepresented in politically powerful institutions such as the Central Committee and Politburo of the CPSU but were represented in far greater numbers in symbolic structures such as the Supreme Soviet. As institutions like the Supreme Soviet became less symbolic and more authentic in the late 1980s, women's participation in such institutions atrophied. Both in the Soviet Union and in the Russian Federation in the 1990s there was little place for women in institutions, membership of which implied influence in foreign policy decision making.

Finally, Russian foreign policy elites were far more likely to have been members of the CPSU than were respondents in surveys of mass publics. In the 1995 and 1999 mass samples, 13 percent of the respondents (17 percent in the 1993 survey) said they had been members of the CPSU. Somewhat fewer than a quarter of the university attendees in the national sample in the 1995 and 1999 surveys (23 and 21 percent respectively) said they had been a member of the Party. (In 1993 the reported figure was 31 percent.) Nearly three-quarters in the three elite surveys (74 percent in 1995 and 1999; 70 percent in the 1993 elite survey) indicated they had been members of the Party and nearly a fifth (19 percent) of the elite respondents said they had held positions as a *raion* (district) secretary or higher in the Party apparatus.

It would be easy to imagine that persons in the former Soviet Union might be reluctant to acknowledge membership in the former CPSU, especially if they occupied elite positions in Russia in the 1990s. There was some indication, though, that a fairly good number of former Soviet citizens answer questions about their prior Party membership truthfully. Brian P. Silver has reported the results of panel surveys conducted in Estonia in 1979 and 1991—by 1991 it was no longer fashionable to have been a communist in the Soviet Union, most especially in Estonia.[15] It turned out that almost everyone (94 percent) of those who had said in 1979 that they were members of the Party again said in 1991 that they had been or were currently a member of the Communist Party of the Soviet Union. In like fashion, of those who said in 1979 that they were not members of the CPSU, 94 percent stated in 1991 that they had never been nor were they currently members of the Party. Moreover, in the three elite surveys nearly all the officers interviewed reported they had been CPSU members. All those born before 1950 indicated they had been members of the Party.

The Attentive Public

Beginning with Gabriel Almond, scholars have assumed that it makes sense analytically to distinguish between those among the citizenry who were most "informed and interested"[16] in politics and those who were not "plugged in" to the world outside their immediate milieu. It is to the informed and interested that elite messages are primarily targeted. These are the people who are most likely to serve as observers of intra-elite disputes.

To those who have thought about mass publics and foreign policy anywhere, it will not come as news that observers have taken multiple paths in constructing indicators of those who are politically aware. There are many pitfalls regardless of the direction the researcher takes. One might, as Almond did in 1950, simply define those with university education as the attentive public. Another tack has been to take at face value respondents' assertions that they were very interested in politics. A third is to focus on respondents' knowledge about the world around them.

Probably the simplest approach taken in distinguishing among levels of awareness in surveys of mass publics has been to distinguish between those with university education and those without. It represented a reasonable approximation of those to whom elite messages were primarily targeted in the United States at mid-century when Almond wrote *The American People and Foreign Policy* or in the 1960s when Philip Converse wrote his classic papers.[17] It is of far less relevance for the United States at the begin-

---

[15] Brian P. Silver, "Evaluating Survey Data from the Former Soviet Union," Manuscript, George Washington University, Washington, D.C., 1992.

[16] Almond, *The American People*, p. 138.

[17] See, especially, Converse, "The Nature of Belief Systems."

ning of the twenty-first century, given the proportion of persons pursuing higher education.

The proportion of university attendees in Russia in the decade after the formation of the Russian Federation was more like that of the United States after World War II than the United States currently. In that respect one might feel comfortable in using university attendance as an indicator of political awareness. Nevertheless, choosing to use education as an indicator of awareness, even for Russia in the 1990s, remains problematic. University attendance in Russia covers a multitude of experiences, from correspondence courses to training in world-class programs. There is scarcely any doubt that university attendance and knowledge about politics correlate. Nevertheless, sizable numbers of persons reporting university attendance do not know obvious facts concerning the outside world, do not profess a strong interest in politics, and do not report behaviors indicative of an interest in politics such as regular reading of newspapers.[18]

Another conventional way to approach the identification of an attentive public has been to ascertain respondents' reported interest in politics. The surveys of mass publics on which this book is based followed conventional practice in asking respondents to tell the interviewer whether they were interested in politics. I share the unease of John Zaller about using self-reported interest in politics inasmuch as such reports may themselves be highly context dependent, but I have used it when, as in the case of the 1999 survey, the items used in ascertaining factual knowledge about the outside world were unavailable.[19] In this book I have elected to emphasize the role of factual knowledge about the outside world. Like Zaller, my preference has been to define the attentive public as those who know a good deal about the world of politics.

To measure knowledge of the world outside Russia, I combined three indicators. I asked respondents to link five leaders with their respective countries: the United States, Great Britain, Germany, France, and Spain. Responses were divided into those that got two or fewer right, those that got three or four right, and those that got them all right.[20] In addition

---

[18] The correlation between university attendance and interest in politics in the 1995 survey was a rather weak Pearson $r = .18$ ($p < .001$), while university attendance and knowledge of foreign events was a more robust $r = .32$, $p < .001$.

[19] John Zaller, "Political Awareness, Elite Opinion Leadership, and the Mass Survey Response," *Social Cognition* 8 (1990): 25–53.

[20] In addition, respondents were asked about "William Zimmerman." Less than 11 percent in the 1993 European Russia survey and fewer than 9 percent in the 1995 nationwide survey associated him with any country. The fact that overwhelmingly Russian respondents said they did not know or refused to hazard a guess as to my identity was an important indicator of the internal validity of the surveys and the seriousness with which respondents answered questions.

respondents were asked whether they had ever heard of the International Monetary Fund and, if so, whether Russia was a member. If they answered yes, they were then asked when Russia had become a member. Distinctions were made between those who had never heard of the IMF or who said Russia was not a member, those who thought Russia a member but were unable to date its membership approximately, and those who knew that Russia had become a member in the 1990s. Likewise, respondents were asked whether "at this time Crimea [was] a part of Russia, part of Ukraine, or of neither" and, if they knew Crimea belonged to Ukraine, when this had occurred. (In pretests we noticed that Russians often answered something to the effect that "it belongs to Ukraine but it should be Russia's." We inserted "at this time" to minimize the probability that Russians would say what they wished was the case rather than what was the case.) Again the responses were trichotomized, this time into those who did not know Crimea belonged to Ukraine, those who said Crimea belonged to Ukraine but who had basically no idea when Crimea had become a part of Ukraine (1954), and those who placed this occurrence in the 1950s or said it had happened "during [Nikita] Khrushchev's time." This resulted in a simple additive measure that allowed me to distinguish among levels of awareness about the world outside Russia. I have used it in this book in analyzing both the 1993 and the 1995 mass surveys.

As reference again to table 1.1 reveals, this measure covaries nicely with indicators of awareness in the sense of media attention. Those defined as attentive publics by virtue of their knowledge of the outside world are also more attentive in their use of foreign and domestic radio, television, and newspapers as ways of learning about the domestic and international events than are others in the mass public. They are also more likely to talk about politics with friends and family.

Moreover, such measures have the advantage of being objective and the potential of being less influenced by context than self-reported interest, especially for surveys conducted against the backdrop of national elections. But such measures are not context free: exactly how independent measures of knowledge are of contextual effects depends on the questions used in constructing the measure.

Differences in Russia between 1993 and 1995 and the salience of some knowledge about the world outside Russia seem to have affected the relative ability of the 1993 and 1995 respondents to answer the factual questions. Respondents in the 1995 national sample performed less well in answering all three items than did their counterparts in European Russia in 1993. They did particularly poorly in comparison with the 1993 sample in their answers to the IMF and Crimea questions—items most open to the charge of contextual contamination. They did best, relatively speaking, in their ability to identify the five Western leaders, though even here there was a weak but statistically significant difference across the two data sets.

The consequence of this is that, as table 1.2 indicates, the proportion of those in the attentive public in the 1993 and 1995 surveys differs. In the 1993 survey almost 22 percent of the respondents are coded that way, while only 11 percent of the 1995 survey are considered to be the attentive public. The alternatives were less attractive. To set the threshold lower was to render the distinction between the attentive public and others fundamentally meaningless. In statistical terms those who received 7, 8, or 9 in the combined score were about one and a half or more standard deviations from the mean. Those who received a 6 were only three-quarters of a standard deviation from the mean. Substantively, drawing the line at those who scored a 7, 8, or 9 usually meant that the respondent had demonstrated that he or she knew all five Western leaders and knew that Russia was a member of the IMF and that Crimea belonged to Ukraine. This seems a reasonable standard and one below which it would be difficult to maintain that the person should be included among the internationally aware. Many 1993 respondents also knew when Russia had become a member of the IMF and/or that Crimea belonged to Ukraine, something an aware Russian was much more likely to know in 1993, only two years after Russia had joined the IMF and at a time when the issue of Crimea was front-page news, than in 1995. Such knowledge was less likely to be expected of an aware Russian in 1995. It does seem reasonable to define an aware Russian in 1995 as someone who could link Western leaders with their respective countries and who knew Crimea belonged to Ukraine and that Russia was a member of the IMF, with such people occasionally being coded in that way if they knew roughly when Russia had joined the IMF or when Crimea had become part of Ukraine and only connected four of five Western leaders with their respective country.

The Public at Large

Should we concern ourselves with the public at large? The literature on the role of mass publics in American foreign policy is divided. Students of American public opinion will recall that the traditional perspective on mass publics was that they were ill informed, their views were highly volatile, and their role in public opinion was counterproductive to rational policy formation.[21] Holsti, in his survey of the Almond-Lippmann consen-

[21] Walter Lippmann, *Public Opinion* (New York: Macmillan, 1922); Almond, *The American People*; Kennan, *American Diplomacy*. For detailed commentary on the shifting American consensus, see Holsti, "Public Opinion."

Table 1.2.
Distribution of Respondents by Knowledge of World outside Russia,
1993 and 1995

	Standard Deviations from Mean	*1993 European Russia*	*1995/96 Russian Panel*	*Total*
Completely unaware (all "don't knows"or wrong)	−1.32	14% (174)	21.3% (588)	19% (762)
Unaware	−.63	19.5% (242)	25.6% (707)	23.7% (949)
Moderately unaware	.06	25.3% (314)	25.9% (716)	25.7% (1030)
Moderately aware	.75	19.3% (240)	16.2% (448)	17.2% (688)
	1.44	11.9% (148)	8.3% (230)	9.4% (378)
Attentive public	2.13	5.7% (71)	2.2% (61)	3.3% (132)
	2.82	4.3% (54)	.5% (13)	1.7% (67)
Total		100% (1243)	100% (2763)	100% (4006)

Sources: The 1993 data derive from a survey of European Russia conducted by ROMIR. The 1995 data were based on survey drawn from a national sample and conducted by Demoscope.

Note: Actual number of respondents for particular cells shown in parentheses.

Items used to indicate knowledge of world outside Russia:
Now, I'll read you the names of several political figures. Tell me, please, which country do they represent?

    François Mitterrand [Jacques Chirac]
    John Major
    Juan Carlos II
    George Bush [Bill Clinton]
    William Zimmerman (not included in measure)
    Helmut Kohl

Have you heard of the International Monetary Fund [IMF]?
    [If yes] Is Russia a member of the IMF?
    [If yes] In what year did Russia become a member of the IMF?

Of which state is the Crimea at this moment a part? Is it part of Russia, part of Ukraine, or neither?
    [If Ukraine] Do you know, even approximately, in what year Crimea became part of Ukraine?

sus, reminds us that Bernard Cohen was just one of many students of American foreign policy in the 1970s who argued that the reason we should not let this finding be of concern was that at the end of the day, presidents could do more or less whatever they wanted in foreign policy and hence the role of public opinion was quite limited.[22]

In the 1990s, by contrast, the scholarly reading on public opinion and foreign policy altered substantially. A strong strand of scholarship began to emphasize the impact of public opinion in American foreign policy.[23] Although it may be the economy that often drives the selection of the president, it is also the case that in the United States a major component of the answer to the question "Is the incumbent doing a good job?"—the sort of general-will question that Rousseau thought most suitably addressed by mass publics—has frequently turned on evaluations by the public of its leaders' foreign policy performance.

Beyond this, there have been several correlational studies showing a generally strong association between public preferences and policies, most notably in the realm of foreign policy. Perhaps most compellingly in this regard, Thomas Graham's intensive study of four arms control cases constitutes the most plausible argument that the correlations others had observed were not spurious.[24] As Holsti reports, Graham concludes that "public opinion had an important impact on decisions at all stages of the policy process, from getting on the agenda, through negotiation, ratification, and implementation."[25] As a result, there is less reason at the beginning of the twenty-first century than there was three decades ago to harbor the suspicion that public opinion is extraneous to the foreign policy process in well-established democracies like the United States.

The good news this time is that, parallel to these studies, there has been a proliferation of studies, noted in the introduction, showing that mass publics in the aggregate evidence more or less rational dispositions toward foreign policy. No one disputes the proposition that American mass publics are often woefully ignorant of basic facts about the world outside the United States.[26] Nevertheless, a sizable body of literature now emphasizes

[22] Holsti, "Public Opinion," p. 444.

[23] Ibid., p. 452; Graham, "The Politics of Failure." On the link between public opinion and military spending in the United States, see Knopf, "How Rational Is," p. 549; Larry Bartels, "Constituency Opinion and Congressional Policy Making: The Reagan Defense Buildup," *American Political Science Review* 85, no. 2 (June 1991): 457–74; Thomas Hartley and Bruce Russett, "Public Opinion and the Common Defense: Who Governs Military Spending in the United States," *American Political Science Review* 86, no. 4 (December 1992): 905–915.

[24] Graham, "The Politics of Failure."

[25] Holsti, "Public Opinion," p. 454.

[26] For an inventory, see Michael X. Delli Carpini and Scott Keeter, *What Americans Know about Politics and Why It Matters* (New Haven: Yale University Press, 1996), esp. chap. 2.

that mass publics do seem to have some rough and ready way of assessing events that permits them in the aggregate to make sense out of a complicated world, thus compensating for their meager knowledge of events and for the relatively inchoate structure of their belief systems in comparison to those of elites.

The role of mass publics in Russian foreign policy is an empirical question. Viewed in a broad perspective, a profound change in the role of mass publics overall took place first in the last decade of Soviet power and subsequently in the post-Soviet Russian Federation. To write about what is now ancient history, it is clear that after Stalin Soviet leaders acted with some consideration in mind of the *reactive* mood of the Soviet public. It certainly made sense in assessing the post-Stalin Soviet period to pay attention to *The Domestic Context of Soviet Foreign Policy*[27]—to use the title of the first major book-length study (published only in 1981) on that topic. By and large, however, while Soviet legitimacy increasingly turned on policy successes, the Soviet leaders' accountability, as Alexander Dallin remarked at the time, remained to a narrow selectorate—a "circumscribed elite rather than a mass public."[28] Only with the initiation of genuinely competitive elections, with the empowerment of previously meaningless institutions such as the Supreme Soviet, with the emergence of a relatively open press, with the activization of the nationality movements, and with the rehabilitation of empirical survey research in the late 1980s could one talk meaningful of mass publics playing a *proactive* role in the policy process.

That transformation of mass politics has been one of the truly salient features of the shift from Soviet to post-Soviet Russian politics. To Mikhail Gorbachev's everlasting credit, he consciously encouraged the development of authentic participation by breathing life into those institutions, such as the Supreme Soviet, that had been moribund throughout the Soviet period. He also acquiesced in the emergence of the autonomous political actors—interest associations, *neformaly* (the informals), political movements, and the like—characteristic of civil society in modern, nonauthoritarian states.

Inasmuch as his actions ultimately resulted in the demise of the state of which he was the president, it would have to be said that he succeeded. The burgeoning of authentic participation during the Gorbachev era changed the internal political situation radically. New players emerged. Attention to public opinion grew rapidly; newspapers such as *Moskovskie novosti* began regularly to report the results of surveys, including those

[27] Seweryn Bialer, ed., *The Domestic Context of Soviet Foreign Policy* (Boulder: Westview, 1981).
[28] Ibid., 351.

dealing with foreign policy. Public opinion now mattered and the leadership recognized this fact.

This condition persisted in the early years of post-Soviet Russia. However successful the institutionalization of democracy in Russia was at the start of the twenty-first century, it is exceedingly unlikely that the phenomenon of active mass participation in politics could be completely reversed. Policy makers will have to grow accustomed to operating in a new environment, even in an area like foreign policy where it has often been maintained that the role of mass publics and their opinions is limited in thoroughly institutionalized pluralist systems such as the United States or Great Britain. V. A. Savel'ev, in 1993 the director of the Ministry of Foreign Affairs' Bureau [Upravlenie] for Ties with the [now defunct] Supreme Soviet, had it right when he observed that "with the development of democratic processes, with the growing role of public opinion in international affairs, diplomats today have a wider spectrum of obligations: in explaining policy, they have to deal with the legislative organs, with parties, with authorities at various levels (from local to republic), with society in general, with the press, radio, and television."[29] Or, as the chief of the Information and Press Department of the Foreign Ministry, G. P. Tarasov, said in 1997, "The implementation of foreign policy is inconceivable without understanding and conscious support from public opinion."[30]

What is going to be at issue concerning mass publics in post-Soviet Russia is not whether they play a role. Rather we are likely to witness in a more compressed time frame a dialogue that bears a striking resemblance to that which has taken place about American foreign policy over the last half century.

For the present, the actual role of mass publics in the foreign policy process remains problematic. Our knowledge about the concrete impact of mass publics on Russian foreign policy remains limited. Until someone does studies of the links between mass attitudes and actual Russian foreign policy decision making comparable to Graham's studies of American foreign policy, students of Russian foreign policy will be in the same boat students of American foreign policy in the 1980s found themselves in.

Absent such studies, we can nevertheless assert confidently that in any event, the role of general and attentive publics in Russian foreign policy will be greater than it was for virtually all the Soviet period—with the possible exception of the last five years of Soviet power—and, literally, infinitely more than the neglible role Almond accorded Soviet publics in 1950. We have the direct testimony of Savel'ev that the democratization

---

[29] V.A. Savel'ev, *Diplomaticheskii vestnik,* nos. 9/10 (May 1993), at p. 57.
[30] *Rossiiskaia gazeta,* June 10, 1997, as cited in FBIS-SOV-97–163.

of Russia has meant that public opinion has become a force to be reckoned with by the Foreign Ministry: "Without analysis and forecasts of new forces and factors [brought on by the emergence of civil society], in many cases an effective foreign policy may become impossible."[31]

It is, though, a kind of backhanded recognition, rather reminiscent of Walter Lippmann's lament that "the unhappy truth is that the prevailing public opinion has been destructively wrong at the critical junctures."[32] Just as the Almond-Lippmann consensus bemoaned the "instability of mass moods, the cyclical fluctuations which stand in the way of policy stability"[33] in American foreign policy, Savel'ev worries that "chaotic" shifts in domestic policies can " 'leap over' into foreign policy as well."[34] Public opinion is in this vision something to be led and shaped, not something to be followed: "Operating on a knowledge of the attitudes and dispositions of forces on 'the internal front,' the government will be able to act externally with more freedom and greater maneuverability."[35] This view of mass publics in the foreign policy process parallels almost exactly Bernard Cohen's 1973 observation that State Department officials, when they thought at all about the public, viewed it as something to be " 'educated.' "[36]

Whether Savel'ev's view of the role of public opinion in Russian foreign policy is correct remains to be determined. Anecdotal evidence suggests it to have been a somewhat more active factor in the last years of the Soviet Union and in the Russian Federation's first decade, though still less than in the United States. An attention to public opinion was important in the implementation of Gorbachev's new thinking during the very last years of the Soviet period. We know that survey results made available to the staff of former Minister of Foreign Affairs Eduard Shevardnadze, which indicated the absence of substantial domestic opposition to the pullback from Eastern Europe or even to the unification of Germany, contributed substantially to the Soviet leadership's crucial determination to withdraw from the center of Europe.[37]

An interesting indication that the masses were important players in the Russian policy process in the first decade after the collapse of the Soviet Union was contained in a long and important 1994 article by Emil' Pain,

[31] Savel'ev, *Diplomaticheskii vestnik*, p. 56.
[32] As cited in Holsti, "Public Opinion," p. 442.
[33] Almond, *The American People*, p. 239.
[34] Savel'ev, *Diplomaticheskii vestnik*, p. 56.
[35] Ibid.
[36] Holsti, "Public Opinion," p. 444.
[37] William Zimmerman, "Intergenerational Differences in Attitudes toward Foreign Policy," in Arthur Miller et al., *Public Opinion and Regime Change* (Boulder: Westview, 1993), pp. 259–70 at pp. 267–68.

at that time a member of the Presidential Council and director of the research section of the Analytic Center attached to the President of the Russian Federation. Pain's concern was with the possibility of reconstituting the former Soviet Union. Drawing heavily on survey data, he found that, while there was considerable nostalgia for the old Soviet Union, citizens of Russia reacted extremely negatively to the idea of using Russian armed forces to bring such an occurrence about. In an election, he contended, a majority would back a "supporter of the independent development of Russia" whereas only a quarter would support a candidate endorsing "the creation [*vossozdanie*] of the [Soviet] Union." This, in his view, was a major part of the reason why "the reintegration of the republics of the USSR" was not a live option: "There aren't the necessary resources— the political will of the leadership, the psychological preparedness of the population—for its realization in Russia."[38]

The surveys on which this book is largely based provide mixed evidence about the role of mass publics in the foreign policy process. Chapter 4 develops a strong argument that views about Russia's relations to the outside world correlate well with orientation to the political system—which in turn predicted on almost a one-to-one basis how persons voted in the July 1996 presidential election. Unless one believes there to be absolutely no relationship to policy preferences expressed before an election and behavior once in office, mass publics clearly influenced the direction, in broad outlines, that Russian foreign policy would take after the 1996 Yeltsin–Ziuganov contest by choosing to vote for Yeltsin and against the more anti-Western, confrontational Ziuganov.

At the same time, it should be stressed that Savel'ev was not alone; the elite participants in the 1995 and 1999 surveys did not attach a great role in the making of foreign policy to mass publics. Elites were asked to characterize the relative influence of various sectors of society and institutions in the making of foreign policy. These were public opinion, the regional leaders, the Duma, the Ministry of Defense, the business community, the Ministry of Foreign Affairs, and the president. The elites' assessment was that public opinion played a modest role indeed, as table 1.3 reveals. In their judgment, the president, the Foreign Ministry, and the Ministry of Defense (in that order) counted most, and public opinion (in both 1995 and 1999) and regional leaders (in 1995) mattered least.

What may have given public opinion a somewhat greater role in the mid-1990s than the perceptions of foreign policy elites might suggest, though, is that in 1995 it was seen by these same elites as occupying an intermediate position on at least one key dimension concerning Russia's foreign policy between the Ministry of Defense and the Duma, on the one

---

[38] *Segodnia* (July 22, 1994).

Table 1.3.
Elite Perceptions of Influence of Various Players in Russian Foreign Policy,
1995–1999 (level of influence: 1, lowest; 7, highest)

	Perceived Influence: Mean (S.E.)	
	1995	*1999*
President	6.16 (.10)	5.70 (.11)
Ministry of Foreign Affairs	5.06 (.13)	5.28 (.10)
Ministry of Defense	4.43 (.12)	4.59 (.10)
Business elite	4.19 (.11)	4.55 (.11)
Duma	3.45 (.10)	3.90 (.08)
Regional leaders	3.25 (.10)	4.10 (.09)
Public opinion	2.94 (.12)	3.01 (.09)

Sources: As in table 1.1.
Question wording:
I am going to show you a list of organizations, institutions, and individuals; tell me to
what degree they can influence current foreign policy. . . . In this instance, 1 will mean little
influence and 7 the most influence.

hand, and the president and the Ministry of Foreign Affairs, on the other.
In the 1995 survey, elites were asked to position the sectors enumerated
in the previous paragraph along a seven-point continuum ranging from
extremely isolationist to extremely internationalist. In quarrels between
the go-it-alone dispositions of the regional leaders, the Ministry of Defense, and the Duma, on the one hand, and the markedly more internationalist business community, the president, and the Ministry of Foreign
Affairs (table 1.4), on the other, the public was situated exactly in the
middle.[39] This would have permitted them to play a role akin to the swing
voter in determining the outcome of political struggles.[40] This becomes a
particularly interesting speculation when we examine the perceived internationalism scores reported in 1999. The business elites and the Ministry
of Foreign Affairs were still seen as being the most internationalist of the
players, though they were perceived in 1999 as being less internationalist

[39] A less optimistic view of this finding would be that elites were in effect stating that they
thought mass publics had no views. Even on that reading, mass publics might still be available for mobilization by elites that do.
[40] My former research assistant Bear Braumoeller, first noticed this result in analyzing the
data for his dissertation," Isolationism in International Relations.

Table 1.4.
Perceived Internationalism of Various Players in Russian Foreign Policy,
1995–1999 (level of internationalism: 1, lowest; 7, highest)

	Perceived Internationalism: Mean (S.E.)	
	1995	*1999*
Ministry of Foreign Affairs	5.21 (.13)	4.72 (.09)
President	4.65 (.12)	3.76 (.13)
Business elite	4.58 (.15)	4.37 (.14)
Public opinion	4.05 (.10)	4.19 (.09)
Duma	3.69 (.11)	3.79 (.10)
Ministry of Defense	3.50 (.13)	3.47 (.10)
Regional Leaders	3.30 (.12)	3.21 (.10)

Source: As in table1.1.

Question wording:

I am going to show you a list of various organizations, institutions, and individuals. On a scale of 1 to 7, tell me, please, where you would locate each [of them]? In this instance, 1 would signify a strongly isolationist orientation and 7 a strongly internationalist orientation.

then than they had been in 1995. The regional leaders, the Ministry of Defense, the Duma, and public opinion not only were ranked in the same order they were in 1995 but were positioned in about the same places on the 1 to 7 scale. The major change was in the perception of the president, who was seen to be far more isolationist in 1999 than he was perceived to be in 1995, the result being that he was in 1999 viewed by elites as being statistically indistinguishable from the Duma. If the foreign policy elites' perceptions are correct, one would have to think Yeltsin's shift was prompted at least in part by a regard for the political mood in the country as expressed both in the Duma and in public opinion.

In sum, we know that Russian elites, the Ministry of Foreign Affairs, and staff people in the office of the president view mass publics as setting limits on what can be done. We know, too, that elections matter in the Russian Federation and, as we shall see below, that such elections can turn importantly on mass orientations to Russia's role in the world, as they did in 1996. What we do not know is how mass opinion affects concrete specific decisions. The study of American foreign policy suffered from that weakness for years. And yet it developed in important ways during the period beginning with the publication of Almond's *American People and Foreign Policy* and extending up to the 1980s, the years that Holsti associates with the initial challenges to the Almond-Lippmann analysis. We could in good conscience examine mass attitudes in a detailed fashion, knowing full well that they should be viewed as something with which leaders must at a minimum deal, even if we were content with leaving to future research the question of the magnitude of that impact. One of the goals of chapters 3 and 4, however, is to move some way in the direction of assessing the impact of mass publics on policy outcomes. These chapters analyze, respectively, the extent to which mass responses to policy questions cohere sufficiently as to be thought of as attitudes, the relevance of mass views about the international system to electoral preferences, and the circumstances when elites encounter resistance to their preferences and are not able even to influence attentive or knowledgeable publics, much less reach that part of the mass public that is fundamentally unaware of elite preferences.

Elites, attentive publics, mass publics: these are the conventional actors in the drama of foreign policy making in open political systems everywhere. They are the actors in the drama of Russian foreign policy making as well. The next chapter examines the differences among mass publics, attentive publics, and elites in their orientations to the new post-Soviet Russian political economy. As it turns out, these differences are often huge. Part of the task of that chapter is to assess why this is so and to enter some judgments as to how these differences influence the prospects for democracy and markets in Russia. Subsequent chapters examine the interactions among these three analytical groupings. When do publics take cues from elites and when are they nonresponsive? When the latter occurs, what consequences does this have for elite orientations? This in turn leads us to explore how orientations to Russia's political economy among elites and mass publics bear on Russia's relations with the outside world and what impact Russia's foreign policy will have on its prospects for democracy and marketization.

2

Politics and Markets

with Judith Kullberg

As a result of the collapse of the Soviet Union and of Soviet power, we are witnessing a social transformation of potentially enormous significance. In starkest terms, Russia is deciding whether it will have a broadly market or a broadly statist economy and whether its political system will be democratic or authoritarian. A thorough exploration of this topic would entail a book-length treatment.[1] What this chapter does is provide evidence, drawn largely from the surveys described in the introduction, that sheds some light on the likely outcome of these processes. While my overall assessment of the prospects for democracy in the short term is guarded, the data in hand do allow us to gain some purchase on factors that are relevant to the larger task of evaluating the long-term prospects for the marketization and democratization of the Russian Federation. Doing so allows us to consider, and reject, some key notions that are relevant to that task. Among these are the following: Is it true that Russians and Westerners do not have a common understanding of democracy? Who are the supporters, and who the opponents, of markets and democracy? What are the predictors of favorable orientation—how crucial is the disparate structure of opportunities and differential access to information for Russians' orientations to the political economy? How substantial is the support for markets and democracy? Is support a mile wide and an inch deep?[2] Is it opportunistic and contextual[3]—in particular, does the desire

---

[1] Among book-length treatments, see Andrei Mel'vil', *Demokraticheskie tranzity: Teoretiko-metodologicheskie i prikladnye aspekty* (Moscow: Moskovskii obshchestvennyi nauchnyi fond, 1999); Colton; *Transitional Citizens*; Michael McFaul and Sergei Markov, *The Troubled Path of Russian Democracy* (Stanford: Hoover Institution Press, 1993); McFaul, *Russia's Troubled Transition from Communism to Democracy: Institutional Change during Revolutionary Transformations* (Ithaca, N.Y.: Cornell University Press, 2001); Timothy J. Colton and Jerry F. Hough, eds. *Growing Pains: Russian Democracy and the Election of 1993* (Washington, D.C.: Brookings Institution Press, 1998); Stephen White et al., *How Russia Votes* (Chatham, N.J.: Chatham House Publishers, 1997).

[2] For part of a continuing conversation in this vein see Gibson, "A Mile Wide but an Inch Deep (?)."

[3] A recurrent theme concerning "First" President Boris Yeltsin in David Remnick, *Resurrection: The Struggle for New Russia* (New York: Random House, 1997).

for order dominate the enthusiasm for democracy? Does support reflect, instead, fundamental changes in elite and mass preferences that are a component of a cultural shift?[4]

Russian Conceptions of Democracy

Russians, the mass media sometimes alleges, do not even have the same understanding of democracy as do Westerners. Whether such is or is not the case is an empirical question. In a 1996 national omnibus survey of 1049 respondents conducted by ROMIR and in the November 1995 and November 1999 surveys of Russian foreign policy elites, Russians were told that "democracy is interpreted differently by various people" and then presented with ten statements and asked to identify those that corresponded to, almost corresponded to, were far from, and totally did not correspond to, their understanding of the concept of democracy. The ten were:

> A country's leaders are chosen in free elections.
> Competition for power exists among various political parties.
> The state does not intervene in the economy.
> People conduct themselves responsibly so that the government can operate effectively.
> People have the right to express themselves freely, even if they sharply criticize the government.
> Workers themselves decide where they work.
> People, if they wish, can participate in any organization.
> A country's leaders act in correspondence with the wishes of the people.
> The people themselves make decisions.
> Citizens have both rights as well as duties.[5]

Survey items that take the form above—where respondents are not presented with choices (Some people think that. . . . Others say. . . . What do you think?)—often engender affirmative-set response; that is, respondents

---

[4] On culture shift, see Ronald Inglehart, *The Silent Revolution* (Princeton: Princeton University Press, 1990).

[5] These items were generated in conversations with Lowell Barrington and are related to those used by Robert Putnam, *The Beliefs of Politicians* (New Haven: Yale University Press, 1973), to explore the differing conceptions of British and Italian politicians (including, in the latter case, Communists). "The rights and duties" question was an attempt, largely unsuccessful, to capture the rights-*and*-duties flavor of Soviet constitutions. Not only did Russians not divide systematically on this item as I had hypothesized, but a distinguished American Russian specialist reviewer of this manuscript asked "Aren't they all rights-and-duties constitutions?"

agree far more often than they would if presented with choices. Doubtless there is some of that in this instance, given the largely positive impression each of the ten items conveys. We should therefore be particularly cautious in attaching significance to the absolute proportions of the responses given by those interviewed.

The likely affirmative set response to these items does not, however, preclude our differentiating between those items virtually all Russians associate with the conception of democracy and those that far fewer respondents connect with it. The range of responses across the ten items was considerable and the items do not uniformly covary.

Among elites (table 2.1), competitive elections ("A country's leaders are chosen in free elections"), competition among parties ("Competition for power exists among various political parties"), free speech ("People have the right to express themselves freely, even if they sharply criticize the government"), the ability to choose one's place of work, and the right to join any organization were all characterized by more than 90 percent of the elite respondents in 1995 as corresponding to their conception of democracy, as was the proposition that citizens have both rights and duties.

A slight drop was noticed in the elite responses favoring all these items in 1999. Nevertheless, with the exception of the right to participate in organizations—which in 1999 was characterized by 79 percent of the elite respondents as meshing with their conception of democracy—more than 85 percent of those elites interviewed said that competitive elections, competition by parties for power, free speech, the right of workers to choose their place of work, and citizens' having both rights and duties corresponded to their conception of democracy.

What they least associated with democracy among the items listed were the classical liberal conception of state nonintervention in the economy and the Rousseauian conception of democracy as a system where "the people themselves make decisions" (table 2.1).

What about mass publics? With a couple of exceptions, elite and mass conceptions were basically congruent. The mass publics' response was overwhelmingly favorable to four propositions. Roughly 90 percent of the mass sample interviewed by ROMIR in 1996 stated that free elections, party competition for power, free speech, and the right to participate in any organization were propositions that corresponded or almost corresponded to their conception of democracy (table 2.1). Similarly, 80 percent or more of the respondents in the 1996 mass survey associated the individual worker's right to decide where to work and the proposition that citizens have both rights and duties with their concept of democracy. Fewer than a third indicated that the statement "The state does not intervene in the economy" either corresponded or almost corresponded to their

Table 2.1.
Conceptions of Democracy among Mass Publics in 1996 and Foreign Policy Elites
in 1995 and 1999

Statements	Mass 1996 ROMIR Omnibus Survey[a]	Elites	
		1995	1999
Democracy means that[b]			
A country's leaders are chosen in free elections.	87% (869)	95% (169)	87% (182)
Competition for power exists among various political parties.	89% (861)	94% (169)	87% (181)
The state does not intervene in the economy.	28% (251)	34% (60)	23% (48)
People conduct themselves responsibly so that the government can operate effectively.	62% (559)	74% (126)	71% (143)
People have the right to express themselves freely, even if they sharply criticize the government.	88% (879)	97% (173)	87% (183)
Workers themselves decide where they work.	80% (786)	97% (173)	87% (172)
People, if they wish, can participate in any organization.	92% (893)	91% (161)	79% (162)
A country's leaders act in correspondence with the wishes of the people.	60% (575)	83% (148)	68% (139)
The people themselves make decisions.	50% (478)	50% (86)	43% (86)
Citizens have both rights and duties.	83% (818)	97% (173)	89% (186)

Sources: The mass survey was based on a national sample conducted by ROMIR, which also conducted the two elite surveys.

Note: Actual number of respondents for particular cells shown in parentheses.

[a] Total number of participants in October 1996 mass survey–1049. Elite respondents' total for 1995–180; for 1999–210.

[b] Combines those who said "fully corresponds" and "corresponds."

definition of democracy. Likewise, only half of the mass respondents affirmed that democracy entailed that "the people themselves make decisions." Endorsing an individual's right to decide where to work and recognizing that citizens have both rights and duties may be notions somewhat more likely to be associated with democracy by people with a Soviet past. Nevertheless, the fact that Russian elites and mass publics were virtually unanimous in associating free elections, competition for power among political parties, free speech even if sharply critical of the government, and the right to join any organization with their own concept of democracy suggests strongly that Russian elites and mass publics do have an understanding of democracy commensurable with that of their Western counterparts. They may attach different weights to particular rights, but they have comparable conceptions of democracy.[6] Perhaps the most noteworthy elite and mass response divergence in the mid-1990s concerned the observation that "a country's leader act in correspondence with the wishes of the people." More than four of five elite respondents in 1995 associated governmental responsiveness with their conception of democracy, whereas only three in five among the mass respondents did. In 1999 the number of elite respondents associating governmental responsiveness with democracy had dropped to 68 percent (table 2.1). A plausible construction of these figures is that elites were slower in recognizing the actual lack of responsiveness by the Russian government than were those with less attractive opportunity structures, many of whom had experienced diminished state capacity on a first-hand basis.

[6] Paul Goble reports high percentages in a VTsIOM survey of respondents defining democracy as a "system of government that provides rights for all," "having the opportunity to influence the government in the interests of the people," "the right to choose leaders in free elections," and a system where there are "opportunities for expressing one's own opinion and criticizing the authorities." But, Goble continues, when they are asked what human rights are "most important," Russians give responses indicating that they largely respond by referring to social welfare rights: free education, medical care, and old-age support. "Entitlements, Rights, and Democracy," www.rferl.org/newsline, October 4, 1999.

In the Colton-McFaul survey conducted after the March 2000 presidential election, respondents were shown a battery of items and asked whether each of them was "a necessary sign" of democracy. More than 90 percent of those who responded identified free speech ("People have the right to say what they think), and "The leaders are freely elected" as necessary signs, while 89 percent said "There is a real leader." Intriguingly, such was also the case in regard to the statement "There is a strong army." (Evidently, we did not all lose the cold war.) "People fear the authorities" received a positive endorsement by 16 percent of those who answered, while 29 percent said that "The courts are subordinated to the authorities" was an attribute of democracy. Large numbers (89 percent) agreed that a necessary sign is that "The state provides good schools, health care, and pensions." Perhaps most relevant for the point at issue here is that Russians divided almost evenly, 55–45, between those who agree and disagree that "there are no big differences in income among people"—far less than those who associate free speech and free election of leaders with democracy.

Table 2.2.
Common Statements about Democracies

Country (Year)	Do Little, Talk Much	Poor Economic Performance	Handles Order Poorly
US (95)	42%[a]	26%	24%
Japan (95)	44%	21%	23%
Finland (96)	61%	45%	34%
Switzerland (96)	94%	28%	28%
Sweden (96)	62%	31%	26%
Slovenia (95)	71%	49%	53%
Bulgaria (98)	60%	45%	45%
Hungary (96)	48%	26%	33%
Poland (96)	83%	37%	76%
Ukraine (96)	61%	43%	55%
Russia (95)	78%	60%	71%
Russia (99)[b]	47% (46%)	32% (28%)	54% (48%)

Sources: World Values Surveys and 1999 national survey of Russia conducted by Demoscope.

[a] Percentage agreeing or strongly agreeing.

[b] The 1999 Russian survey presented the respondents with an intermediate option between strongly agreeing and agreeing, on the one hand, and disagreeing and strongly disagreeing, on the other. The figures in parentheses are those for the proportion of respondents agreeing or strongly agreeing divided by the number taking committed positions. The figures outside parentheses are those agreeing or strongly agreeing plus half of those who said they were ambivalent as a percentage of the total number of valid responses.

This difference notwithstanding, Russian elites and masses converge in most of their core understandings of what democracy entails. These convergent views generally parallel common Western understandings of democracy. For Russian elites and mass publics, democracy primarily calls to mind contestation, participation, free speech, and individual control of work-location decisions. Evidently the notion that Russians, ordinary and otherwise, and Westerners do not even speak a common language does not withstand serious scrutiny.

This is borne out by comparisons of four observations pertaining to the conception of democracy presented to respondents in the December 1999 post-parliamentary election survey. One of these called for Russian citizens to assess whether they thought that democracy better offered citizens "opportunities for controlling their leaders than nondemocratic systems." Three-quarters (77 percent) of those who expressed a definite opinion agreed or agreed completely. Three other items were partially factual, partially normative, questions that have been asked as part of the large-scale, comparative World Values Survey.[7] Table 2.2 helps to place Russian responses in a broader context by comparing the assessments of these three assertions in the 1999 Russian survey with a 1995 survey of Russia conducted by ROMIR for Ronald Inglehart and with those from five developed democracies and five European post-communist systems. Russians were asked whether or not they agreed that under democracy "there is little accomplished and too much empty talk," "the economy develops poorly," and "the maintenance of order" is not handled "very well." These observations may be thought of as empirical conceptions of democracy, although they are heavily value laden as well. In comparison with citizens from either other formerly communist European states (other than Poland) or from the developed democracies, Russians in 1995 were more disposed to express agreement with the assertion that there is much talk and little action in a democracy, and much more prone to associate democracy with poor economic performance, than people from either developed democracies or formerly communist European states. Likewise, they were far more likely than persons from developed democracies or formerly communist European states (with the exception of respondents from Poland) to agree with the assertion that "democracy is not very good for the maintenance of order."

By contrast, the proportion of Russians agreeing in 1999 with the assertion that democracies accomplish little and generate much empty talk was about that of respondents from the United States and Japan (and Hungary) and noticeably less than in the other countries in table 2.2. Similarly, Russian responses in the 1999 survey concerning economic performance in democracies were not distinctive in comparison with those of respondents from the other states in table 2.2, whether reference is made to developed democracies or to formerly communist European countries. Where Russian response patterns remained in 1999 quite distinct from those of established democracies was with regard to the notion that democracy and the maintenance of order were incompatible.

The typical Russian responses about democracy and the maintenance of order, however, no longer set them apart from the bulk of responses from other formerly communist European states. In general, though, we can conclude that Russians share with Americans and Europeans some common understanding of the notion of democracy, albeit the responses to the 1999 survey pertaining to order remind us that there is a place for context in assessing mass conceptions of democracy in Russia and elsewhere.

[7] I am indebted to my colleague of many years, Ronald Inglehart, for sharing these data with me.

That observation needs, however, to be qualified in turn, lest readers be lulled into too hopeful an assessment of the prospects for democracy on the basis of the materials presented in this section. There was a fourth assertion concerning democracy included in the battery asked of Russians, which is not so much a conception of democracy as an overall normative claim about democracy that readers will recognize as a survey-research paraphrase of a famous Churchillian *bon mot*. Respondents were asked their reaction to the assertion that "while there can be problems under democracy in any country, nevertheless democracy is better than any other form of rule." The good news and the bad news is that of those taking an explicit position in the 1999 survey, 70 percent (67 percent of the total, apportioning half of the waverers to the agree/strongly agree respondents) agreed or agreed completely that democracy is on balance the best system. The reason this is good news is that in the 1995 Russian component of the World Values Survey only 57 percent agreed. The bad news is that at 70 percent Russia remains at the very bottom of the fifty or so countries surveyed in the World Values Survey during the years 1996–1999.[8]

Identifying the Supporters of Liberal Democracy

If there is a common core to Russian and Western basic concepts about democracy, it becomes possible to make some progress in sorting out the supporters of liberal democracy in Russia in terms understandable to Western readers. For the basic choices facing Russia and other post-communist countries in Europe and Eurasia remain democracy versus authoritarianism and market versus obligatory (as opposed to indicative) state planning. A natural way to think of these issues is to build on Charles Lindblom's categorization of states in *Politics and Markets*.[9] So doing yields a simple but robust two-by-two table, familiar to readers of Lindblom's work, which allows us to identify four basic orientations to the Russian Federation's emerging politicoeconomic system. They are (a) market or liberal democrats, (b) market authoritarians, (c) social or socialist democrats, and (d) socialist authoritarians. With the important qualification (discussed below) that even those classified as liberal democrats in the Russian context

[8] It should be emphasized that truly nondemocratic countries rarely tolerate mass surveys in their respective countries.
[9] Charles Lindblom, *Politics and Markets* (New York: Basic Books, 1977).

are more prone to endorse state ownership of heavy industry than would be the case for citizens in any North American or Western European country, Russian liberal democrats are persons who would be recognizably identified as such in Western contexts and who would endorse many of the core principles of Western liberal democratic thought.[10] Market authoritarians, as the label implies, might be thought of as those who would convert Russia into a Eurasian Singapore or into a Pinochet Chile. Social democrats are those who share much common ground with European social democracy. In another era they would have been members of the Second International, not the Third, Communist, International (Comintern). I have termed persons in the fourth category "socialist authoritarians" primarily for logical consistency but in part to use (relatively) value-neutral terms in referring to them. These are persons whose orientation is fundamentally congruent with traditional Soviet communist orientations to politics and economics. Whether or not they were members of the CPSU under the old regime or are attached to the contemporary Communist Party of the Russian Federation or one of the other current communist parties is in this instance immaterial. These are people who in the Soviet Union would have been recognized as ideological Leninists, though their commitment to (small n) national and (small s) socialism might render them as either right- or left-wing statist authoritarians in contemporary Russian politics.[11]

In our samples, all four logical possibilities concerning individual Russians turned out to be empirical possibilities as well (table 2.3)—unlike Lindblom's categorization of states, which revealed that, as he defined the terms, the cell that combined a statist or planned orientation to the economy and a democratic (polyarchic, in his terms) political system was devoid of cases.

	Democracy	*Authoritarianism*
Market	Liberal democrats	Market authoritarians
State	Social democrats	Socialist authoritarians

[10] J. Roland Pennock, *Democratic Political Theory* (Princeton: Princeton University Press, 1979); Dahl, *On Democracy.*

[11] Donna Bahry, "Comrades into Citizens? Russian Political Culture and Public Support for the Transition," *Slavic Review* 58 (Winter 1999): 841–53, reminds us that "hybrids are the norm rather than the exception" (p. 853). I am painting in broad strokes here. The cells within the typology used herein encompass sizable regime variation. The Japanese and American political economies are quite different, but both are liberal or market democracies. Pinochet's Chile was quite distinct from the regimes of East Asia, but I have no problem in lumping them under the rubric "market authoritarianism."

Table 2.3.
Elite and Mass Orientations to the Political Economy

	Distribution Including All Respondents					
				Mass		
	Elites			European Russia,	Russia,	Russia,
	1993	1995	1999	1993	1995	1999
Liberal democrats	74.0%	72.8%	64.8%	27.4%	21.9%	24.9%
	(148)	(131)	(136)	(341)	(621)	(459)
Market authoritarians	5.0%	5.6%	5.7%	7.2%	5.8%	6.1%
	(10)	(10)	(12)	(89)	(164)	(113)
Social democrats	6.0%	7.8%	9.0%	18.2%	16.7%	18.5%
	(12)	(14)	(19)	(226)	(473)	(340)
Socialist authoritarians	4.5%	3.9%	10.0%	14.8%	13.7%	15.3%
	(9)	(7)	(21)	(184)	(388)	(282)
Ambivalent	7.5%	9.4%	9.5%	16.7%	27.4%	25.8%
	(15)	(17)	(20)	(207)	(779)	(475)
Unmobilized	3.0%	0.6%	1.0%	15.8%	14.6%	9.4%
	(6)	(1)	(2)	(196)	(414)	(173)
Total	100%	100%	100%	100%	100%	100%
	(200)	(180)	(210)	(1243)	(2839)	(1842)

	Distribution Excluding "Ambivalent" and "Unmobilized"					
				Mass		
	Elites			European Russia,	Russia,	Russia,
	1993	1995	1999	1993	1995	1999
Liberal democrats	82.7%	80.9%	72.3%	40.6%	37.7%	38.4%
	(148)	(131)	(136)	(341)	(621)	(459)
Market authoritarians	5.6%	6.2%	6.4%	10.6%	10.0%	9.5%
	(10)	(10)	(12)	(89)	(164)	(113)
Social democrats	6.7%	8.6%	10.1%	26.9%	28.7%	28.5%
	(12)	(14)	(19)	(226)	(473)	(340)
Socialist authoritarians	5.0%	4.3%	11.2%	21.9%	23.6%	23.6%
	(9)	(7)	(21)	(184)	(388)	(282)
Total	100%	100%	100%	100%	100%	100%
	(179)	(162)	(188)	(840)	(1646)	(1194)

Sources: ROMIR conducted the three elite surveys and the 1993 mass survey of European Russia. The 1995 and 1999 surveys were based on national samples and conducted by Demoscope.

Note: Actual number of respondents for particular cells shown in parentheses.

The indicator of orientation to the political system was composed of five items.[12] Construct scores were calculated for all respondents who responded to at least three of the five. Taken together, these items assess the extent of respondents' acceptance of core tenets and practices of liberal democracy—political contestation, the presumption of innocence, the rights of the individual versus society, the free exchange of ideas, and philosophical pluralism. The specific questions were "Competition among various political parties makes our system stronger." "The rights of the individual should be defended even if guilty persons sometimes remain free." "The interests of society should be protected even if innocent people sometimes end up in prison." "In any society it will always be necessary to prohibit the public expression of dangerous ideas." "It is apparent that of all the existing philosophies, there is only one that is clearly correct." The last three items, obviously, were reversed in computing the measure.

Economic orientation was assessed by combining attitudes toward essential features of the market economy: economic competition, private ownership of heavy industry, income inequality, and economic risk. Four items were used in constructing the scale: "Competition among various enterprises, organizations, and firms benefits our society." "All heavy industry should belong to the state and not be in private hands." "It's normal when the owner of a prosperous enterprise, using the labor of his workers, becomes richer than many other people." "There's no sense in beginning a new business inasmuch as it might fail." Scores were calculated for individuals who responded to at least two of the four questions. Once again, as in the indicator of orientation to the political system, two items, the heavy industry ownership and new business questions, were reversed to provide uniform directionality in creating the scale.

For each statement in the three elite surveys and in the 1993 mass survey used to construct the typology, respondents were given four possible response categories ranging from "completely" and "somewhat" agree to somewhat and completely disagree. In the 1995 and 1999 mass surveys, respondents had a fifth, intermediate, choice between agree and disagree, "I hesitate to say [*koleblius'*]." I coded the strongly agrees and disagrees in all surveys as +2 and −2, respectively. The ambivalent position was coded as 0, midway between +2 and −2. In order to make the 1993 and the 1995 and 1999 mass scales roughly comparable, the response categories in the three elite surveys and the 1993 mass survey were adjusted so that "some-

---

[12] In earlier work ("Markets, Democracy, and Russian Foreign Policy," *Post-Soviet Affairs* 10 [April–June 1994]: 107–108, and "Synoptic Thinking and Political Culture in Post-Soviet Russia," *Slavic Review* 54 [Fall 1995]: 637–38), only three questions dealing with individual rights, political competition, and the market place of ideas were used. The use of five items produces somewhat more coherent distinctions between orientation to democracy and to authoritarianism.

what agree" and "somewhat disagree" were .66 and −.66, respectively. This retained equal intervals between all responses within surveys, but to compensate for the absence of a true middle position, weakened the somewhat agree and somewhat disagree responses in questions that had four alternatives.

Placement of respondents was done by aggregating the political and economic liberalism scores. Those persons whose aggregate scores on both the political and the economic dimensions were greater than 0 were treated as liberal democrats; those whose political liberalism score was below 0 and whose economic liberalism score was above 0 were treated as market authoritarians. Those whose political liberalism score was above 0 and whose economic liberalism score was below 0 became social democrats. Those below 0 on both scores were categorized as socialist authoritarians. Respondents with 0 scores on either scale were treated as ambivalent and those for whom scores could not be calculated because of the number of question refusals were termed 'unmobilized.'

I recognize immediately that typologies in general and this one in particular are rather blunt instruments; the chief advantages in this instance are two.[13] First, the typology employed here parsimoniously captures the central choices—plan versus market, democracy versus dictatorship—that have faced decision makers and mass publics in post-communist transitions. Second, empirically it correlates well with the actual system preferences of respondents. Among the mass respondents interviewed in the third wave of the election study in July 1996, more than three-quarters (76 percent) of those categorized as liberal democrats indicated that they thought either "the present political system" or "democracy of a Western type" most suitable for Russia, as did more than two-thirds (67 percent) of those categorized as market authoritarians. Almost two-thirds (64 percent) of those identified as socialist authoritarians and 58 percent of the social democrats answered that the "Soviet system before *perestroika*" was most suitable for Russia. (The correlation between categorization in the typology for those taking committed positions in 1999 and political system suitability for Russia was Pearson $r = -.41$.)[14]

Those coded as ambivalent were truly ambivalent: In 1996 exactly half (49 percent) favored the old Soviet system and half (51 percent) preferred the present system or Western-style democracy. The same question was

---

[13] For a brief but sensible discussion of the pros and cons of typologies and dimensions, see Holsti, *Public Opinion*, pp. 48–49.

[14] In the 1999 surveys the respondents were also asked the question concerning the suitability of alternative political systems for Russia a second time. In this instance respondents were offered a fourth option, "the Soviet system, but in another, more democratic form." The correlation between the views of the committed in the typology and the suitability of alternative political systems for that item was Pearson $r = -.46$.

asked twice in the pre- and post-parliamentary elections surveys in 1999. In one instance, though, respondents were given the additional option of describing as suitable for Russia "the Soviet system, but in another, more democratic, form." I combined these two questions into a simple additive scale ranging from 2 to 7, with 2 being those who opted for the Soviet system before *perestroika* in both instances and 7 those, relatively few, who chose Western-style democracy both times. Eighty-five percent of those coded as socialist authoritarians were scaled as 2 or 3, as were 29 percent of the liberal democrats. Fifty-four percent of the liberal democrats and only 7 percent of the socialist authoritarians gave responses to the two questions about the system most suitable for Russia that summed to scores of 5 through 7.

The central point to be made here is that throughout the 1990s, support for the admixture of economic and political liberalism constituting market democracy was far greater among elites than among mass publics. This is demonstrated by table 2.3, which displays the distributions of the elite and mass samples across the categories of the typology in 1993, 1995, and 1999. In all three instances, elites were overwhelmingly committed to the market. Likewise, elite commitment to democracy is high in all three surveys. There was, however, a noteworthy decrease in elite commitment to liberal democracy in 1999 when compared with both 1993 and 1995. That change is noticeable both with and without those elites coded as ambivalent or unmobilized, and shows up largely in an increase in support for social democracy and socialist authoritarianism (table 2.3). It is worth stressing, moreover, that much of the explanation for the drop turns on the responses of the military. In 1993 and 1995, 58 and 60 percent of the officers interviewed were coded as liberal democrats, whereas only 27 percent were in 1999. As a consequence, excluding the armed forces officers from the elite sample in 1993 and 1995 has the effect of increasing the proportion of liberal democrats among the foreign policy elite from 74 to 78 percent for 1993 and from 73 to 75 percent in 1995. Excluding the military from the 1999 elite respondents brings the liberal democratic component of the foreign policy elite up from 65 to 71 percent.

In comparison with the high overall levels of foreign policy elites throughout the 1990s, the proportion of mass respondents (including all respondents) who could be labeled market democrats was well less than half the proportion found among elites throughout the 1990s (table 2.3). Conversely the proportion of nondemocratic illiberal respondents (market and socialist authoritarians) among mass respondents was approximately twice as great throughout the decade. Overall a clear majority of the mass respondents taking committed positions were political liberals in 1993, falling into either the market or the social democrat category, and a majority with committed positions continued to favor political liberalism in

1995 and 1999. A slight majority with committed positions (46 percent overall) were economic liberals (market democrats or market authoritarians) in 1993. That number dropped to less than half among those with committed positions (under 30 percent overall) in 1995 or 1999. Among those with committed positions in 1995 and 1999, political liberals (market democrats and social democrats) constituted a majority, and economic liberals (market democrats and market authoritarians) represented less than a majority among both those with identifiable positions and overall. In 1993, 1995, and 1999, liberal democrats outnumbered socialist authoritarians overall but the ratio of those identified as liberal democrats to those termed socialist authoritarians was lower in 1995 and 1999 than in 1993. Thus mass support for political liberalism was considerably greater than support for the market throughout the 1990s, and aggregate levels of support for economic liberalism had diminished somewhat over the decade. While support for political liberalism diminished between 1993 and 1995, the increase in the proportion of respondents coded as social democrats between 1995 and 1999 left it unclear whether there had been a change in aggregate support for political liberalism between 1993 and 1999 (table 2.3). The central point remained, though, that elites were far more supportive of liberal democracy, and the market, than were mass publics throughout the Russian Federation's first decade.

To bring home the extent and character of the gap between elites and mass publics, the levels of response on specific measures used in our construction of ideological orientation are displayed in table 2.4. To display a large quantity of data efficiently, I report here the mean score for both elites and mass publics for each item on the scale used to construct the typology, that is, with −2 representing "strongly disagree" and +2 representing "strongly agree" and with the adjustments described above. Higher scores represent greater support for the market or democracy, as the case may be. No striking trends are seen in mass responses to the economic components of the aggregate political economy score (table 2.4). The data do demonstrate once again one of the most stable findings in the study of the Soviet Union and Russia, namely, that mass publics always endorse the proposition that all heavy industry should be state owned and not in private hands.[15] One notes some tendency across the decade for mass publics to be more aggravated by income inequality and thus less likely in 1999 than they had been in 1993 to endorse the proposition that "it's normal when the owner of a prosperous enterprise, using the labor of his workers, becomes richer than many other people." They

---

[15] Alex Inkeles and Raymond Bauer, *The Soviet Citizen* (Cambridge: Harvard University Press, 1961); James Millar, ed., *Politics, Work, and Daily Life in the USSR* (Cambridge, UK: Cambridge University Press, 1987), especially the chapter by Donna Bahry.

Table 2.4.
Elite and Mass Responses to Individual Items in Political Economy Typology, 1993–2000

	Elites			Masses		
	1993	1995	1999	1993	1995	1999
A. Economy						
Competition among various enterprises, organizations, and firms benefits our society.	1.20	1.17	1.02	.80	.81	.70
It's normal when the owner of a prosperous enterprise, using the labor of his workers, becomes richer than many other people.	1.13	.79	.79	.11	−.01	−.06
There's no sense in beginning a new business inasmuch as it might fail. [R]	1.04	.90	.87	.15	.16	.40
All heavy industry should belong to the state and not be in private hands. [R]	−.10	−.08	−.45	−1.20	−1.14	−1.27
B. Political System						
Competition among various political parties makes our system stronger.	.58	.61	.42	.06 [.08]	.13	.09
The rights of the individual should be defended even if guilty persons sometimes remain free.	.77	.60	.26	.37	.22	.22
In any society it will always be necessary to prohibit the public expression of dangerous ideas. [R]	.39	.02	−.20	.08	−.32	−.19
The interests of society should be protected even if innocent people sometimes end up in prison. [R]	1.13	.95	.75	.60	.62 [.46]	.51
It is apparent that of all the existing philosophies, there is only one that is clearly correct. [R]	1.57	1.47	1.37	.56	.34 [.29]	.35

Sources: For the figures outside of brackets, as in table 2.3. The figures in brackets are based on reinterviews of those in the 1995/96 national sample conducted after the 2000 presidential election.

Note: As explained in the text, means were computed from responses ranging from −2 to 2, with 2 indicating strong agreement with a proposition favorable to democracy or markets and −2 being highly unfavorable. Those items with [R] after them were reversed in constructing the typology so that positive scores were always favorable to democracy or markets.

The bracketed numbers are the scores in 2000 for respondents from the 1995/96 sample who were re-interviewed after the 2000 presidential election.

For the elite responses, the standard errors were all less than .10; for the mass publics, they were all less than .05.

were less likely in 1999 than they had been in either 1993 or 1995 to endorse the benefits of economic competition—though this remains the proposition about markets mass publics are most prone to endorse—but more disposed to entrepreneurship.

With respect to the political system, mass publics throughout the decade have supported individual rather than societal rights, though somewhat less strongly in 1999 than in 1993. The same has been true, among those expressing a view, about the lack of support for the proposition that there is only one right philosophy. Intolerance—as expressed in the failure of a majority to challenge the proposition that the state has an obligation to protect society from the public expression of dangerous views—was a concern in 1993 from the viewpoint of the prospects for democracy in Russia.[16] In 1999, it remained one. With the exception of the marginally different response pattern with respect to political competition, liberal responses received less support in 1999 than they did in 1993.

Table 2.4 reinforces the conclusion that elites were far more committed to economic and political liberalism than were mass publics. Across surveys in 1993, 1995, 1999, and when we reinterviewed those interviewed in the 1995 mass survey in 2000, we observed only one instance in which foreign policy elites were not more liberal than were mass publics. That pertained to the decreased support for the tolerance of dangerous ideas recorded in 1999. Moreover, in general the elite scores reflected fairly strong support for markets, except with respect to private ownership of heavy industry, and moderately to fairly strong support for political liberalism, except, especially in 1999, with respect to toleration for the public expression of dangerous ideas.

At the same time, it bears noting that for elites the scores for all nine items that make up the political economy typology were lower, that is, less liberal, than they were in 1993 and that in several instances the change has been monotonic, with the scores in 1995 reflecting a less liberal overall perspective than in 1993 and the response patterns in 1999 less liberal than in 1995. This is the case with respect to the support for the benefits of economic competition, entrepreneurship, individual over societal rights, philosophical pluralism, and free speech. Elites and mass publics remain sharply divided, with masses exhibiting a greater proclivity to economically socialist, politically illiberal ideologies and elites being more supportive both of markets (especially) and of democracy. A clear preponderance

---

[16] For divergent perspectives on the implications of Russian intolerance, see James Gibson and Raymond Duch, "Political Intolerance in the USSR: The Distribution and Etiology of Mass Opinion," *Comparative Political Studies* 26 (1993): 286–329, and Donna Bahry et al., "Tolerance, Transition, and Support for Civil Liberties in Russia," *Comparative Political Studies* 30 (1997): 484–510.

of elites had accepted market liberalism by 1993, and the bulk continued to support it at the dawn of the twenty-first century. One hesitates to speak of trends with what are in effect three data points—1993, 1995, and 1999—stretched out over seven years. After a decade highlighted by a declining economy and high crime rates, elites were less supportive of liberal democracy in 1999 than they were in 1993. If there is a trend, it is that elite dispositions have moved in the direction of mass attitudes, though the gap remained large between what are largely liberal elites and what are largely socialist masses.

The Bases of Orientations to the Political Economy

Who supports democracy and markets? Explanations should emphasize two different dimensions of the post-Soviet experience: asymmetries in opportunity and asymmetries in knowledge of the world outside Russia. Judith Kullberg and I have emphasized that the ideological positions of elites and mass reflect their respective opportunity structures.[17] Elites, with their greater opportunity to acquire property and engage in profitable business activity, were virtually unanimous in their support for most elements of market liberalism in 1993. Consensus continued to exist among elites throughout the decade that economic competition was beneficial, that entrepreneurial enrichment was normal, and that it was worth the risk to open a new business. In contrast, members of the mass public, with their more limited opportunities and greater likelihood of bearing the costs rather than the benefits of reform, were less positive about the various facets of the market economy. However, in their attitudes toward the various elements of democratic reform, particularly individual rights, masses were more positive.

Thus Kullberg and I showed there was a gap in both 1993 and 1995 in the disposition of men and women to the political economy, with women scoring significantly lower on the economic liberalism scale. Increases in level of education predicted very well to increased attachment to market liberalism, and it was also the case that younger age categories were more economically liberal. Further, we found a strong, linear relationship between socioeconomic status, as measured by occupation, and support for market liberalism in the 1993 data, and a similar, though less linear, pattern of variation in the 1995 data. In both years, people who filled the categories of manager and highly qualified professionals were relatively pro-market, while mean scores for other categories indicated adherence

---

[17] Kullberg and Zimmerman, "Liberal Elites." This and the next two paragraphs borrow heavily from that article.

to more anti-market or socialist orientations. Agricultural workers and unskilled laborers displayed the lowest levels of economic liberalism. Finally, community size also was a factor shaping economic liberalism. In both 1993 and 1995, considerably higher levels of economic liberalism were present among residents of Moscow and cities with populations exceeding one million; considerably lower levels were present in smaller communities. While in 1993 there was much less support for economic liberalism in medium-sized to fairly large cities than in either smaller towns or large cities, in 1995 the relationship between community size and economic liberalism was nearly linear.

The intuition that economic opportunity structure also affects individual support for liberal democracy was confirmed by variation across most of the same factors in average political liberalism scores. Occupational status and education were positively correlated with support for political liberalism, while age was negatively correlated. Such findings are consistent with the considerable body of comparative and single-country studies regarding the effect of upward social mobility, generational change, and material "satisfaction" on support for democratic values. We again found a significant difference between men and women, with women less inclined toward political liberalism, and a corresponding pattern in the case of city size, with the larger cities more drawn to political liberalism.

The data from the 1999 Duma election provided the opportunity to test the stability of Kullberg's and my findings. Table 2.5 shows the proportion supporting economic liberalism—those coded as either market democrats or market authoritarians—and political liberalism—market or social democrats—in 1999, controlling for age, sex, education, and city size, among respondents taking a committed position. Men were somewhat more inclined to support market liberalism and modestly more supportive of political liberalism as well. Education and orientation to both economic and political liberalism were tightly linked. Age too continued to be an important correlate of support for both economic and political liberalism, as did city size—though with regard to political liberalism the relation was not monotonic but rather reflected a rural-urban divide.

Table 2.6 illustrates what the more robust bivariate relations signify in percentage terms for orientation to liberal democracy per se. It excludes those coded as ambivalent or unmobilized. Of those born before 1950, fewer than a quarter in 1999 were coded as liberal democrats. Forty-five percent of the respondents born from 1950 to 1959 were so classified, and 55 percent of those interviewed born in 1960 or after were market democrats. Among those without university education, less than a third gave responses resulting in their being classified as liberal democrats, while almost three in five of those with some or complete university education were coded as such.

Table 2.5.
Correlates of Economic and Political Liberalism, 1999

	Supports Market Liberalism	*Supports Political Liberalism*
Male	56 % (246)	71% (314)
Female	43% (326)	64% (485)
	Tau$_c$ =.12, $p < .001$	Tau$_c$ =.06, $p < .05$
Born before 1950	32% (165)	57% (299)
1950–1959	53% (128)	73% (177)
1960 +	66% (274)	76% (317)
	Tau$_c$ = .33, $p < .001$	Tau$_c$ = .19, $p < .001$
Less than university education	42% (385)	63% (576)
Some or complete university	66% (184)	80% (221)
	Tau$_c$ = .17, $p < .001$	Tau$_c$ = .12, $p < .001$
City size < 25k	40% (132)	57% (187)
25k to < 100k	39% (75)	69% (132)
100k to < 500k	56% (115)	73% (152)
500k to < 1m	54% (112)	70% (147)
> 1m	57% (127)	71% (158)
	Tau$_c$ = .16, $p < .001$	Tau$_c$= .12, $p < .001$

Sources: As in table 2.3.
Note: Actual number of respondents for particular cells shown in parentheses.

Table 2.6.
Age, Education, and Support for Liberal Democracy, 1999

Some or Complete University	*No University*	*When Born*		
		Before 1950	*1950–1959*	*1960+*
58%	32%	24%	45%	55%
(162)	(296)	(124)	(108)	(227)
Tau$_b$ = .23, $p < .001$		Tau$_c$ = −.29, $p < .001$		

Sources: As in table 2.3.
Note: Actual number of respondents for particular cells shown in parentheses.

Multivariate analysis, likewise, revealed that city size, education, male versus female, and age all had independent effects in determining support for markets. They were less robust predictors of orientation to political liberalism than to markets, with sex being only significant at $p < .10$. If, though, as Kullberg and I did in assessing the 1993 and 1995 surveys, we view conventional demographic factors having an indirect effect (via the role they have in shaping orientation to market) on support for political liberalism as well as a direct effect, the 1999 data bear out the notion that economic opportunity structure provides an important key on understanding support not only for markets but for democracy in Russia as the twenty-first century begins.[18]

The economic opportunities that Russians either have or think they have bear substantially on their orientation to the economy and to the political system. But this is not to argue that it is such factors that exclusively dominate their orientation to the economic or political system. Knowledge of the outside world represents an additional important and independent effect. Those who are politically attentive are substantially more supportive of market democracy than are those among mass publics who know less about the world outside Russia. In an earlier paper, I utilized the 1993 data to argue that in addition to factors that might be viewed both as contributing to a Russian citizen's economic opportunity structure and as having predictive consequences for that person's orientation to communications networks—city size; proximity to the Baltic states, Finland, and Poland; education, sex, and age—factual knowledge of the world outside Russia contributed substantially to identifying those Russians who supported market democracy.[19] In that instance, I used as my indicator of being "plugged in" the questions testing whether respondents could associate five Western leaders with the correct country and whether the respondents knew that Crimea was part of Ukraine and when that had occurred. In a subsequent paper, and in this book, as we saw in the previous chapter, I have incorporated a further set of questions pertaining to whether respondents knew the Russian Federation was a member of the International Monetary Fund and when it had joined into the indicator of the mass respondents' basic knowledge of the world outside Russia.[20] This in turn I use to distinguish levels of attentiveness among respondents among the mass public.

The 1995 Russia-wide survey bore out the inference drawn from the 1993 survey of European Russia.[21] Those who scored highest with regard to their international awareness—the internationally attentive public—were more prone to support liberal democracy than were those with moderate knowledge or low knowledge, though even they were far less supportive of market democracy than were elites. Table 2.7 shows the relation in 1993 and 1995 between knowledge of the world outside Russia and

---

[18] Ibid.

[19] Zimmerman, "Markets," pp. 112–14.

[20] Zimmerman, "Synoptic Thinking," pp. 630–41.

[21] These questions were not incorporated in the 1999/2000 survey of Russian mass publics.

Table 2.7.
International Attentiveness and Support for Market Democracy, 1993–1995

Year	Elite	Internationally Attentive	Moderately Aware	Moderately Unaware	Unaware	Completely Unaware
1993	83%	59%	44%	35%	26%	24%
	(148)	(126)	(80)	(78)	(40)	(17)
1995	81%	55%	46%	43%	27%	18%
	(131)	(111)	(139)	(198)	(111)	(44)

Sources: As in table 2.3.

Note: For the construction of the attentiveness scale, see the text. The exact question wordings are reported in table 1.2. Those who were unmobilized or ambivalent were excluded from the analysis. Actual number of respondents for particular cells shown in parentheses.

orientation to liberal (market) democracy among mass publics and compares that pattern with the responses of foreign policy elites. Those whom I have termed here "completely unaware" scored a 3 on the additive scale, which ranged from 3 to 9. In practice they did not know that Crimea belonged to Ukraine, that Russia was a member of the IMF, and at best could link only two of the five Western leaders—usually the American president and the German chancellor—to their respective country. The internationally aware received scores of 7 through 9. The latter typically linked all five Western leaders with their respective countries, knew that Russia belonged to the IMF, that Crimea belonged to Ukraine, and sometimes when, roughly, Russia had joined the IMF and/or when Crimea had become part of Ukraine.

Likewise, in multivariate analysis, knowledge of the world outside Russia had a statistically significant and independent effect on Russian mass public respondents' disposition to accept liberal democracy, as table 2.8 illustrates, when I incorporated international political attentiveness in models that included reports about respondents' material position in the past year and demographic factors that correlate with differential economic opportunities—age, sex, size of settlement, and education. In the logistic regression table presented here, I have compared those who were liberal democrats only with those who fit substantive attitudinal categories—market authoritarians, social democrats, and socialist authoritarians—by excluding from the analysis the ambivalent and the politically unmobilized. This exclusion does not affect the analysis.

Moreover, the effect of being relatively knowledgeable about the world outside Russia was also manifest among subgroups who were overall less knowledgeable politically and more disadvantaged economically than

Table 2.8.
Liberal Democracy, International Attentiveness, and Economic
Opportunity, 1995

Variable	Coefficient (B)	Standard Error	Probability (p)
International knowledge	.310	.06	.000
Age	.931	.14	.000
Settlement size	.125	.06	.035
University Attendance	.571	.15	.000
Sex	.398	.14	.004
Income last year	.141	.07	.054
Income next year	.117	.07	.091
Constant	−1.648	.47	.001

Source: As in table 2.3.
Note: Overall $N = 2839$. Cases in analysis: 1136. (Those who were ambivalent or unmobilized were dropped from the equation. Including them does not materially affect the results.)
Initial log likelihood function: −2 log likelihood 1488.03.
Goodness of fit for model: 1131.7
Cases correctly predicted: 70.1%. (Given coding of variables, signs are appropriate for hypothesis.)

their counterparts within various demographic and experiential categories. For respondents who were either situationally disadvantaged economically and relatively less well informed—women, rural dwellers, people over fifty, people with less than university education—or whose estimate of their present or prospective economic situation was relatively poor, support for liberal democracy, while quite modest, almost uniformly increased with knowledge of the world outside the Russian Federation. Table 2.9 summarizes the relevant cross-tabulations for those categories and international political knowledge.

It is important to reiterate that persons in these subgroups were relatively less likely to support economic or political liberalism than were others. Nevertheless, *within* each category those who evidenced greater knowledge of the outside world were substantially more likely to give responses supportive of market democracy than were others (Table 2.9). Thus among those who lived in a village whose ability to answer questions on the world outside Russia resulted in their being coded as members of the internationally attentive public, slightly more than two-fifths in the 1995 sample taking a committed position were coded as liberal democrats;

Table 2.9.
Support for Liberal Democracy in 1995, Controlling for Knowledge of
International Events

	Internationally Attentive	Moderately Aware	Moderately Unaware	Unaware	Completely Unaware
Women	60%	41%	40%	24%	18%
	(43)	(63)	(109)	(61)	(31)
Age over 50	34%	34%	33%	16%	11%
	(23)	(39)	(49)	(27)	(14)
Lived in village or settlement	42%	39%	35%	21%	10%
	(18)	(26)	(47)	(27)	(11)
Did not attend university	46%	38%	39%	25%	17%
	(45)	(67)	(131)	(86)	(37)
Personal economic situation worsened significantly last year	42%	32%	33%	22%	12%
	(22)	(40)	(50)	(33)	(13)
Expect personal economic situation to worsen significantly next year	34%	31%	33%	23%	7%
	(11)	(15)	(29)	(19)	(4)

Sources: As in table 2.3.

Note: As in the preceding tables, this table excludes the unmobilized and the ambivalent. The pattern remains the same if they are included. Actual number of respondents for particular cells shown in parentheses.

of those who were completely inattentive only 10 percent were coded as liberal or market democrats. The same basic pattern is replicated across other relevant categories—over fifty years old, those who thought the economic situation had worsened significantly in the past year, women, and those without university education. Three-fifths of the women with committed positions and classified as internationally attentive were market democrats as opposed to less than a fifth among the completely inattentive. Among those who said the previous year had been significantly worse for their material position, 42 percent of the internationally aware fit into the liberal democrat category whereas only 12 percent of the completely unaware were so categorized. In all instances, within categories, those who were better acquainted with the world outside the Russian Federation were more likely to support market democracy than were those for whom the world was thoroughly mysterious.

Order, Political Culture, and Synoptic Thinking

But how thorough is the commitment to democracy among those whom we have identified as supporting liberal democracy? Two major ways of framing that issue are discussed in this next section: (a) Does the desire for order in practice outweigh support for democracy among those who declare themselves favorable to the latter? (b) How superficial is the support for liberal democracy among those who give politically correct answers to questions about markets and democracy?

One view often encountered is that although Russians favor democracy in the abstract, when push comes to shove they favor order at the expense of democracy. This observation has two corollaries. The first is that support found in survey items for abstract concepts, whether they concern democracy, order, markets, or social justice, is of little relevance to concrete behavior. The second is that order dominates democracy among Russian respondents' preferences in culturally distinct ways that distinguish Russians from mass publics in Western democracies.

In the Russian context I am aware of only one effort to address the first part of this argument, and that is by James Gibson.[22] Gibson reports an interesting experiment that shows fairly convincingly that how Russian respondents orient themselves to general questions does indeed bear strongly on their orientations in specific, concrete settings.

Several Western scholars in the 1990s tackled the other element in this proposition, usually by framing the issue, as Arthur Miller, William Reisinger, and Vicki Hesli did, as one of choosing between "the desire for an orderly society versus more individual freedom."[23] This they did by asking Russians whether they believe "It is better to live in an orderly society than to allow people so much freedom that they become disruptive" or something similar.[24]

Miller and his colleagues use the question as a component part of a multiple-item index measuring respondents' orientation to the pace of political reform in Russia and other parts of the former Soviet Union. This seems to me unexceptional, but the question has the potential for abuse.

The structure of the question, doubtless unintentionally, implies that freedom and order are antinomies, a proposition which, by implying that

[22] James Gibson, "A Sober Second Thought: An Experiment in Teaching Russians to Tolerate," *American Journal of Political Science* 42 (July 1998): 819–50.

[23] Arthur Miller, William Reisinger, and Vicki Hesli, "Understanding Political Change in Post-Soviet Societies," *American Political Science Review* 90 (March 1996): 155.

[24] Arthur Miller, William Reisinger, and Vicki Hesli, "Reassessing Mass Support for Political and Economic Change in the Former USSR," *American Political Science Review* 88 (June 1994): 406.

democratic freedom and order are incompatible, plays into the hand of those who would prefer the old, pre-*perestroika* political system over contemporary Russia or Western-style democracy. Indeed, those who say that the political system before *perestroika* is more suitable for Russia than either the current system or Western-style democracy tend to favor order, regardless of how the question is framed. Questions about order and freedom were asked in two different ways in both the 1995/96 and the 1999 all-Russia surveys conducted by a research team headed by Polina Kozyreva of the Russian Academy of Sciences' Institute of Sociology. One item asked the respondents whether it was "better to live in a society with strict order than to give people so much freedom that they can destroy society." A second item presented respondents with a scale and asked them to situate themselves "where 1 means that order should be imposed at any price even at the expense of infringing on the rights of citizens and 5 means that in no circumstances should the imposition of order infringe on the rights of citizens." For the 1995/96 panel studies each question was asked twice, once at the time of the Duma elections and once after the 1996 presidential elections.

Question effects are enormous in regard to these items. Practically everyone in Russia in the 1990s opposed the infringement of the rights of citizens and practically everyone agreed that order was preferable to freedom that threatens to destroy society. The mean responses for the "order–freedom destroy society" question and the "order at any price–order while preserving rights of citizens" question diverged sharply. Asked whether order was preferable at any cost or whether order should not infringe the rights of citizens, the mean answer was 4 (3.94 in one instance, and 4.03 in the other) in the 1995/96 survey and close to 4 (3.78) in the survey conducted before the 1999 parliamentary elections. The same question was also asked of Russian foreign policy elites in 1999. The mean response was again 4 (3.97) on the same five-point scale. The mean scores for the "strict order" versus "too much freedom" questions were just slightly above 2 (2.15 and 2.25, respectively) for the 1995/96 surveys and exactly 2 in the survey conducted before the December 1999 parliamentary elections. Thought of in conventional scalar terms, where the choices range from strongly agree to strongly disagree on a five-point Likert scale, the median answer in one instance would have been "agree" and in the other "disagree."

On the one hand, in percentage terms, 74 percent at the time of the 1995 Duma election, 71 percent after the 1996 presidential election, and 80 percent before the 1999 Duma election chose 1 or 2—the scalar equivalent of having strongly agreed or agreed—when asked whether they thought that order was preferable to too much freedom.

On the other hand, 69 percent and 72 percent in the 1995/96 surveys and 64 percent in the 1999 pre-Duma survey chose either 4 or 5 as their response when asked to locate themselves along a scale ranging from (1) order at any price to (5) order without infringing on the rights of citizens. Like most people, Russians taken as a whole sought order without infringing the rights of citizens in the first decade of the Russian Federation and were willing to repress freedom should it threaten to destroy society. To be sure, those Russians who were nostalgic for the Soviet system were far more likely to associate themselves with order than were those who thought post-Soviet Russia or Western democracy preferable, but used without great care, responses to questions about order shed little light on Russian support for democracy.

Some comparative data may complicate matters even further. In his studies of cultural shift, Ronald Inglehart has asked persons from all over the globe, "If you had to choose," which do you think is "the most important responsibility of government": "to maintain order in society or to respect freedom of the individual." This question was asked in Russia in 1995 and in many other countries in either 1995 or 1996. The distribution of responses ranged from 90 percent in Taiwan opting for order to 35 percent in Uruguay and 28 percent in the Basque region of Spain. Of the Russian respondents, 45 percent chose order and 55 percent chose respecting freedom. The Russian figures favoring respect for freedom were higher than western Germany, Spain, Japan, the United States, South Africa, Norway, Australia, Finland, Poland, Switzerland, Brazil, and Slovenia, among others. But in these same surveys Russians and others from former communist states in Europe were generally much more disposed than others to rate order as more preferable than items closely associated with democracy, such as free speech.

How are we to ascertain, among those who give survey responses that are indicative of a favorable orientation to markets and political pluralism, whether this putative support for liberal democracy is stable or instead "a mile wide but an inch deep"?[25] The answer to this question raises fundamental issues about our view of the nature of political culture—a group or nation's basic orientations to politics—in Russia.

By one account, culture is a relatively stable, ethnically or spatially specific predictor variable that shapes a nation's political institutions. In one long and honorable tradition in Russian studies, it is an approach that has emphasized the connection between the Russian autocratic past and the similarities in tsarist political institutions before 1917 and Bolshevik insti-

---

[25] Gibson, "A Mile Wide but an Inch Deep."

tutions after 1917.[26] Those attracted by this assessment of political culture are prone to think a statist, authoritarian, political economy in Russia will be a constant regardless of the collapse of the Soviet system in 1991.

The other approach views political culture as being more malleable. It has two variants. One of these two shares with the first approach the assumption that culture is a predictor variable, but emphasizes the effects of secular changes in education and changes in work experience on the distribution of attitudes in a society.[27] Unlike the first approach, in this conception the core attitudes that constitute a political culture are driven by societal and technological change and evolve as the society changes. For those in this intellectual tradition, the transformations in the former Soviet Union and the states of Eastern Europe stem directly from changes in their respective societies. Direct political consequences are seen to flow from the changes in Soviet society from the 1950s to the late 1980s.[28] The Soviet Union in this view was not at all the same place in 1989 as it was in 1959: the proportion of persons with high school education had grown substantially, the number of persons with university degrees had become much larger, and the urban population of the Soviet Union had become as large in absolute terms as that of the United States (though with an additional thirty million people living in rural areas)—and this had consequences for the polity.

Another variant shares the assumption that culture is malleable.[29] But in this perspective political culture is regarded as an outcome variable shaped by institutions and incentive structures. For scholars in this tradition, if you get the institutions right, political culture follows, rather than drives, successful institutionalization. In the event, it remains the case that political culture in this perspective is viewed as being malleable: change the institutions, change the political culture.

In this chapter I do not seek to address the direction of the causal arrows between culture and institutions. Rather, the goal here is to assess the

[26] Merle Fainsod, *How Russia Is Ruled* (Cambridge, Mass.: Harvard University Press, 1953); Zbigniew K. Brzezinski, *Ideology and Power in Soviet Politics* (New York: Praeger, 1962); Stephen White, *Political Culture and Soviet Politics* (London: Macmillan, 1979).

[27] For a good statement of this perspective, see Ronald Inglehart, *Culture Shift in Advanced Industrial Society* (Princeton: Princeton University Press, 1990).

[28] Moshe Lewin, *The Gorbachev Phenomenon* (Berkeley: University of California Press, 1988).

[29] An excellent statement of this view remains Brian Barry, *Sociologists, Economists, and Democracy* (Chicago: University of Chicago Press, 1978). Edward N. Muller and Mitchell A. Seligson, "Civic Culture and Democracy: The Question of Causal Relationships," *American Political Science Review* 88 (1994): 635–52, have written an important paper that largely supports the notion that civic culture results from, rather than causes, democracy. At the same time, they also find that support for gradual reform has a positive impact on the chances for democracy.

relative plausibility of views that emphasize the malleability of political culture and those that emphasize the stability of traditional Russian cultural norms. I do this to gauge the depth of support for liberal democracy among those who give responses favorable in general terms to values associated with support for markets and democracy. Key in this respect is the role of "synoptic" thinking in contemporary Russia. By synoptic thinking, I refer to the kind of thinking that constitutes one of the two fundamental approaches to the manipulability and mastery of political and social reality and, in turn, to the organization of society Lindblom identified in *Politics and Markets*.[30]

What Lindblom termed Model 1—synoptic thinking—"specifies that some people in the society are wise and informed enough to ameliorate its problems and guide social change with a high degree of success."[31] The "intellectual leaders of the society . . . [are] able to produce a comprehensive theory of social change that serves to guide the society." The Leninist and Maoist versions of Marxism were thought to constitute such a theory, an underlying premise of which was that there was only one correct philosophy. That philosophy in turn provided the intellectual wherewithal to guide the society and underlay the claim of "the" Party—that it ought to guide Soviet society, since it had a monopoly on the one truly "scientific" social theory.

Model 2, by contrast, rejects the idea of there being a synoptic theory that produces a comprehensive understanding of the world and how to change it. Lindblom cites John Stuart Mill's observation in *On Liberty* that " 'every one well knows himself to be fallible' " as the paradigmatic assessment of the role of knowledge and political philosophy in understanding the world that is characteristic of Model 2.[32] Those persons disposed to a Model 2 orientation to the world accept the idea that there are only partial truths and multiple philosophies. People are seen as creatures "of limited cognitive capacity to organize . . . [their] society and solve . . . social problems." People in this tradition strongly prefer "problem-solving interactions" rather than to attempt "impossible analytical tasks."[33] As a result, people in this tradition are drawn to market systems in the economy and to analogously competitive systems in the polity,[34] what Lind-

---

[30] Lindblom, *Politics and Markets*; see also Donald J. Munro, "One-Minded Hierarchy versus Interest-Group Pluralism: The Chinese Approaches to Conflict," in William Zimmerman and Harold K. Jacobson, eds., *Behavior, Culture, and Conflict in World Politics* (Ann Arbor: University of Michigan Press, 1993), pp. 247–275.

[31] Lindblom, *Politics and Markets*, p. 249.

[32] Ibid.

[33] Ibid., p. 255.

[34] A nice clarification of the reforms that Soviet leaders after Stalin and before Gorbachev were willing to entertain, which centers on their reluctance to entertain either political or

blom and Robert Dahl termed polyarchy, which has been termed here, more prosaically and less defensively, liberal democracy.

Having an appreciation of the extent to which synoptic thinking is present in contemporary Russia would bear crucially on our judgments about the malleability of political culture in post-Soviet Russia. For the immediate purposes of this chapter, what is more relevant is its bearing on our judgments about the extent to which survey responses favoring generalized propositions about market democracy are associated with fundamental changes in cognition favorable for the middle-run prospects for the institutionalization of political and economic pluralism in Russia. If we found that in post-Soviet Russia people believed overwhelmingly there was only one correct philosophy, this would constitute strong evidence of the long-term and nonmalleable role of political culture. Regardless whether persons in post-Soviet Russia have overtly rejected Leninism, finding that in any event they thought synoptically would indicate that culturally determined patterns of thought had weathered the collapse of the Soviet Union. Marxism-Leninism as a secular religion would have gone the way of all flesh, only to be replaced by an alternative, equally correct, philosophy. (I happened to be in Moscow for the first Easter after the collapse of the Soviet Union. I could not help but notice that the banners across the streets proclaiming that Christ had risen were located precisely where in previous years banners greeting the coming CPSU Congresses had been hung.) The perpetuation of synoptic thinking would strengthen the case for cultural persistence and call into question optimistic scenarios about the prospects for democracy in Russia.

If, though, we found that a substantial fraction of the Russian population strongly rejected the idea that there was only one correct philosophy, this would strengthen the case of those who assume that culture is relatively malleable—whether because what we take to signify culture is altered by institutional changes or because a more literate and urban Russian populace is more likely to reject the notion that any one philosophy has a monopoly on truth.

If we found it was precisely elites and those among mass publics having university education or having the greatest knowledge of the outside world who reject the idea that there is one right philosophy, this would represent a piece of strong evidence for knowledge-driven explanations of a malleable political culture. Similarly, if those who are disposed to orientations that are recognizably liberal democratic in the Western sense are also strongly disposed to reject the idea that there is one correct philosophy, then these dispositions are less likely transient and more plausibly

---

economic markets, is contained in George Breslauer, *Khrushchev and Brezhnev as Leaders* (London: Allen & Unwin, 1982), p. 5.

Table 2.10.
Elites, University Education, and Other Mass Publics and One Right Philosophy
(those who disagreed or strongly disagreed)

			Mass Public					
Elites			1993		1995		1999	
1993	1995	1999	Univ.	No Univ.	Univ.	No Univ.	Univ.	No Univ.
93%	89%	89%	79%	62%	69%	46%	67%	47%
(180)	(159)	(182)	(190)	(381)	(346)	(613)	(232)	(469)
			Tau$_c$ = .17		Tau$_c$ = .17		Tau$_c$ = .17	
			$p < .001$		$p < .001$		$p < .001$	

Sources: As in table 2.3.
Note: Actual number of respondents for particular cells shown in parentheses.
Question wording:
It is apparent that of all the existing philosophies, there is only one that is clearly correct.

construed as a component part of a broader way of thinking about the world. Findings in this vein would increase our confidence that support for economic and political competition in Russia is evidence of an erosion of attitudes rooted in an authoritarian past.

As it turns out, with respect to synoptic thinking at least, the latter propositions are the right answers: elites and those favorably oriented to the market are strongly disposed to reject the notion that there is a single correct philosophy. This has important implications for our judgments about Russian political culture at the onset of the twenty-first century and for assumptions about the long-term prospects for economic and political pluralism in Russia.

Table 2.10 reports the distribution of responses among elites, those who were university attenders, and the general public in the 1993, 1995, and 1999 surveys to the statement "It is apparent that of all the world's philosophies there is only one that is clearly correct."[35]

Elites, university attenders, and those who knew a great deal about the world outside Russia or who were generally politically attentive overwhelmingly rejected the idea that there was only one right philosophy (table 2.10). Three-quarters in 1993 and 1995 and more than two-thirds

---

[35] The number of "don't knows" and "no responses" requires some comment. A sizable minority in the mass surveys either did not answer or said they did not know when asked whether there was only one right philosophy, even when they were presented, as in the 1995 and 1999 surveys, with the option of stating that they are ambivalent. Three out of eight respondents (36 percent and 38 percent, respectively) without university education in the 1993 and 1995 mass surveys said they didn't know.

in 1999 (68 percent) of the elite respondents who answered the question disagreed *fully* with the proposition.

Similarly, large proportions of those in the mass survey with university education disagreed, half strongly, in 1993. The propensity of university attendees to register intense disagreement with the assertion that there was only one right philosophy may have diminished considerably by 1995, when only 14 percent with university education said they disagreed strongly. Much of this is largely an artifact. In the 1995 and 1999 surveys respondents were given five choices, including an intermediate "I hesitate to say [*koleblius'*]," whereas in the 1993 mass survey only four options (strongly agree . . . strongly disagree) had been presented. In the event in 1995, 1999, and again in 2000 among those interviewed in 1995 and reinterviewed, two-thirds (67 percent in 1995 and 1999) of those with university education expressed disagreement in some form with the statement.

The same finding generally obtains when we look at the association between orientation to the market and disposition to reject synoptic thinking. The market oriented among the elites were more likely than other elite respondents to reject completely the idea that there was only one right philosophy. Among those elites committed to market solutions, 80 percent in both 1993 and 1995 and 78 percent in 1999 disagreed fully with the proposition.

Among university attendees, those who were market oriented, regardless of their orientation to democracy, were more likely to reject synoptic thinking as well. In 1993, 88 percent and in 1995 and 1999, more than three-quarters of those market-oriented university attendees who expressed a view disagreed with the proposition that there was only one right philosophy in comparison with roughly three-fifths (62 percent in 1993; 57 percent, 1995, 55 percent in 1999) of the statist—including both social democrats and socialist authoritarians—university attendees who expressed a view.

Fewer among those in the mass public lacking university education were prone than elites or university attenders to assert that there was only one philosophy. Nevertheless, it was still the case that throughout the 1990s among those without university education about 20 percent more of those who were market oriented disagreed with the proposition that there was only one right philosophy than did those who had statist economic orientations. In short, we observe the same trend among the general public as we do among elites and university attenders.

Moreover, multivariate analysis designed to identify those disposed to reject the idea that there was only one right philosophy reinforced the conclusion that such a response was part of a larger normative package. In logistic regressions using the 1993 and 1995 data, variables were employed that distinguished the market oriented from socialists of whatever stripe; those who accepted and rejected the proposition that Stalin is blamed for things he didn't do; those who were and were not "plugged in" to the world outside Russia; and among people according to the size of the settlement in which they lived, and all were statistically significant. Those oriented to the market, who did *not* agree that Stalin is blamed for things he didn't do, who lived in large urban areas, and who were reasonably attuned politically were all more likely than those who did not fit these categories to disagree, often strongly, with the proposition that there is only one clearly right philosophy.

These are significant findings both for what they imply for the prospects for economic and political pluralism in Russia and for what they suggest about our understanding of political culture in Russia. The fact that in the decade after the formation of the Russian Federation it was precisely elites, university attendees, and those well informed about the world outside Russia who overwhelmingly rejected the notion of there being only one right philosophy lends support for the idea that culture is relatively malleable. Similarly, the association we found in the mass surveys between knowledge of politics and dwelling in a large urban area, on the one hand, and disposition to reject completely the proposition that there is one right philosophy, on the other, suggests that attitudes core to a political culture are knowledge driven and not constant.

Moreover, the connection between orientation to the market, especially, and to a lesser extent to the political system, and the disposition to reject the idea that there is only one right philosophy reinforces the view that those who support notions congruent with liberal democracy are not simply giving lip service to such a conception. Rather, they seem to have bought into the idea of ideological and philosophical pluralism, what Lindblom characterized as Model 2.

Much further research and the passage of far more time will be necessary before it will be possible to assess fully the magnitude and significance of Model 2 thinking in Russia. Already, however, the overwhelming rejection of synoptic (Model 1) thinking among elites and among university attenders indicates that a culturally dependent fatalism about the continuance into the future of synoptic and nonpluralist thinking is inappropriate. It also suggests a commitment to intellectual and normative pluralism among liberal democrats that is incompatible with a view that interprets their responses to queries exclusively as transitory cue taking or merely as a momentary reaction to the failures of the Soviet system.

At the same time, the substantial number of people who answer that there is a single right philosophy (along with those who express no opinion in this regard) is also significant. Writing in 1977, Lindblom spoke of a great divide in the aftermath of the French Revolution and the Paris

Commune as a result of which liberal democratic and socialist thought divided.[36] One might equally well date that divide with the split occurring in the latter half of the nineteenth century and the beginning of the twentieth century between the West European democratic socialists, exemplified by the revisionist Eduard Bernstein, and the radical Marxists, located primarily in Russia and typified by Lenin. Unlike Marx, Bernstein thought socialism morally right, independent of whether it was scientific and historically inevitable. The radical Marxists, by contrast, modified specific empirical projections of Marx (for example, that revolution would occur where development was greatest). They did this, though, in order to retain what they considered the essence of Marxism, namely that it was *the* truly scientific method that unified theory and practice.[37]

In either event, throughout most of the twentieth century a divide separated the West and what used to be the world communist movement. At the beginning of the twenty-first century, that split now divides Russia with respect to whether a single right philosophy exists. Among the Russian general public, those who were drawn to markets were much more likely to reject, either partially or fully, the idea that there was one correct philosophy and, by implication, favor Model 2. Those who had attended university and those who (regardless of their level of formal knowledge) knew a good deal about the world around them were among those in the mass public most inclined to reject Model 1. The less-educated respondents, the respondents who were less knowledgeable about the world outside Russia, and the respondents who were economic statists were more prone to synoptic thinking and to endorse the proposition that there was just one right philosophy.

What is most striking is that Model 2 persons among the general public were joined in that rejection by an overwhelming proportion of the political elites. Indeed, in the 1990s it was precisely Russian elites, especially but not *exclusively* those who were market oriented, who, in keeping with Model 2, were "increasingly skeptical of man's capacity to reshape his world" and "turned toward institutions that would hold fallible leaders responsible but would not grant them authority to create 'correctly' an egalitarian world."[38]

What this suggests is that for Russian elites and for some, but scarcely all, ordinary citizens (notably those drawn to the pluralism of the market) commitment to democracy is not a mile wide and an inch deep. Whatever the burdens of Russia's tsarist and Soviet authoritarian past, a nonmallea-

[36] Lindblom, *Politics and Markets*, p. 253.

[37] Alfred G. Meyer, *Marxism: The Unity of Theory and Practice* (Cambridge, Mass.: Harvard University Press, 1954).

[38] Lindblom, *Politics and Markets*, p. 253.

ble Russian political culture does not preclude these Russians from re-
jecting the kind of synoptic thinking alien to political pluralism.

The Burden of the Past and the Onus of the 1990s

Another way to explore the impact of political culture on Russian attitudes
to democracy is to address the hypothesis that orientations to the political
system are invariant across age cohorts. The worry that the Soviet experience would have profound negative effects on post-communist Russia has
been a persistent theme since the collapse of the Soviet Union.[39] In the
immediate aftermath of the collapse of Soviet power, scholars expressed
the concern that mass orientations would continue to manifest the authoritarian values associated with the Soviet system. Analogous arguments may
be found in more recent studies of the prospects for successful economic
and political transformation in Russia, a burgeoning cottage industry to
which broad-gauge comparativists and Russian specialists alike have contributed.[40] More recently, there has been a propensity to explain the problems of contemporary Russia as carryovers from the not-too-distant communist past.[41]

These are arguments that can be addressed by data drawn from interviews of Russian elites and mass publics. If Russian political culture is not
malleable, we should observe relatively similar patterns of responses to
questions pertaining to orientations to the political system across age cohorts. By the same token, were it the case that persons who reach political
maturity are prone to accept the dominant views of the political system at
the time when they reach maturity, one should witness sharp differences
across age cohorts in orientation to the political system. Those who
reached political maturity under Soviet power would be more acceptant
of the traditional Soviet model. Those who came of age politically during
perestroika and after the collapse of the Soviet system would be more ame-
nable to the present Russian system or Western democracy. If socialization

---

[39] Examples include Kenneth Jowitt, *The New World Disorder* (Berkeley: University of
California Press, 1992), and George Schopflin, "Culture and Identity in Post-Communist
Europe," in Stephen White, Judy Batt, and Paul Lewis, eds., *Developments in East European
Politics* (London: Macmillan, 1993).

[40] For example, Juan Linz and Alfred Stepan, *Problems of Democratic Transition and Con-
solidation* (Baltimore: Johns Hopkins University Press, 1996); Frederic Fleron and Richard
Ahl, "Does the Public Matter for Democratization in Russia?" in Harry Eckstein et al., eds.,
Can Democracy Take Root in Russia? (Lanham, Md.: Rowman & Littlefield, 1998), pp. 287–
330; Bahry, "Comrades into Citizens?"

[41] This section in general and the above paragraph in particular draw heavily on Kullberg
and Zimmerman, "*Perezhitki proshlogo.*"

in turn persists in shaping people's orientation to politics throughout their life, it follows that persons in the same age cohort should have roughly the same orientation to the political system regardless of their subsequent economic opportunities or their contemporary level of political awareness. Finally, if a major source for identification with the past was the differential economic opportunities of Russians in the first decade after the formation of the Russian Federation, then we should observe within age groups greater support for the present system and Western democracy among those who have better economic opportunity structures. Support for the Soviet system before *perestroika* should accordingly be higher within age groups for those with relatively poorer economic opportunities.

Through analysis of the 1995/96 and 1999/2000 survey data we can test the validity of various cultural and economic opportunity structure hypotheses regarding stability and/or change in the political orientations of Russians. If culture is as persistent and powerful a force as its strongest adherents claim, we should find strong, stable, and largely undifferentiated dispositions among the Russian mass public for Soviet values and institutions. Further, if the dominant explanatory factor is an authoritarian political culture rooted in Russian national experience, this bias should be relatively uniform across the population, independent of factors such as age, level of education, and occupation.

If, on the other hand, social structural change accompanying industrialization did indeed provide "culture shifts" over time in a more liberal direction, identification with things Soviet should be a function of standard demographic variables such as age, urbanization, and education. Specifically, those citizens who came of political age during Soviet times, at least prior to the latter years of the Brezhnev era—the years of stagnation (*zastoi*)—and born twenty years earlier should be much more likely to support the socialist system than subsequent political generations, while those who came of age subsequently should be more disposed to the present system or Western-style democracy. If respondents' opportunity structures in the 1990s played a major role in determining orientation to the political system, we should find major differences *within* age cohorts when controlling for how relatively well-off the respondents thought they were as well as when controlling for those demographic variables that obviously have an impact on people's economic opportunities. Males and those who live in more urban settings, have higher incomes, and have higher education should be more disposed to regard the present system or Western-style democracy as suitable for Russia than others, *within* age cohort.

If the relative level of economic opportunity is an important factor influencing the evolution of Russian culture, we should find the highest levels of support for Soviet values and institutions among those groups in the population who have benefited least from the economic transforma-

Table 2.11.
Decade Born and Assessed Suitability of Political System for Russia (1 = Soviet system before *perestroika*; 2 = present system; 3 = Western-type democracy)

When born:	1995 Mean (S.E.)	1999 Mean (S.E.)	2000[a] Mean (S.E.)
1918–1927	1.35 (.04)	1.12 (.03)	1.25 (.05)
1928–1937	1.36 (.03)	1.24 (.04)	1.29 (.05)
1938–1947	1.64 (.04)	1.33 (.04)	1.43 (.05)
1948–1957	1.78 (.04)	1.55 (.05)	1.58 (.04)
1958–1967	1.89 (.04)	1.68 (.06)	1.72 (.05)
1968–1977	2.05 (.05)	1.90 (.06)	1.80 (.07)
1978–	N.A.	1.95 (.11)	N.A.

Note: Those born before 1918 excluded from analysis. N.A. = Not applicable.

[a] The figures in the 2000 column are for respondents from the 1995/96 sample who were reinterviewed in 2000, after the March presidential election. For the other sources, see table 2.3.

Question wording:

What political system, in your opinion, is most suitable for Russia?

tion or perceive themselves as having benefited least from the post-Soviet changes. Conversely, we should find the lowest levels of attachment to the Soviet past among segments of society that have benefited or perceive themselves as having benefited the most.

These issues are treated in tables 2.11 and 2.12, which nicely illustrate the independent role of age, and by extrapolation, exposure, to alternative patterns of socialization and historical experience, when account is taken of factors relevant to the respondents' opportunity structures. Table 2.11 shows the proportion, by decade born, of respondents saying that one or another political system is most suitable for Russia. (The two decades 1920–1929 and 1930–1939 were collapsed to increase the numbers in each of the subcategories in the subsequent tables.) Respondents were asked whether the Soviet system before *perestroika*, the current system, or Western democracy was "the most suitable political system for Russia." The mean responses across age cohorts are reported in Table 2.11.

Table 2.12 reports the mean scores across decades for the respondents' identification of the political system most suitable for Russia, controlling for family income, sex, respondents' assessment of their personal economic situation in the past year, and their overall satisfaction with life (subjective well-being). In this instance, the means reported are for responses to four options: the Soviet system before *perestroika*; the Soviet system but in another, more democratic form; the current system; or democracy of a Western type.

The pattern is striking. Table 2.11 undermines the argument that identification with the Soviet political system is stable across age cohorts. The decade respondents were born and the answer respondents gave to the question pertaining to the political system most suitable for Russia were related in a straightforwardly linear relation. It is easy to tell a story about culture shift as a result of diverging historical experiences, growing levels of education, and changes in occupational profiles that meshes well with these data.

The subsequent table (table 2.12) reveals two additional points. First, as table 2.12 indicates, the broadly linear relation between decade of birth and orientation to the political system holds when controls for income, sex, personal economic situation during the past year, and overall satisfaction with life are taken into account. In each instance, a uniformly or almost uniformly monotonic relation was observed within each columnar category. Thus a linear relationship is observed, as the columns in part I of table 2.12 indicate, between decade of birth and orientation to the political system for those who in 1999 said their economic situation had remained the same, had worsened, or had worsened significantly. Only among those who reported that their situation had improved was the linear relationship not perfect. When the same respondents were interviewed after the March 2000 presidential election, the same unambiguously linear relationship was observed for those who said their situation had remained the same or worsened significantly, with the relation between decade born and disposition to the political system being nearly linear for respondents who said their economic situation had improved and those who said it had worsened (table 2.12, I).

In several other instances, support for the Soviet system as the political system for Russia decreases with each decade, and the number of partisans of a more democratic Soviet system, the current political system, or Western democracy increases correspondingly. Thus among men and women in 1999, those earning less than R4000 in December 1999 and the same after March 2000 (the ruble-dollar exchange rate in December 1999 was about 25 to 1 and in March 2000 about 28 to 1), and those who in 1999 were dissatisfied or very dissatisfied with their life overall, there is a linear relation between decade born and response pertaining to the political system most suitable for Russia. For the others categories in table 2.12 the pattern is not completely uniform across age cohorts, but the trend is clear. Those born and socialized under Soviet power were more likely in 1999, as they had been in 1995, to assert that the Soviet political system before *perestroika* was the one most suitable for Russia.

Table 2.12.
Respondents' Assessment of System Most Suitable for Russia, 1999–2000 Election Surveys
(1 = Soviet system before *perestroika*; 2 = Soviet system of another, more democratic type; 3 =
present system; 4 = Western-type democracy)

| | I. Change in Economic Situation | | | | |
Decade Born[a]	Improved[b]	Remained the Same	Worsened	Worsened Significantly	Total
			1999—Mean (S.E.)		
1920–1939	1.69 (.12)	1.60 (.05)	1.78 (.08)	1.68 (.06)	1.67
1940–1949	1.90 (.12)	1.90 (.11)	1.92 (.13)	1.89 (.09)	1.91
1950–1959	2.10 (.13)	2.10 (.08)	2.12 (.10)	1.99 (.09)	2.07
1960–1969	2.60 (.15)	2.19 (.10)	2.28 (.12)	2.01 (.12)	2.23
1970+	2.55 (.17)	2.51 (.09)	2.41 (.12)	2.47 (.14)	2.48
			2000—Mean (S.E.)		
1920–1939	2.15 (.09)	1.83 (.06)	1.76 (.09)	1.68 (.11)	1.88
1940–1949	2.46 (.12)	2.01 (.07)	1.76 (.14)	1.93 (.18)	2.04
1950–1959	2.37 (.12)	2.26 (.07)	2.22 (.11)	1.95 (.13)	2.22
1960–1969	2.49 (.11)	2.36 (.08)	2.35 (.13)	2.00 (.18)	2.35
1970+	2.63 (.09)	2.55 (.08)	2.37 (.15)	2.27 (.15)	2.51

| | II. Sex of Respondent | | |
	Male	Female	Total
		1999—Mean (S.E.)	
1920–1939	1.78 (.06)	1.62 (.04)	1.67
1940–1949	1.96 (.11)	1.88 (.06)	1.90
1950–1959	2.15 (.08)	2.01 (.06)	2.06
1960–1969	2.30 (.10)	2.19 (.07)	2.33
1970+	2.58 (.09)	2.41 (.08)	2.47
		2000—Mean (S.E.)	
1920–1939	1.97 (.07)	1.83 (.05)	1.87
1940–1949	2.03 (.12)	2.04 (.06)	2.04
1950–1959	2.37 (.09)	2.13 (.06)	2.22
1960–1969	2.35 (.10)	2.37 (.07)	2.36
1970+	2.63 (.08)	2.44 (.07)	2.51

Table 2.12.

Respondents' Assessment of System Most Suitable for Russia, 1999–2000 Election Surveys (1 = Soviet system before *perestroika*; 2 = Soviet system of another, more democratic type; 3 = present system; 4 = Western-type democracy) (*cont'd*)

Decade Born:	III. Family Income in Rubles		
	Under R4000	R4000 and Up	Total
	1999—Mean (S.E.)		
1920–1939	1.66 (.03)	2.33 (.27)	1.68
1940–1949	1.84 (.06)	2.20 (.17)	1.89
1950–1959	2.03 (.06)	2.22 (.13)	2.06
1960–1969	2.12 (.07)	2.51 (.15)	2.20
1970+	2.39 (.07)	2.71 (.15)	2.46
	2000—Mean (S.E.)		
1920–1939[c]	1.85 (.04)	2.38 (.22)	1.87
1940–1949	1.98 (.06)	2.28 (.15)	2.01
1950–1959	2.14 (.06)	2.40 (.11)	2.19
1960–1969	2.21 (.06)	2.77 (.12)	2.33
1970+	2.39 (.07)	2.67 (.12)	2.44

Decade Born	IV. Respondent Subjective Well-being (Overall Satisfaction with Life)			
	Satisfied[d]	Dissatisfied	Very Dissatisfied	Total
1920–1939	2.05 (.14)	1.64 (.04)	1.59 (.06)	1.68
1940–1949	2.19 (.10)	1.91 (.07)	1.71 (.08)	1.90
1950–1959	2.47 (.12)	2.02 (.07)	2.00 (.09)	2.07
1960–1969	2.40 (.13)	2.17 (.08)	2.11 (.13)	2.34
1970+	2.54 (.10)	2.38 (.08)	2.59 (.15)	2.47

Sources: As in table 2.4.

[a] Those born before 1920 omitted.

[b] Between four and six respondents *per decade* stated that their economic situation had improved very significantly in the past decade. They are not included in the table.

[c] Virtually all of those born before 1920 reported earning less than R2000.

[d] A total of eleven of the respondents reported being "fully satisfied" with life on the whole.

Question wording:

What political system, in your opinion, is most suitable for Russia? (Unlike the figures reported in table 2.11, respondents in this case had four options, the Soviet system before *perestroika*, the Soviet system but in another, more democratic form, the present system, and democracy of a Western type.)

The second major point is that for the 1999 survey *within* age groups, the pattern along the tabular rows is by and large linear as well. In most instances, the mean scores were lower—closer to the Soviet system end of the scale—as disadvantage or dissatisfaction increased. The weakest relationship pertains to respondents' reported personal economic situation in the past year, where the differences within age cohort were quite modest overall. This is not surprising, at least for those born before 1950. Among those born before 1940, 96 percent reported incomes of less than R4000. Of those born between 1940 and 1949, 86 percent had incomes of R4000 or less. Whatever the changes in a middle-aged or older Russian's material status in the year prior to 1999, that person's situation was much like others of his or, primarily, her age group —and it was desperate.

Within all age cohorts, the means for 1999 were lower for women than for men, though the pattern is less clear cut for the same respondents interviewed after the March 2000 presidential election. As for income, both in late 1999 and after March 2000, within age cohort, those making R4000 or more always had higher mean scores than those who reported family incomes of less than R4000. The same was true in most instances for assessment of overall satisfaction with life. Within age cohort, the more satisfied respondents said they were overall, the less likely they were to be nostalgic for Soviet system before *perestroika*.

The changes across age cohort bespeak culture shift, not a stable Russian political culture. Those citizens born after the Revolution and who came of political age during the heyday of Soviet power were more prone to persist in their identification with Soviet symbols than were their successors. Conversely, regardless of the impact of individual opportunity structures, the more recently Russians were born, the more likely they were not to identify with Soviet institutions.

For those born before 1950, how one did last year was almost irrelevant to how one answered the question which political system was most appropriate for the Russian political system. Regardless of these respondents' personal experience in the past year, they shared the views of their age cohort—though it should be stressed that those whose incomes were higher and whose overall satisfaction with life was higher were less drawn to the Soviet model than were others in their age cohort. What this suggests—this is an argument Kullberg and I developed prior to my obtaining the 1999/2000 data—is that it was the reality of the 1990s along with prior socialization that has fueled nostalgia for the Soviet system.[42] It is the onus of the present—one that has been unevenly experienced—of Russia in the first decade after the collapse of Soviet power as much as the

[42] Ibid.

recollection of the past that drove orientation to the political system and nostalgia for the Soviet system as the twenty-first century began. For those roughly fifty or over, a return to the past seemed far preferable. Those who were younger and had more relevant skills were far more disposed to endorse the present system or to envisage democracy of a Western type as suitable for Russia; this development has produced an evolution in political culture in Russia over time.

That evolution notwithstanding, strong identifiers with traditional Soviet symbols exist. They were more prevalent in 1999 than they were in 1995. Rather, when one looks at the proportion of those saying in 1999 that Western-style democracy or the current system is more suitable than the Soviet system before *perestroika*, there was much to be concerned about with regard to the prospects for democracy. It can hardly be good news for democracy in Russia that, when asked, prior to the December 1999 parliamentary elections, to choose among Soviet system before *perestroika*, the present system, or Western democracy, that two-thirds of a national sample asserted in 1999 that of those choices the Soviet system before *perestroika* was more suitable than the present system or democracy of a Western type.[43] Likewise, there is more bad news in learning that more than three-quarters of that same sample regarded the old Soviet system or what to Westerners might seem an oxymoronic "Soviet system in another, more democratic form" more suitable than the present system or "democracy of a Western type."

Some solace at first glance may be taken in the fact that 55 percent of the 1999 survey respondents at the same time took a Churchillian perspective on democracy when asked if they agreed or not that "while there can be problems under democracy in any country, nevertheless democracy is better than any other form of rule." Moreover 70 percent of Russian respondents in the same survey in which two-thirds of them had said that the Soviet system was most suitable for Russia also answered that "a democratic political system" is "very suitable or suitable for our country." Almost certainly question effects play an important role in explaining these seemingly incompatible results. In this instance respondents were not presented with a choice among alternative political systems (the Soviet system before *perestroika*, the present system, Western-style democracy). In any event, as readers will recall, when placed in a cross-national context the 70 percent figure is worrisome. That proportion represents less support for democracy in general than in any of the over fifty surveys implemented

---

[43] There were many who refused to answer or volunteered some other answer. A sizable proportion of these respondents chose "the Soviet system but in another, more democratic form" when that additional option was presented to them in a survey conducted after the 2000 parliamentary election. See also Mel'vil,' *Demokraticheskie tranzity,* pp. 77–82.

by the World Values Survey in the period 1995–1999, even though it was up some from a survey in 1995 conducted as part of the project.

The substantial increase in mass responses between 1995/96 and 1999 asserting that the old Soviet system before *perestroika* was more suitable for Russia than the present system or Western democracy, coupled with the finding that Russian mass publics, viewed in a global perspective, remain comparatively less supportive of democracy, casts a dark cloud on several of the more optimistic findings reported in the first part of this chapter. (I have in mind the fact that Russians have an understanding of democratic concepts comparable to that of Westerners, the enormous, though declining, support for democracy and markets among civilian elites—including the rejection of synoptic thinking—and the relatively stable, though clearly weaker, support for democracy among mass publics as measured against our constructed political economy typology.)

There was, however, a silver lining that was barely visible in the December 1999 survey but became somewhat more evident after the March 2000 presidential election. Although Russians remained pessimistic in 1999 about their own economic prospects for the coming year—as they had been throughout the 1990s—they were on the average disposed to assert that the overall economic situation would improve. Of those giving an answer in late 1999, slightly more than a majority (53 percent) answered that they thought the economy would improve or improve significantly and 13 percent answered that it would get worse or significantly worse, with the balance answering it would remain the same.

Even more answered that the economy overall would improve after the presidential elections in March 2000—and they were right: the economy was improving.[44] Moreover, Russians were increasingly disposed to respond that the economic upturn would benefit them as well. Almost twice as many (22 percent in December 1999, 37 percent after the March 2000 election) said they thought their own economic situation would improve. This was paralleled by a modest decrease (from 77 to 67 percent) in the proportion of respondents saying that the Soviet system before *perestroika* was the system preferable for Russia.

These changes take on greater import when it is recognized that the same pattern observed with respect to assessments of the respondents' economic situation or their relative opportunities obtains with regard to their views about their prospective assessments both for themselves and for the Russian economy. As table 2.13 shows, the younger respondents are (overall and controlling for whether they answer that the economy will improve, stay the same, or worsen), the less attracted they were to the

[44] A good survey is Jacques Sapir, "The Russian Economy: From Rebound to Rebuilding," *Post-Soviet Affairs*, 17 (2001): 1–24.

Table 2.13.
Respondents' Assessment of System Most Suitable for Russia, 1999, Controlling for Views about Russia's Economic Prospects (1 = Soviet system before *perestroika*; 2 = Soviet system of another, more democratic, type; 3 = present system; 4 = Western-type democracy)

	Economic Situation in Russia in Coming Year		
Decade Born[a]	Improve or Improve Significantly	Stay the Same	Worsen or Worsen Significantly
	1999—Mean (S.E.)		
1920–1939	1.96 (.06)	1.47 (.05)	1.51 (.07)
1940–1949	2.05 (.07)	1.77 (.10)	1.70 (.15)
1950–1959	2.26 (.07)	1.81 (.07)	1.97 (.16)
1960–1969	2.46 (.09)	2.03 (.12)	2.04 (.18)
1970+	2.62 (.09)	2.26 (.11)	2.26 (.17)
	2000—Mean (S.E.)		
1920–1939	2.21 (.06)	1.61 (.07)	1.53 (.12)
1940–1949	2.31 (.07)	1.84 (.11)	1.44 (.16)
1950–1959	2.56 (.07)	1.96 (.11)	2.18 (.18)
1960–1969	2.60 (.07)	2.12 (.09)	1.92 (.18)
1970+	2.63 (.07)	2.34 (.12)	2.58 (.26)

Sources: As in table 2.4.

[a] Those born before 1920 omitted.

Question wording:

As in tables 2.11 and 2.12.

Soviet system before *perestroika*—though the absolute values emphasize how many would like to combine the social safety net features of the Soviet system with democracy. Within age cohort there are no systematic differences between those who respond that the economy will remain the same and those disposed to say it will worsen. In every case, both in 1999 and in 2000, those who answered that the Russian economy would improve or improve significantly in the forthcoming year were less nostalgic for the Soviet past and more inclined to assert that the present system or Western-type democracy is the political system most suitable for Russia. Russia may be another case of sociotropic thinking.[45] Whether that is so or not, nostalgia for the Soviet Union decreased in the brief span between

[45] Donald R. Kinder and D. Roderick Kiewiet, "Sociotropic Politics: The American Case," *British Journal of Political Science* 11 (1981): 129–61.

the Duma elections in 1999 and the presidential elections in March 2000 across all age cohorts as perceptions of the economy shifted.

Conclusion

This chapter by design has been a *tour d'horizon* concerning Russian attitudes to democracy and the market. It has, I hope, put to rest some widely held beliefs about Russian attitudes to key issues of politics. It is clear that in the 1990s Russians did not have conceptions of democracy that were radically at variance with Western notions. Overall support for democracy is distributed quite unevenly across Russian society. Elites, who have benefited enormously from the turn to the market and democracy, turn out, not surprisingly, to be more committed to the overt symbols of democracy than are mass respondents. Elites' endorsement of such symbols extended beyond superficial endorsement of political majoritarianism. They were also strongly disposed to the kind of philosophical pluralism requisite for democracy summarized by the rejection of the proposition that there is only one right philosophy.

Among mass publics there are systematic differences in various Russians' orientation to the market and democracy. Those who view the market favorably tend to extend the competition and pluralism inherent in markets to the arena of politics as well. Among Russian mass publics, likewise, younger cohorts, those with greater educational attainment, and the more politically knowledgeable were strikingly less imbued with Soviet orientations than were others.

In a longer frame of reference the decrease in support for the Soviet system across age group was a product of the social-structural transformation that accompanied continued development in the post–World War II period, liberalization and relaxation of control following the death of Stalin, and the general loss of faith induced by the faltering performance of the system in the 1970s and 1980s. As a result, by the early 1990s the general direction of change was away from adherence to Leninist tenets and values. Given that the strongest supporters of the Soviet system are those born prior to 1950, a reasonable extrapolation at the time of the collapse of the Soviet Union would have been that, given the natural process of generational replacement, Soviet political values would rather quickly vanish—especially in light of the gruesome decline in life expectancy among Russian males.

This picture of a natural process of the transmutation of values through generational change has to be tempered substantially by an awareness of the economic crisis in Russia and Russia's political experience in the 1990s. The asymmetries in income grew enormously in those years. Until the very end of the decade the economy declined precipitously. Across all age groups, a poor material situation and limited economic opportunity have dampened support for the new order. Correspondingly, they have strengthened attachment to the old, especially on the part of those socialized for the longest time into Soviet norms. Should the optimism about the prospects for the economy observed first in December 1999 and then in greater amounts after the March 2000 presidential election prove to be justified over the longer haul, it is possible that attachment to the old order will diminish, notably among those born after 1950.

Support for many but not all attributes associated with markets and democracy in Russia is sufficiently great at the beginning of a new millennium that it would be folly to write off as futile a partly free Russian political system and a grave mistake to attribute the bulk of Russia's present political difficulties to its past political culture. Many, especially among elites and the more market oriented and well informed among mass publics, reject the synoptic thinking one might encounter if some key dimensions of Russian culture were not malleable. Support for markets and democracy is, however, selective: Russians are less inclined to endorse tolerance for the public expression of dangerous ideas than for other aspects of democracy. Even those generally disposed to markets remain strongly committed to state ownership of heavy industry in ways that would be understood by some in Western Europe but are alien to virtually all Americans and British. Those who hope for markets and democracy in Russia have reason to be profoundly worried about how the economic crisis of the 1990s apparently has rekindled identification with the Soviet system, the Soviet Union, and the authoritarian, statist, attitudes we correctly associate with the Soviet system among those roughly fifty or older, first among those most adversely affected and by century's end more uniformly across the board. Whether the developments in 1999/2000 that seem to have prompted optimism among a sizable fraction of the Russian population about the prospects for the economy and by 2000 even for their own material position will persist in the first decade of a new century remain to be seen. If they do, the numbers of Russians regarding the Soviet system before *perestroika* as the system most suitable for Russia should diminish, especially if sizable numbers begin to think that not only Russia's but their own personal material situation will improve. Subsequent chapters explore the ramifications of Russia's partly free political-economic system for foreign policy.

3

Elite-Mass Interactions, Knowledge, and Russian Foreign Policy

THE LAST two chapters have described how demographically and behaviorally elites differ from attentive and other mass publics and have presented findings key to assessing the prospects for democracy in the Russian Federation. I turn now to the implications of the opening of the Russian political system for foreign policy. Because the empirical study of foreign policy attitudes has been largely synonymous with the study of American foreign policy, much of what I will be doing is asking whether generalizations about foreign policy orientations that emerge from the study of American foreign policy extend to post-Soviet Russian foreign policy and, if so, which ones.

This chapter advances four arguments. The first is that, just as elites differ importantly from mass publics in their orientation to the political economy, they have somewhat different orientations to foreign policy as well. This is true statistically and, more important, substantively: on balance elites are less isolationist and more internationally inclined than are mass publics. Moreover, at comparable time periods they have been more militantly internationalist (MI) and more cooperatively internationalist (CI) in the more precise sense that Eugene Wittkopf [1] and Ole Holsti[2] have in mind in describing attitudes of American leaders and mass publics.

Second, elites are more constrained, in Converse's terms, in their foreign policy views than are mass publics, both in the sense that the range of ideologically connected beliefs is broader and in the sense that a central notion such as the extent to which the United States is a threat is more systematically related to other policy orientations. The range of foreign policy issues about which attentive and other publics have coherent perspectives is not nearly so broad. As a consequence, the preferences of foreign policy elites are more connected, in terms of both number and complexity.

Third, among mass publics high levels of attentiveness are a stable predictor of the "connectedness" of foreign and domestic policy items,

---

[1] Wittkopf, "On the Foreign Policy Beliefs of the American People."
[2] Holsti, *Public Opinion*, pp. 98–118.

whether one has in mind the degree of ideological constraint or the links between whether the United States is a threat and a limited range of other foreign policy orientations.

Fourth, internationally attentive publics often manifest patterns of responses to survey items that are closer to those of elites than are the responses of the moderately informed or the unaware—though the gap among the responses of all the mass respondents is often narrower than between the very attentive public and the elites. The responses by the attentive public are not merely a function of taking cues from elites but, rather, are associated with the resistance of other mass publics, most relevantly the unaware and the completely unaware, to the cues provided by elites.[3] When elites advocate values that contravene traditional norms, attentive publics show less support for the preferences of the elite majority than would be expected by extrapolation; when elites lean on an open door and advocate views that will resonate among mass publics, a disproportionately large number from the attentive public favor the majority elite perspective.

Elite and Mass Differences in Foreign Policy

Gabriel Almond's seminal *American People and Foreign Policy* sought to develop a normative case for the democratic nature of the foreign policy process in the United States in light of two important empirical realities. The first is that power and competence are asymmetrically distributed in all political systems. The second is that sizable fractions of the public are stunningly ignorant about the world external to their immediate milieu. Almond coped with the first reality by distinguishing empirically between the nature of elites in the United States and in the Soviet Union and with the second by asserting that among mass publics there existed "an attentive public which is informed and interested in foreign policy problems, and which constitutes the audience for the foreign policy discussions among elites."[4] Underlying his approach was the assumption that social standing and attentiveness had profound implications for how people oriented themselves to politics, including foreign policy. One way to address that assumption is to compare orientations to foreign policy in our elite and mass samples in order to ascertain whether positional and knowledge-driven hypotheses point to differences in policy orientations.

---

[3] In the analysis that follows I have lumped the unaware and completely unaware together and referred to them both as "unaware."

[4] Almond, *The American People*, p. 138.

By and large, they do. Certainly, elite status differentiates survey response patterns, though as we see below the roles of knowledge among mass publics and the links between the attentive public, on the one hand, and both elites and the inattentive among the mass public, on the other, are complex. Tables 3.1 and 3.2 reveal the responses by foreign policy elites and mass publics to two sets of questions concerning foreign policy: one about policy orientations, the other, assessments of threats to Russian security. With few exceptions—the most important being whether respondents thought the United States was a threat to Russian security—elites had substantially different foreign policy orientations than did respondents in the mass public in 1993. Thus they were more disposed to send the Russian army in response to a request for military assistance than were persons in the 1993 mass sample. They were far more inclined to assert that Russia's "national interests for the most part extend further than its present territory," though they were less disposed to view the defense of Russians abroad, whether within the Commonwealth of Independent States (CIS) or elsewhere, as an important goal of Russian foreign policy than were mass respondents. (The announcement by the Ministry of Foreign Affairs in March 2000 that Russian foreign policy would pay greater attention to the concerns of Russians abroad was likely a response to the views of the Russian public.) Foreign policy elites in 1993 were far more inclined to reduce military spending and foreign aid than were mass publics.

On matters pertaining to threats to Russian security, foreign policy elites in 1993 also differed from their mass respondent counterparts. Russians were presented with a battery of questions in which they were shown a continuum ranging from 1 to 5. The scale, as presented, identified 1 as the absence of threat and 5 the greatest threat, without labeling the interior scale numbers. I have termed 4 "great" throughout this book. (Many of these items have also been asked by Holsti and Rosenau of American leaders.)[5]

The results are excerpted in table 3.2, which shows the proportion of respondents characterizing a particular item as being either a great or the greatest danger to Russian security. In 1993 Russian foreign policy elites were more relaxed than other Russians about the world outside Russia. They saw the growth of American military power and American involvement in the third world as being less threatening than did other Russians. They were also less concerned about the security implications of the gap globally between rich and poor countries and about global population growth, and less worried about the conflicts on Russia's borders as a threat to Russia's security. Where they meshed with their counterparts in the mass sample was that they were equally concerned about the ability of

[5] Holsti, *Public Opinion*, pp. 106–109.

Table 3.1
Mass Foreign Policy Orientations 1993–2000

	Elites			Mass		
	1993	*1995*	*1999*	*1993*	*1995*	*2000*
U.S. a threat to Russian security	27%	53%	62%	26%	44%	68%
	(52)	(91)	(119)	(288)	(1030)	(908)
Agreed: Russia should "send its army, if asked, to aid countries of the former USSR"	56%	78%	72%	35%	35%	56%
	(106)	(130)	(134)	(396)	(870)	(759)
To aid other countries	35%	53%	39%	19%	16%	26%[a]
	(65)	(84)	(69)	(207)	(399)	(340)
"For the most part the national interests of Russia should extend beyond its current territory"	77%	80%	83%	58%	60%	—
	(149)	(144)	(168)	(614)	(1273)	
Rebuilding Russian economy cannot be done without help of West[b]	57%	46%	30%	31%	28%	17%
	(105)	(87)	(60)	(340)	(690)	(240)
"The defense of Russians abroad in the former republics of the USSR" is a very important foreign policy goal.	69%	72%	64%	79%	74%	81%
	(137)	(129)	(132)	(937)	(1841)	(1204)
In other countries?	38%	48%	34%	53%	38%	49%
	(76)	(86)	(70)	(621)	(925)	(710)
"Obtaining the security of countries friendly to Russia" a very important foreign policy goal	—	14%	12%	—	34%	—
		(24)	(25)		(821)	
"Strengthening . . . the United Nations" a very important foreign policy goal	—	35%	33%	—	49%	54%
		(63)	(68)		(1087)	(693)
"Human rights in other countries" a very important goal	—	20%	20%	—	30%	—
		(36)	(41)		(702)	
Foreign aid should be reduced	87%	67%	69%	75%	89%	—
	(166)	(118)	(138)	(876)	(2382)	
Increase military spending	5%	46%	67%	15%	35%	—
	(10)	(80)	(139)	(180)	(931)	

Sources: The three elite surveys and the 1993 mass survey of European Russians were conducted by ROMIR. Demoscope conducted the 1995/96 national survey. The 2000 mass data are from those re-interviewed from the 1995/96 sample conducted by Demoscope.

Notes: Actual number of representatives for particular cells shown in parentheses. Dashes indicate question not asked.

[a] In the December 1999 mass survey, 66 percent said the United States was a threat; 55 percent agreed that Russia should send its army if asked to aid a country of the former Soviet Union; and 28 percent agreed with regard to sending troops to other countries.

[b] Figures reported are those who disagreed with the proposition that rebuilding the economy can be done without the help of the West.

Question wording for items not quoted directly in the table:

Do you think the United States is a threat to Russian security?

Should Russia send its troops, if asked, to aid other foreign countries?

Russia can resolve its economic problems without the help of the West. (Table shows proportion disagreeing.)

Many believe it necessary to decrease government expenditures in several areas. In which areas, in your opinion, should expenditures be decreased, in which kept the same, and in which increased?

. . .

2. Expenditures for defense and military needs.
3. Expenditures for aid to foreign countries.

Table 3.2
Perceived Security Threats to Russia, 1993–1999

	Elites			Mass		
	1993	1995	1999	1993	1995	1999
"Growth of U.S. . . .power"	20% (40)	50% (94)	60% (127)	40% (461)	62% (1479)	73% (1227)
U.S. penetration in third world	11% (21)	—	—	34% (250)	—	—
Spread of NATO in Eastern Europe	—	64% (115)	59% (122)	—	53% (990)	65% (905)
NATO intervention in European countries	—	—	63% (131)	—	—	72% (1118)
Having "key economic sectors in foreign hands"	—	44% (79)	55% (114)	—	72% (1589)	—
"Increase in the gap between rich and poor countries"	17% (33)	25% (45)	36% (75)	41% (450)	42% (907)	52% (817)
Border conflicts within Commonwealth of Independent States	44% (87)	50% (90)	55% (114)	69% (793)	69% (1517)	70% (1147)
With other countries	22% (44)	37% (66)	36% (75)	52% (577)	72% (1663)	78% (1273)
Russian involvement in conflicts not its concern	36% (71)	42% (74)	34% (71)	62% (718)	71% (1662)	78% (1301)
"Uncontrolled growth in global population"	9% (18)	21% (36)	16% (32)	21% (230)	19% (390)	—
Failure to handle domestic problems	72% (142)	84% (150)	84% (174)	72% (820)	77% (1835)	79% (1313)

Sources: The three elite surveys and the 1993 mass survey of European Russians were conducted by ROMIR. Demoscope conducted the 1995 and 1999 mass surveys based on a national sample of Russians.

Note: Actual number of representatives for particular cells shown in parentheses. Dashes indicate question not asked.

Question wording:

Which of the below represent the greatest threat to the security of Russia and which do not at all threaten it? Evaluate, please, the level of danger of each item listed on a five-point scale, where 1 indicates absence of threat and 5 the greatest danger.

Growth of US military power in comparison with that of Russia.
American penetration in a third world country.
The expansion of NATO to include countries of Eastern Europe.
The increasing gap between rich and poor countries.
Military intervention by NATO in inter-nationality conflicts within European countries
The transfer of key sectors of the Russian economy into the hands of foreign companies.
Russian involvement in conflicts which are not its concern.
Border conflicts of Russia with countries of the CIS, that is, former republics of the USSR.
Border conflicts of Russia with other foreign countries.
The uncontrolled growth of global population.
The inability of Russia to solve its internal problems.

the government to handle the country's domestic problems, which they regarded as by far the greatest threat confronting the country.

Russia's orientation to the world had changed considerably in the two years between 1993 and 1995. The era dominated by those sometimes termed the Atlanticists in Russian foreign policy had passed.[6] Foreign policy elites continued to be more disposed to think of Russia's national interests as extending beyond its territorial confines than did members of the mass public. Among the changes, elites in 1995 were more prepared than they had been in 1993 to respond favorably to a request for armed aid if requested by another state, an enthusiasm not shared by mass publics in 1993 or 1995. The proportion of the latter's response to questions concerning whether "Russia should send its troops if asked" either by a state that had been a member of the former Soviet Union or from elsewhere remained in 1995 essentially unchanged from 1993. (There was some increase in mass support for the use of force within the former Soviet Union in 1999; it remains to be seen whether this change was contextual.)

Elites remained less inclined to assert that the Russian economy could be restored without the help of the West than members of the mass public, though Russians in general, mass publics and elites alike, were more prone to assert that the reconstruction of the Russian economy could be accomplished without Western help than had been the case in 1993. Likewise, in 1995 elites were just as likely as mass respondents to assert that the protection of Russians in other states in the CIS was very important. They were somewhat more likely to regard the protection of Russians outside the confines of the former Soviet Union as a very important goal of Russian foreign policy than they had been in 1993, and fewer advocated reducing foreign aid. (Ironically, mass publics moved in the opposite direction; in 1995 they were almost unanimous in favoring reduced foreign aid and fewer responded that the protection of Russians outside the CIS should be a very important foreign policy goal.) At the same time, while elites were marginally less likely to regard the security of Russia's "friends abroad" as a very important goal, the survey evidence provided the latter scarce comfort. Only a third of the mass public respondents and one in seven among the elite respondents in 1995 stated that the defense of Russia's friends abroad was a very important goal of its foreign policy.

Russian foreign policy elites and mass publics viewed the world in more threatening terms in 1995 than they did in 1993. Table 3.2 reflects a

[6] Celeste Wallander, ed., *The Sources of Russian Foreign Policy after the Cold War* (Boulder: Westview Press, 1996); Alexei Arbatov, "Rossiia: natsional'naia bezopasnost' v 90-e gody," *Mirovaia ekonomika i mezhdunarodnye otnosheniia*, 1994, no. 7, pp. 5–18, nos. 8–9, pp. 5–18; Arbatov, "Russia's Foreign Policy Alternatives," *International Security* 18 (Fall 1993): 5–43.

context in which the initial euphoria after the collapse of the Soviet Union had begun to be clouded by issues such as NATO expansion and Russian sales of nuclear technology to Iran. Russians across the board were more concerned about the U.S. threat to Russian security and the growth of U.S. power in 1995 than in 1993. There was a huge shift in the direction of favoring increased military spending. In 1993, mass publics, doubtless fearful of job loss, had resisted reductions. In 1995, elites had moved beyond the mass publics in advocating increased spending for defense. In 1993, 59 percent of the foreign policy elites who responded had favored decreased military spending and 5 percent had supported increasing it, with the balance of answers being to keep it at the same level. Two years later, less than a quarter (23 percent) of the elite respondents wanted to reduce military spending and almost half (46 percent) indicated that it should be increased. They saw the prospects of border conflicts as more threatening, and more of them were concerned about Russia's becoming involved in conflicts of no concern to it.

At the same time, elites for the most part continued to be distinct from mass publics in being *relatively* less concerned about a broad spectrum of issues, with the exception of the American threat to Russian security and NATO expansion. The proportion of elites choosing 4 or 5 on a five-point scale where 1 represented absence of threat and 5 the greatest threat increased from 20 to 50 percent from 1993 to 1995 regarding the growth of U.S. military power. Nevertheless, the proportion of elites characterizing the growth of American military power as a great or the greatest danger remained lower than that of respondents among the mass public. Similarly, they were proportionately less inclined to give responses indicating that they were fearful of foreign firms controlling sectors of the Russian economy, less likely than mass publics to be concerned about the security threat of involvement in a conflict about which Russia should have no concern, and less concerned about global distributional issues.

I was unable to ask of mass publics in 1999 all the questions asked in 1993 and 1995, though they were posed to elites. Consistent with the 1993 and 1995 surveys, elite and mass public assessments of the threat to Russian security by the United States grew more or less in tandem in 1999, and the proportion of each regarding the United States as a threat increased correspondingly.[7] Items concerning the growth of American

---

[7] Responses to questions about the American threat are highly contextual. There was, for instance, an appreciable drop in the proportion saying that the United States was a threat between December 1995 and the summer of 1996. For links between these changes and the 1996 election, see chapter 4. The Russian public opinion firm VTsIOM, similarly, reported in September 1999 that 49 percent of a Russian sample thought "badly" or "very badly" of the United States in March. In August the negative assessments had dropped to 32 percent. RFE/RL Newsline, 3, 172, September 3, 1999.

power and NATO expansion indicated that in 1999 elites were somewhat less likely to give answers indicative of alarm about such matters than were ordinary Russian citizens—even though surveys in 1997 had revealed that a sizable fraction of the latter had not even heard about plans for NATO expansion.[8] For both elites and mass publics, responses in 1999 to questions about American power were radically different from those given in 1993. Table 3.1 brings this home in more detail. It suffices here to observe that in 1993 one in five respondents from among Russian foreign policy elites and two of five of the mass public in European Russia had termed the growth of U.S. military power a great or the greatest threat to Russian security. At century's end, three of five among the elite and three of four (73 percent) in the Russian national mass sample considered it such.

At the same time, mass publics were more disposed to the use of force, especially within the former Soviet Union, in 1999 than in 1993 or 1995, probably in the context of the early stages of the renewed war in Chechnya. (The differences in responses in 1999 and in 1993 and 1995 to the use of force in the former Soviet Union and elsewhere were statistically significant, though in the latter instance the relationship was a weak one.) Elites were likely somewhat less disposed than they had been in 1995 to use force outside the former Soviet Union (table 3.1). It remained the case, though, as it had been in 1993 and 1995, that foreign policy elites were markedly more likely to agree that Russia should send troops if requested by another state than were ordinary folk. As Immanuel Kant observed two hundred years ago, it is not leaders who fight wars. Russian elites persisted in 1999, as they had in 1993 and 1995, in being far less concerned about Russia's involvement in conflicts that were not its concern, about the dangers of border conflicts either within the CIS or elsewhere, and about the gap globally between rich and poor countries (table 3.1).

Militant and Cooperative Internationalism

One should not, however, regard elites in Russia—or mass publics, for that matter—as being in any way monolithic on foreign policy issues. Drawing in somewhat general terms from the work of Wittkopf and Holsti, we can identify two dimensions in Russian foreign policy orientations, what Wittkopf has described as "militant internationalism" and "cooperative internationalism." The Russian data do not permit us to replicate exactly the measures Wittkopf and Holsti employed to create these scales, but a reasonable approximation of the spirit of each internationalist strand may be captured.

[8] See chapter 6.

In the American foreign policy literature, militant internationalism largely refers to whether persons perceive another great power as constituting a major threat to their nation's security and whether they are prepared to use their armed forces in the pursuit of various foreign policy goals.[9] To get at this disposition, I combined three questions, one that asked explicitly whether "the United States was a threat to Russian security" and two others that called for respondents' views as to whether in one instance, "Russia should send its army, if asked, to aid countries of the former USSR," and in the second, ". . . to aid other foreign countries, if asked." For the 1993 and 1995 mass surveys and the three elite surveys I used a single question to get at Russia's proclivity for economic cooperation in the first decade or so after the collapse of the Soviet Union, namely, whether respondents agreed that "Russia could resolve its economic problems without the help of the West." This question was not asked in the 1999 mass survey, but was used in 2000 when those interviewed in 1995/96 were reinterviewed. What the 1999 survey did have was an item that identified much the same hostility to economic cooperation: "It is necessary to defend our industry from foreign firms that wish to seize Russian markets." This question was also asked in the 1995 mass survey but not in the 1993 survey of European Russia.[10] Use of one or the other item turns out basically not to affect the measure. The results for 1995 were essentially the same as were those for the December 1999 parliamentary survey and the reinterviews after the March 2000 presidential election of those who had been interviewed in 1995/96. (See, for instance, table 3.5 below.)

Combining the indicators of economic cooperation with the two use-of-force questions and the U.S. threat question produces an approximation of the militant/cooperative internationalist typology (MI/CI) that has proved fruitful in depicting elite and mass attitudes in the United States. Those in this scheme who are high on the militant-internationalist dimension and high on the cooperative dimension as well have been termed in the literature on American foreign policy "internationalists." Those who are high on militant internationalism and low on international economic cooperation are "hard-liners." Those who are low on militant internationalism because of their views about whether the United States is a threat and the use of Russian armed forces abroad and who favor Western aid to ease Russia's economic needs are "accommodationists."

---

[9] Holsti, *Public Opinion*, pp. 98–105.

[10] I considered combining this item with one calling on the respondents to say whether they thought "Russia needs to attract foreign capital into the economy." But using two items presented me with an arbitrary cut-point choice for which there was no substantive basis and had profound consequences for what was reported as the distribution of respondents on the scale.

Finally, "isolationists" are those who agree with hard-liners that Russia can deal with its economic problems without the help of the West but score low on militant internationalism.[11]

Using this scheme we can compare Russian foreign policy elite attitudes across time and with Russian mass publics, and, in some respects, with the attitudes of American foreign policy leaders. Table 3.3 presents the elite responses to several foreign policy items and to a battery of questions dealing with threats to Russia's security. To enlarge the number of respondents, I have aggregated the elites from the 1993, 1995, and 1999 surveys, excluding the responses the second time they were interviewed of those who had been reinterviewed. (I did the analysis with and without duplication and the differences in the percentage distributions were trivial.) As inspection of table 3.3 reveals, the predictive potency of the MI/CI scheme is rather strong with regard to security measures traditionally conceived and to economic issues ranging from fears of Western economic dominance of Russia to the putatively growing global divide between rich and poor countries. Unlike American leaders, however, the range of issues for which the scheme provides powerful differentiation does not extend to matters such as the environment or the possibility of a global population crisis.[12]

This is indicated in table 3.3 in two ways. To take an illustrative example, Russian elites were fundamentally divided in the 1990s on the matter of military spending. This division is evidenced in table 3.3 by the proportion favoring increased military spending. Less obviously, reference should also be made to the superscripts. The superscripts for each item are intended as a shorthand way to indicate that one group is statistically distinguishable at the .05 level from one or more of the other three.[13] Thus the reference to 63%[2,3,4] of the hard-liners advocating increased military spending represents, obviously, the proportion favoring increased spending. It also indicates that as a group the hard-liners are statistically distinguishable from the internationalists in column 2, the accommodationists in column 3, and the isolationists in column 4. Over the three surveys, only 16 percent of the accommodationists favored increased military

[11] I am uncomfortable with the normative connotations of the categories identified in the text but have chosen to use them to enhance comparability with the dispositions of American elites.

[12] Holsti had 2312 in his sample; the three Russian elite surveys together conducted 590 interviews including re-interviews. The difference in sample size, at a minimum, qualifies comparative statements about the relative range of issues that the MI/CI typology predicts to for the two elites.

[13] I employed analysis of variance in discriminating among the categories and employed the so-called Bonferroni test. It is analogous to employing multiple t tests and discriminates among group means at the .05 level.

Table 3.3
Militant and Cooperative Internationalism among Elites, 1993–1999

	1 Hardliners	2 Inter-nationalists	3 Accommoda-tionists	4 Isolationists
Increase military spending	63% [2,3,4] (90)	36%[3] (31)	16%[4] (16)	31% (27)
Reduce foreign aid	65%[3] (94)	70% (60)	82% (81)	79% (69)
". . . National interests of Russia extend beyond its current territory"	89%[3,4] (129)	85% (74)	69% (66)	73% (62)
Security threat:				
Border conflicts within the Commonwealth of Independent States	61% (90)	50% (44)	45% (45)	42% (36)
Elsewhere	42% [2,3,4] (61)	23% (20)	29% (29)	27% (23)
U.S. intervention in third world (1993 only)	24%[3] (8)	23% (8)	3% (2)	5% (2)
NATO expansion (1995 and 1999 only)	75% [3,4] (92)	64% (38)	37% (18)	53% (26)
NATO intervention in European countries (1999)	79%[3,4] (52)	71% (15)	42% (8)	46% (17)
Growth of U.S. military might	71%[2,3,4] (104)	43%[3] (38)	13%[4] (13)	37% (32)
Having "key economic sectors in foreign hands" (1995 and 1999)	57%[3] (67)	52%[3] (31)	25% (12)	40% (22)
"Involvement in conflicts that don't concern" it	28%[3] (42)	33%[3] (29)	55%[4] (55)	31% (27)

spending, when presented with choices of increasing, reducing, or keeping military spending the same. (It should be noted that virtually no one among the foreign policy elites interviewed, including the military officers, favored increased military spending in 1993.) By contrast, the hardliners are, well, hard-liners: They were far more likely than any of the other elite respondents to regard the growth of American military power as a great or the greatest threat to Russian security. Hard-liners similarly were more likely to be concerned about NATO expansion in Eastern Europe and the possibility of NATO's repeating its experience in Yugoslavia by

Table 3.3 (*cont'd*)
Militant and Cooperative Internationalism among Elites, 1993–1999

	1 Hardliners	2 Inter- nationalists	3 Accommoda- tionists	4 Isolationists
"Environmental pollution" (1993)	35% (55)	36% (32)	47% (47)	49% (34)
"The greenhouse and other negative effects on the earth's climate" (1993)	29% (10)	29% (10)	27% (16)	23% (8)
Global gap between rich and poor countries	38%[3] (56)	26% (23)	17% (17)	24% (21)
"Uncontrolled growth in global population"	13% (19)	15% (13)	13% (12)	12% (10)
"Inability . . . to resolve domestic conflicts"	80% (118)	80% (70)	77% (77)	75% (63)

Sources. The three elite surveys were conducted by ROMIR. The *n*'s vary because not all questions were asked in all three surveys.

Notes. Those who were interviewed in 1993 and reinterviewed in 1995 and those who were interviewed in 1995 and reinterviewed in 1999 are counted only once, the first time they were interviewed. Actual number of representatives for particular cells shown in parentheses.

Items used to construct militant internationalist/cooperatively internationalist (MI/CI) scale:
Should Russia send its troops, if asked, to aid countries of the former USSR?
Should Russia send its troops, if asked, to aid other foreign countries?
Do you think the United States is a threat to Russian security?
Russia can resolve its economic problems without the help of the West.
It is necessary to defend our industry from foreign firms that wish to seize Russian markets.
Question wording.

For the exact wording of the items not in direct quotes, see table 3.2 of this chapter.

intervening militarily in a European state to address an interethnic conflict than were other elites, and were statistically separable from both accommodationists and isolationists. More than twice as many (76 percent) of the hard-liners as the accommodationists viewed NATO expansion into Eastern Europe as major threat to Russian security. Seventy-one percent of the hard-liners had grave misgivings about the growth of American military power, whereas only 13 percent among those coded as accommodationists considered it a great or the greatest danger. By contrast, accommodationists were almost twice as likely as hard-liners to regard the possibility of Russia's involvement in conflicts that are none of its affair as representing a major threat to Russia's security (table 3.3).

Both hard-liners and internationalists were far more concerned than either accommodationists or isolationists about the prospects of key economic sectors falling into foreign hands. Accommodationists presumably

Table 3.4
Militant and Cooperative Internationalism among Elites, 1993–1999

	1993	1995	1999
Hard-liners	20%	39%	47%
	(34)	(56)	(71)
Internationalists	21%	27%	14%
	(35)	(39)	(22)
Accommodationists	36%	20%	13%
	(61)	(29)	(20)
Isolationists	22%	13%	26%
	(37)	(18)	(39)

Source: See table 3.3, where the wording for the items used in constructing the MI/CI measure may be found.
Note: Actual number of respondents for particular cells shown in parentheses.

were simply not concerned that key economic sectors might fall into the hands of foreigners. To say the least, isolationists do not favor increased economic interdependence. They may reason, however, that since they were disposed to think that Russia could handle the restructuring of its economy without the help of the West, there was little likelihood of key economic sectors falling into foreign hands, and thus on this score they were relatively less worried than hard-liners and internationalists.

Which constructed group or groups prevail at a particular time has clear implications for Russian foreign policy at that moment. Comparing these groups is also one useful way of assessing the changes in Russian foreign policy in the 1990s and of comparing Russian and American elites. Table 3.4 shows how the distribution among accommodationists, isolationists, hard-liners, and internationalists among elites changed over the decade of the 1990s. It captures the broad outlines of the evolution of Russian foreign policy in that time period. In 1993, accommodationists constituted the dominant, though not the majority, viewpoint among Russian elites, with each of the remaining constructed groups constituting about a fifth of the elites sampled. By century's end, hard-liner perspectives occupied a preeminent position. We have three data points over a bit less than a decade, so one wishes to be careful in extrapolating to the first decade of the new century. But East-West relations were palpably different in 1999 than they were in 1993 and 1995, and those differences are evident in this table.

Obviously, the relative distribution of groups at any one time has important implications for Russian foreign policy behavior at a particular juncture. The MI/CI typology also reinforces the basic point that elites are both more militantly internationalist and more cooperatively interna-

Table 3.5
Militant and Cooperative Internationalism among Mass Publics, 1993–2000

	1993 European Russia	1995/96 Panel A^a	1995/96 Panel B^b	1999 Panel	2000 Reinterview
Hard-liners	15% (131)	18% (347)	19% (391)	39% (489)	40% (421)
Internationalists	7% (65)	9% (168)	7% (136)	9% (115)	9% (90)
Accommodationists	24% (215)	19% (367)	17% (346)	10% (133)	8% (86)
Isolationists	53% (472)	54% (1032)	57% (1039)	42% (533)	44% (464)

Sources: ROMIR conducted the 1993 mass survey of European Russians. The remaining surveys were conducted on the basis of a national sample by Demoscope. The figures for 2000 are drawn from Demoscope's reinterviews after the presidential election of those surveyed in 1995/96.

Note: The wording of the items in the MI/CI measure may be found in table 3.3.

[a] Corresponds to scale for 1993. For a description, see text.

[b] Corresponds to scale for 1999. For a description, see text.

tionalist than are mass publics. The fundamental instinct of mass publics is isolationist. Tables 3.4 and 3.5 compare the distribution of groups for the 1993, 1995, and 1999 elites and the1993, 1995, and 1999 mass surveys, along with the reinterviews in 2000 of those interviewed in 1995/96. In 1993 the proportion of elites who were hard-liners and internationalists was higher than among the mass sample, and the proportion of accommodationists among the elites was also noticeably higher. In 1995 the proportion of elite accommodationists was slightly greater than in the mass sample, and the proportion of hard-liners and internationalists was much greater. In 1999 again—allowing for the fact that the elite and mass measures are not the same—elites were composed of a higher proportion of hard-liners than the mass public despite the latter's sharp increase in hard-liners since 1995 (as well as in internationalists and accommodationists). In 1999 and 2000, as they had been in 1993 and 1995, the mass publics were more isolationist than were the elites, though they were significantly more hard-line than they had been in 1993 and 1995. Russian elites are both more militantly internationalist and more cooperatively internationalist than are mass publics.

In cross-national terms, Russian elites were not, however, as prone to accommodation and internationalism as were their American counterparts, even in the early 1990s when such sentiments were highest among

Russian elites. By Holsti's reckoning, only 5 percent of the American elite in 1992 was isolationist, in comparison with 22 percent of the Russian elites in 1993, and only 9 percent of the American elites were hard-liners, as opposed to 20 percent of the Russian elites. Even in 1993 at what was the peak of Russian elite accommodation in the 1990s, three in eight Russian elites were accommodationists and one-fifth were internationalists (table 3.4), whereas among the American elites at approximately that juncture (1992) more than half (53 percent) were, by Holsti's coding, accommodationists and exactly a third were internationalists.[14]

Belief Systems and Knowledge

The neatness with which we can make the point about the sharp and nearly uniform distinction attitudinally between elites and others is less evident, using Almond's theoretical division within the mass sample, when we compare attentive publics with others. Against a knowledge-based criterion, we usually notice a continuum ranging from the responses to foreign policy items of the unattentive to those of foreign policy elites, with the moderately unaware, moderately aware, and attentive public situated between—though the responses of the attentive public were often closer to those of the unaware than to those of the foreign policy elites. Thus the responses of the attentive public are part of an overall pattern ranging from the responses of the inattentive through those of the foreign policy elites on matters, here aggregating the responses to the 1993 and 1995 surveys, such as use of force abroad, the need (or lack thereof) for the West's help in rebuilding the Russian economy, fear of foreign control over key economic sectors, support for Russia's friends abroad, and the growth of American military might. But the pattern is not monotonic with regard to whether Russia's national interests are broadly conceived, whether the United States is a threat, whether aid for Russians abroad is a high priority, and the importance of the United Nations. Clearly, on some matters attentive publics respond to elite cues and on others they do not. The simple notion that attentive publics can be mobilized by elites and that they in turn mobilize the remainder of the citizenry did not capture the reality of leader-citizenship interactions in Russia in the 1990s (table 3.6).

But there are other ways that elites and attentive publics have been thought to differ from the remainder of a country's citizenry. One, by now conventional, way to differentiate among the three groups is to consider the extent to which the former two groups have constrained (coher-

[14] Holsti, *Public Opinion*, p. 109.

ent) belief systems, while the latter, especially those who are least informed, have "nonattitudes."[15] I define the correlation of attitudes across
a broad set of questions as the relative constraint in a person's belief system. As Converse did, I divided individuals' belief systems about politics
into two broad categories, foreign policy–related beliefs and domestic policy beliefs.[16] Not surprisingly, by this criterion elites turn out to have more
coherent belief systems about the domestic political economy—here using
the nine items employed to construct the political economy typology in
chapter 2—than do others. Similarly, those we have identified as attentive
publics—whether identified by university attendance or by their level of
knowledge of the external world—occupy second place (table 3.7).

The same is true for foreign policy. Using items that identify orientations to military intervention, if requested, within a state that is a former
member of the Soviet Union, protection of Russians abroad, national interest domain, need for help from the West, and the U.S. threat, elites
did indeed have more constrained belief systems than do others by the
conventional measure. Whether the attentive public is defined by using a
measure based on international knowledge or by the cruder indicator of
university attendance, the Russian attentive public had more constrained
foreign policy beliefs than others among the mass public. Those with some
knowledge (combining those who were moderately unaware and those
who were moderately aware) had in turn more constrained beliefs than
the unaware and the completely unaware.

An additional approach to thinking about whether and how attentive
publics differ from other publics is to return to an idea in Converse's classic
1964 paper to which neither Converse nor the legion of scholars since have
devoted anything like the attention that his ideas on range have received in
thinking about belief constraint, to wit the notion of centrality.[17] Table
3.8 explores the extent to which the battery of items pertaining to threats
to Russian security to which reference has been made previously links to
the central question of whether the United States is seen as constituting
a threat to Russian security.

The pattern is striking. Elites link a wide range of security matters to
the perceived threat by the United States. Nine of the eleven items in table
3.8 correlate with elites' reported perception of the American threat to

---

[15] Converse, "The Belief Systems."

[16] I employed the standard method for measuring the conception of constrained belief
systems, which involves running bivariate correlations for several questionnaire items, sum-
ming the absolute values generated by the correlation matrix, and computing an average
interitem correlation. For an alternative approach, see Ole Holsti and James Rosenau, "The
Domestic and Foreign Policy Attitudes among American Leaders," *Journal of Conflict Resolution*, 32 (1988): 248–94.

[17] Converse, "The Belief Systems," p. 208.

Table 3.6
Knowledge and Foreign Policy Preferences, 1993–1995

	Unaware	Moderately Unaware	Moderately Aware	Attentive	Elites
Agreed: Russia should "send its army, if asked, to aid a country of the former USSR"	29% (435)	36% (335)	40% (251)	43% (224)	65% (207)
To aid other countries	13% (187)	17% (161)	19% (117)	25% (132)	42% (131)
"The defense of Russians abroad in the former Soviet Union" is a very important foreign policy goal	74% (1064)	76% (745)	78% (524)	78% (442)	72% (241)
In other countries	42% (599)	44% (420)	44% (295)	41% (231)	42% (143)
"Strengthening. . . the United Nations" a very important foreign policy goal (1995)	47% (427)	51% (314)	49% (205)	48% (137)	35% (63)
"For the most part the national interests of Russia should extend beyond its current territory"	57% (634)	61% (542)	57% (347)	60% (325)	79% (261)
Military spending should be decreased	21% (318)	25% (244)	28% (182)	35% (196)	44% (143)
Aiding Russia's friends abroad a very important foreign policy goal (1995)	36% (367)	33% (270)	33% (143)	30% (87)	14% (24)
Foreign aid should be reduced	84% (1312)	83% (829)	87% (572)	86% (484)	77% (252)
Rebuilding Russian economy can be done "without help of West"	77% (1053)	68% (630)	68% (424)	64% (343)	48% (152)
U.S. a threat to Russian security	43% (574)	31% (309)	37% (227)	33% (540)	39% (126)

Russian security. These include matters about which we would be aston-
ished if they were not significantly correlated to the perceived threat to
Russia by the United States, such as NATO expansion in Eastern Europe
and the control of key sectors of the Russian economy. But we also observe
weaker, but statistically significant, relations between whether the United
States is a threat and concerns about the global gap between rich and poor

Table 3.6 (*cont'd*)
Knowledge and Foreign Policy Preferences, 1993–1995

	Unaware	Moderately Unaware	Moderately Aware	Attentive	Elites
The following are a great or the greatest threat to Russian security:					
Border conflicts within the Commonwealth of Independent States	71% (923)	70% (659)	69% (448)	66% (375)	46% (155)
With other countries	72% (916)	66% (608)	61% (391)	56% (320)	28% (94)
"Involvement in conflicts that don't concern" it	71% (954)	67% (630)	69% (437)	63% (275)	37% (122)
"Inability. . .to resolve domestic conflicts"	74% (1000)	76% (715)	77% (505)	77% (432)	76% (254)
"Increase in the gap between rich and poor countries"	46% (565)	42% (374)	39% (240)	32% (175)	21% (71)
"Spread of NATO to Eastern Europe"(1995)	50% (354)	54% (284)	52% (187)	58% (163)	64% (115)
"Uncontrolled growth in global population"	22% (353)	19% (165)	19% (114)	16% (86)	14% (45)
"Growth of U.S. military power"	63% (857)	53% (506)	50% (322)	44% (251)	34% (112)
Having "key economic sectors in foreign hands" (1995)	74% (660)	73% (448)	71% (285)	66% (192)	44% (79)

Sources. The 1993 mass data are from a survey of European Russia conducted by ROMIR, as are the 1993 and 1995 elite surveys. Demoscope conducted the 1995/96 survey, drawing on a national sample.

Notes. Actual number of respondents for particular cells shown in parentheses. Those elites reinterviewed in 1995 are counted only once for the questions asked both in 1993 and 1995.

Question wording. for those foreign policy items not in direct quotes, see the notes to tables 3.1–3.3.

The construction of the scale used to indicate knowledge of world outside Russia is described in chapter 1. The questionnaire items are repeated here:

Now, I'll read you the names of several political figures. Tell me, please, which country do they represent?

    François Mitterrand [Jacques Chirac]   George Bush [Bill Clinton]
    John Major   William Zimmerman (not included in measure)
    Juan Carlos II   Helmut Kohl

Have you heard of the International Monetary Fund [IMF]?
    [If yes] Is Russia a member of the IMF?
    [If yes] In what year did Russia become a member of the IMF?

Of which state is the Crimea at this moment a part? Is it part of Russia, part of Ukraine, or neither?
    [If Ukraine] Do you know, even approximately, in what year Crimea became part of Ukraine?

Table 3.7
Interitem Correlates of Domestic and Foreign Policy, 1993–1999

	Unaware	Aware[a]	Attentive	Elite
Domestic				
1993	.12	.11	.15	.21
1995	.09	.117	.121	.19
1999	—	—	—	.17
	Nonuniversity	University		
1993	.11	.15		
1995	.10	.12		
1999	.12	.13		
	Unaware	Aware	Attentive	Elite
Foreign				
1993	.05	.06	.09	.12
1995	.06	.07	.09	.15
1999	—	—	—	.14
	Nonuniversity	University		
1993	.06	.12		
1995	.06	.07		

Sources: For the elites, see table 3.1; for the mass surveys, see table 3.2.
Note: Dashes indicate question not asked.
[a] Includes those who were "moderately unaware" and "moderately aware."

Question wording:

For the domestic questions used in computing the scores, see table 2.4. The foreign policy items were:

Should Russia send its troops, if asked, to aid countries of the former USSR?

Which goals of Russian foreign policy, in your opinion, are very important and which less important?

... Defense of the interests of Russian citizens living in the former republics of the USSR.

There exist various opinions about Russia's national interests. Which of the two assertions below is closer to your point of view?

For the most part the national interests of Russia should be limited to its current territory.

For the most part the national interests of Russia extend beyond its current territory.

We can solve our economic problems without the help of the West.

Do you think that U.S. policy is a threat to the security of Russia?

Table 3.8
Centrality of U.S.-Russia Relationship? (Correlations with U.S. Threat to Russian Security)

	1993/1995[a] Elites	Attentive Public 1993–1995	Other 1993–1995
Growth of U.S. military	−.59 (.001)[b]	−.40 (.001)	−.31 (.001)
NATO East European expansion (1995 only)	−.40 (.001)	−.36 (.001)	−.22 (.001)
U.S. involvement in third world (1993 only)	−.35 (.001)	−.28 (.001)	−.28 (.001)
Key economic sectors in foreign hands (1995)	−.33 (.001)	−.24 (.001)	−.16 (.001)
Gap between rich and poor nations	−.29 (.001)	−.20 (.001)	−.14 (.001)
Border conflicts not in CIS	−.14 (.001)	−.09 (.05)	−.13 (.001)
Involvement in conflicts none of Russia's concern	−.12 (.05)	−.05 (n.s.)[c]	.05 (.05)
Inability to solve domestic problems	−.12 (.05)	−.11 (.001)	−.04 (.05)
Uncontrolled population growth	−.08 (n.s.)	−.09 (.05)	−.17 (.001)
Border conflicts CIS	−.03 (n.s.)	−.01 (n.s.)	−.05 (.005)
	N = max 337	N = max 577	N = max 3429

Sources: See table 3.1.

[a] Omits those reinterviewed in 1995.

[b] Two-tailed probability in parentheses ($p \leq$).

[c] In this and subsequent tables, I observed the standard convention n.s. = not significant.

Question wording:

For exact wording of questions, see the notes to tables 3.1–3.3.

countries, involvement in conflicts that are not Russia's concern, and even whether Russia can solve its domestic problems. (Readers should note that there also is a statistically significant relation between these items and the U.S. security threat for the aggregated nonknowledgeable mass public, but this includes almost 3500 cases. With that number, it is difficult for things not to correlate.) For these nine items, correlation coefficients for the elite respondents are uniformly higher than for other respondents. Nearly the same pattern is observed for the attentive public. Again, nine of the eleven security-related questions correlate. But the correlations are always less than for the elites. In all but one instance (where the correlations are identical), the attentive public correlations for those items that are most closely tied to assessment of the U.S. threat (the first five items in table 3.8) are higher than they are for the remainder of the mass publics. In this respect, elites have more coherent conceptions of foreign policy than do attentive publics. The latter's views in turn are more centrally organized around the threat by the United States than are those of the remainder of the mass public (table 3.8).

From the perspective of centrality, therefore, attentive publics could play the role expected of them in a democracy of serving as the intermediary between elite and mass foreign policy dispositions, but whether this happened for Russia during the 1990s is not at all certain. As the examples cited above indicate, there were instances when the distribution of responses among attentive publics about foreign policy were more akin to those of others in the mass public and not evidently responsive to the predominant strands in elite orientations. This is important for understanding the links between democratization and foreign policy; a minimal precondition for effective elite-citizenry interaction is that knowledge drives some important policy orientations of at least some segments of the citizenry. A minimal precondition for mass publics to play a role in the foreign policy process is that they are in some way able to match up their policy orientations to those of key leaders and that their orientations to foreign policy have enough coherence that candidates will be concerned about the effects of policy choices on mass orientations. I consider the first of these issues in the next section and the second in the following chapter. What is clear at this juncture, though, is that mass involvement in the post-Soviet foreign policy process, however modest, constitutes a drag on both the more militantly internationalist and the cooperatively internationalist propensities of Russian foreign policy elites.

Knowledge and Value Acceptance in Russian Public Opinion

Recent years have witnessed a burgeoning literature on the effects of knowledge on political attitudes, or at least on what scholars often take as the equivalent to attitudes, the responses given by interviewees to items from a survey instrument.[18] In this section I borrow from that literature to lay out an argument about when, in the aftermath of major political transformations, internationally attentive publics are more responsive than others in the mass public to the dominant strand in elite orientations to domestic and foreign policy and when attentive publics converge more with the views of ordinary folk. It is an argument that has implications

---

[18] See, especially, Zaller, *The Nature and Origins.*

for thinking about democracy and democratic transitions as well as for the role of public opinion in policy making.

Major political transformations are accompanied by corresponding transformations in elite values. The success of the political transformation depends to a large extent on whether elite views diffuse throughout the society or whether the values associated with the old order persist. Some parts of the elite agenda may involve formulations that a sizable fraction of the population can associate themselves with or at least do not resist. Other aspects encounter resistance, a resistance that takes the form of articulating traditional values or, especially among those who know little about the outside world, in refusals to answer or "don't know" responses when surveyed.[19] Those among mass publics who are most aware of the political realm are those most disposed to share the predispositions of the elite. Those who have no or virtually no awareness of the world outside Russia are similarly least likely to give responses that accord with the views embraced by the majority of the elite. Those who know least will express their resistance by dividing a sizable fraction of their responses to survey questions between ones characteristic of the value system of the prior order and by behaviors, whether by refusing to answer categorically or indicating that they don't know, that reveal that their lack of factual knowledge carries over into the realm of values and predispositions as well.

Many of those who are moderately attuned will also favor prior values. Others among these respondents will attempt to integrate in some way the newly dominant elite values with those of the prior order, rather than tuning out the world around them in the way that those who know little seem to do. Relatively few, at least during the putative transition, will endorse the package of values as a whole embraced by the elites. Those who are aware, by contrast, will include the greatest proportion of those among mass publics who do not endorse the traditional value system. Rather, they will be relatively more prone either to share the predispositions of the majority from among the elites or to entertain some mix of old and new values.

At the same time, there is a connection between the response patterns of those in the mass public who know least and those who know most. When those who know least are *relatively* predisposed to associate themselves with elite-embraced values, a relatively higher proportion of those who are aware—the attentive public—will generally be more prone than on high-resistance topics to express responses that correspond to the majority views among the elites. Items that produce high resistance among the unaware will result in the proportion of the attentive public giving responses corresponding to the views of the majority among the elite

[19] Ibid., pp. 121–22.

being less than would be expected if one were simply to extrapolate from the gap between the elite and the unaware. Where resistance among the unaware is low, the distribution of responses among the attentive public will be such that a larger proportion of responses by attentive publics will have views like the majority among the elite than expected by simple extrapolation. Moreover, these propositions, which seem a priori primarily relevant to attitudes toward the domestic political economy—the responses that are core to the values of new elites—extend to the foreign policy predispositions of attentive publics as well.

In partly free (and, I would expect, free) societies, the interaction between knowledge and acceptance of elite predispositions seems to be a general phenomenon. When resistance is high and acceptance low among mass publics—when the unaware show little predisposition to share elite responses—the attentive public differs less in its response patterns from other, less aware, segments of the mass public. When acceptance is high for mass publics, the politically aware manifest a distribution of attitudes that more nearly approximates that of the elite.

As we saw in chapter 2, in the 1990s elites in Russia were overwhelmingly committed to liberal democratic norms, orientations that contrasted sharply with what I have termed socialist authoritarian responses, responses that nicely captured traditional Soviet and Marxist-Leninist orientations to politics and economics. Persons endorsing these values were likely, in the political climate of the 1990s, to be drawn ideologically either to leftist "red" or rightist "brown" political parties and leaders. Table 3.9 illustrates the link in the mass public between knowledge and orientation to the political economic system on the part of liberal democrats and socialist authoritarians, omitting not only the unmobilized and ambivalent but also the market authoritarians and the social democrats—those who identify with some third way between traditional Soviet orientations and liberal democracy.

Overall orientation to the political economy, it will be recalled, was based on attitudes to five questions about politics and four about the economy. The five relating to the polity concerned the desirability of political competition; whether individual rights should take precedence over societal rights, even if the guilty go free; whether the rights of society should prevail even if the innocent are sometimes imprisoned; the state's obligation to protect society from the expression of dangerous ideas; and the notion that there is one right philosophy. The four relevant for the economy were the desirability of economic competition, whether the state should own heavy industry, whether it is normal for an owner of a prosperous enterprise to make more money than others, and whether it is senseless

Table 3.9
Knowledge and Political Economy Preference among Market Democrats
and Socialist Authoritarians, 1993 and 1995 Surveys

	Unaware[a]	Moderately Unaware	Moderately Aware	Attentive	Elite
Market democrats	12%	27%	32%	41%	73%[b]
	(212)	(276)	(219)	(237)	(247)
Socialist authoritarians	16%	14%	11%	10%	4%
	(277)	(147)	(78)	(58)	(15)

Sources: See table 3.1.

[a] As noted in the text, in these and subsequent tables "unaware" refers to those who were completely unaware or "merely" unaware.

[b] Excludes those foreign policy elites reinterviewed in 1995.

to start a new business when it might fail. (The exact wording of the items may be found in table 2.4.)

The proportion of liberal democrats among the mass publics increases steadily as we move from the unaware (bracketing here, as noted above, the completely unaware and the unaware) to the moderately aware to the attentive publics. At the general level of orientation to the political economy, clearly, attentive publics were relatively more disposed to accept the new norms than were others in the mass public, whereas the proportion of those accepting traditional socialist authoritarian attitudes increased with the inability to identify basic facts about the world outside Russia.

At the same time, when we unpack the nine variables that were used to construct the political economy typology, it becomes evident that the public has responded quite differently to the individual items that, taken together, constitute the basis for that typology and for defining support for liberal democracy. On some items, even the most unaware were rather favorable, while on others the resistance—whether expressed as explicit disagreement or in the propensity to refuse to answer—was high.

It is the relative disposition of the unaware to give the same answer on a survey item as that favored by a majority among the elite that defined the measure of acceptance. I assumed that acceptance—the predisposition to associate oneself with new values or generalizations—was approximated by dividing the percentage supporting an item among the unaware (U) by the percentage supporting the item among the elite (E). In this instance, because refuse-to-answer and don't know "responses" are viewed as evidence of resistance, the proportions reported are the percentage favoring an item divided by the *total* number of respondents within the relevant group. High U/E ratios signified high acceptance and low resistance; I defined no resistance to exist in those instances when the favorable responses on an item (or a combination of items) by the unaware equaled or exceeded those of the elite, thus resulting in an acceptance ratio equal to or greater than 1.0.

Table 3.10 reports the pattern of responses across levels of knowledge for particular items relevant either to the economy or to the political system. Those among the mass public who were most aware were those whose views the distribution of which usually most approximated those of the elites. Similarly, those who were least aware were least likely to give responses that accorded with the values of the elites. They were also most likely to refuse to answer or to respond that they did not know to the individual items used to make up the political economy scale. Table 3.11 shows the dramatic difference in the propensity to respond about attitudinal questions among those who either did not know or declined to answer questions about the world outside Russia.

The overall pattern is clear. A majority of the elite respondents gave answers to most individual items Western observers would categorize as supportive of liberal or market democracy. For 1993, there was one exception. Even among the elite sample, only a minority favored the privatization of heavy industry. A majority (54 percent) responded that heavy industry should be in the hands of the state and not in private hands. This remained true when I excluded the military from the elite sample. Indeed, there was no majority favoring private ownership of heavy industry in the subsamples of any of the sectors—the institutes, the media, those in the economy, the government itself, or the military—used to constitute the elite sample in 1993. In 1995 and 1999 a majority among the elite again agreed that heavy industry should be owned by the state and in addition asserted that the state had an obligation to protect society from the public expression of dangerous ideas.

The connection between the dispositions of the majority among elite respondents and the response patterns of the unaware is suggested by table 3.11, which shows the "don't knows" or "no answer" responses for each of the nine items in the political economy typology. In every instance, those knowing the least were most prone not to answer or to respond that they did not know. The aware, similarly, declined to answer more frequently than did the attentive public, and with rare exception, the attentive public declined to answer more frequently than did the elite.

What is most relevant in this context, though, is that in the case of the ownership-of heavy-industry question—the item where elites were least disposed to pose a challenge to traditional values—the unaware were most likely to give some answer. Only one in seven of the unaware (14 percent) failed to give an answer to the question about the state ownership of heavy

Table 3.10
Awareness and Mass Responsiveness to Elite Preferences, 1993–1995

	1993				
	Unaware[a]	Aware	Attentive	Elite	U/E Ratio
State ownership, heavy industry (agree)	79% (79)	81% (71)	79% (62)	54% (54)	1.46
Individual rights	49% (49)	60% (57)	71% (65)	73% (73)	.67
Economic competition beneficial	57% (57)	71% (68)	85% (79)	90% (90)	.61
Defend society (disagree)	48% (48)	63% (59)	68% (70)	81% (81)	.59
Prevent expression dangerous ideas (disagree)	30% (30)	40% (39)	48% (49)	58% (58)	.52
Political competition beneficial	33% (33)	43% (46)	54% (60)	73% (73)	.435
Richer	37% (37)	53% (53)	66% (70)	86% (86)	.43
Senseless start new business (disagree)	31% (31)	49% (48)	58% (65)	82% (82)	.38
Only one right philosophy (disagree)	26% (26)	51% (47)	66% (69)	90% (90)	.29
State ownership, heavy industry (disagree)	7% (7)	13% (19)	16% (31)	43% (43)	.16

industry in 1993 (table 3.11). By contrast, almost half (table 3.11) of the unaware in both 1993 and 1995 either gave no answer or replied they did not know to a relatively abstract question about whether there was one right philosophy, and two in five in 1993 and one in three in 1995 declined to answer or said they didn't know in response to a question calling on them to assess whether political competition among parties was favorable for society (table 3.11).

If there is a connection between the pattern of responses by the unaware and the dispositions of the majority among elite respondents, there is also a relationship between the response patterns of those who were unaware and those among the mass publics who were the most well informed about the outside world. A way to identify this linkage is to examine the acceptance of new ways of thinking among mass publics and then to explore the association between that propensity among the least aware and the

Table 3.10 (*cont'd*)
Awareness and Mass Responsiveness to Elite Preferences, 1993–1995

	1995				
	Unaware	*Aware*	*Attentive*	*Elite*	*U/E Ratio*
State ownership, heavy industry	71%	76%	71%	53%	1.34
(agree)	(71)	(65)	(59)	(53)	
Defend society (disagree)	59%	66%	70%	75%	.79
	(59)	(64)	(69)	(75)	
Prevent expression dangerous ideas	41%	43%	47%	53%	.77
(agree)	(41)	(46)	(50)	(53)	
Economic competition beneficial	49%	72%	84%	91%	.54
	(49)	(63)	(77)	(91)	
Individual rights	34%	47%	49%	71%	.48
	(34)	(46)	(59)	(71)	
Senseless start new business (disagree)	33%	47%	51%	78%	.42
	(33)	(48)	(63)	(78)	
Richer	25%	40%	54%	74%	.34
	(25)	(42)	(58)	(74)	
Political competition beneficial	24%	42%	57%	73%	.33
	(24)	(60)	(57)	(73)	
Only one right philosophy (disagree)	24%	40%	52%	88%	.27
	(24)	(45)	(67)	(88)	
State ownership, heavy industry	4%	8%	14%	46%	.09
(disagree)	(4)	(18)	(32)	(46)	

Sources: ROMIR conducted both the 1993 and the 1995 elite surveys as well as the mass survey in European Russia in 1993. Demoscope conducted the national survey in 1995.

Note: As indicated in the text, the first row in each case refers to the actual percentages and the second represents the extrapolated percentages. U = unaware; E = elite.

[a] For this table and tables 3.11 and 3.12, "unaware" includes those who were completely unaware, and unaware and the "aware" includes those who were "moderately unaware" and "moderately aware."

Question wording for the items in the table:

All heavy industry should belong to the state and not be in private hands.
The rights of the individual should be defended even if guilty persons sometimes remain free.
Competition among various enterprises, organizations, and firms benefits our society.
The interests of society should be protected even if innocent people sometimes end up in prison.
In any society it will always be necessary to prohibit the public expression of dangerous ideas.
Competition among various political parties makes our system strong.
It's normal when the owner of a prosperous enterprise, using the labor of his workers, becomes richer than many other people.
There's no sense in beginning a new business inasmuch as it might fail.
It is apparent that of all the existing philosophies, there is only one that is clearly correct.

Table 3.11
Proportion of "Don't Knows" and "Refused to Answer" Responses by Level
of Knowledge

	1993			
	Unaware	*Aware*	*Attentive*	*Elite*
State ownership, heavy industry	14% (58)	6% (33)	4% (11)	4% (7)
Individual rights	21% (88)	8% (44)	6% (16)	5% (9)
Defend society	22% (91)	10% (53)	5% (13)	3% (6)
Richer	23% (97)	8% (45)	6% (17)	2% (3)
Economic competition beneficial	26% (110)	12% (65)	4% (10)	2% (4)
Prevent expression dangerous ideas	29% (119)	9% (50)	5% (14)	3% (5)
Senseless start new business	30% (123)	12% (64)	8% (23)	5% (9)
Political competition beneficial	40% (166)	18% (98)	8% (22)	4% (7)
Only one right philosophy	47% (196)	28% (154)	14% (37)	4% (7)
	1995			
State ownership, heavy industry	16% (208)	5% (60)	5% (15)	1% (2)
Individual rights	20% (262)	7% (87)	4% (11)	6% (11)
Defend society	16% (211)	6% (76)	5% (15)	4% (7)
Richer	19% (249)	7% (77)	7% (21)	2% (4)
Economic competition beneficial	28% (357)	8% (92)	1% (2)	2% (3)
Prevent expression dangerous ideas	23% (291)	9% (108)	6% (17)	1% (1)
Senseless start new business	26% (336)	9% (109)	5% (15)	1% (2)
Political competition beneficial	33% (422)	14% (162)	4% (11)	3% (5)
Only one right philosophy	46% (597)	28% (322)	14% (3)	1% (2)

Sources: See table 3.10
Note: Actual number of respondents for particular cells shown in partentheses.
Question wording:

For exact wording of questions, see table 3.10.

response patterns of the attentive public. Table 3.10 once again provides
the proportion favoring the elite-endorsed response for the elite and for
those among mass publics with various levels of knowledge.

The table also reports two other findings. The first is the predisposition
to accept elite-endorsed responses, computed by simply dividing the proportion among those who know least endorsing a proposition by the proportion of elite respondents endorsing that same proposition. Thus, for

instance, 57 percent of the unaware in 1993 agreed or strongly agreed that "competition among various enterprises, organizations and firms benefits our society," a statement endorsed in some fashion by fully 90 percent of the elite respondents. This results in an acceptance, or perhaps more precisely an absence-of-resistance, score of 0.61. In addition, table 3.10 also includes in parentheses the values for each category we would expect to find were it the case that the pattern of responses increased by equal amounts from the unaware to the moderately aware to the attentive public to the elite.

For those instances where resistance is high—and the acceptance score is relatively low—the attentive public's actual response was at or below the extrapolated response pattern and not very close to that of the elite respondents. Where acceptance is high and resistance low and the acceptance score is relatively high, the attentive public's propensity to endorse views endorsed by the majority of the elite exceeded the extrapolated proportion of favorable responses.

From the perspective adopted in this chapter, it is the attitude of the elite majority, not government policy, that matters in assessing mass "acceptance." Support for state ownership of heavy industry is a traditional Soviet value that has been endorsed by a majority of respondents in Soviet and Russian surveys over many years.[20] As such, it was a dimension along which mass publics were already predisposed.

All three subsets of the mass sample—the unaware, the moderately aware, and the attentive public—were far more disposed to agree with the proposition that heavy industry should be owned by the state than were the elite respondents. The support among the unaware (79 percent in 1993, 71 percent in 1995) was far greater than among the elite sample (54 percent in both 1993 and 1995), yielding an acceptance ratio of 1.46 in 1993 and 1.34 in 1995. In this instance, the attentive public (along with the other respondents in the mass public) actually was more favorably inclined to agree with the proposition than were the elite respondents.

But privatize—after a fashion—in the early 1990s, the Russians did.[21] For completeness, therefore, I have also computed the acceptance score in 1993 for private ownership of heavy industry, notwithstanding the fact that even among elites it did not have majority support in 1993. The acceptance score is very low, 0.16—strong evidence of resistance among all the

[20] Donna Bahry, "Society Transformed? Rethinking the Social Roots of Perestroika," *Slavic Review* 52 (Fall 1993): 512–54.

[21] Valuable assessments are Gustafson, *Capitalism Russian-Style*, and Solnick, *Stealing the State*.

sectors of the mass public, including the attentive public. The logical corollaries to acceptance of continued state ownership of heavy industry were
enormous resistance to the privatization of heavy industry among the unaware, a very large gap between the extrapolated and observed pattern
of responses favorable to privatization among the attentive public, and a
corresponding gap in responses favorable to privatization between those
in the attentive public and among the elites.

All this suggests that there is an interactive effect between knowledge
and level of acceptance. In conditions of high acceptance and weak resistance the unaware were more inclined to respond in some way and the
attentive public's receptivity to elite cues was relatively greater. The attentive public, by virtue of its knowledge, had the opportunity to latch onto
elite values and, given weak resistance across mass publics, had no motive
not to embrace the notions accepted by a majority of the elite.

How widespread is this phenomenon? Of the items in the political economy typology there is only one incorrect prediction out of eighteen possible over the two years 1993 and 1995. In 1995 the attentive public and
moderately aware were closer to elite values concerning the value of economic competition than the U/E ratio would predict. Otherwise, for
these items the hypothesized relationship holds.

Does it transfer to foreign policy? Table 3.12 shows the responses to
nine items (see tables 3.1–3.3) used to address post-Soviet Russian foreign
policy vis-à-vis the West and in relation to the "near abroad"—those countries formerly part of the Soviet Union on the periphery of Russia. As in
table 3.10, table 3.12 reports (a) the actual proportion of responses given
by elites, the attentive public, the aware, and the unaware; (b) the expected response patterns, were the response patterns between those of the
unaware and the elite to increase by equal increments (in parentheses);
and (c) the acceptance scores.

For those items characterized by low acceptance and high resistance,
the proportion of responses by the attentive public generally fell below
the extrapolated estimates and were closer to those of others in the mass
publics. Use of the Russian army outside the former Soviet Union did not
have majority support from the foreign policy elites in 1993. Rather, a
majority among the elite opposed such action in 1993 but the various
sectors in the mass public were even more opposed. The result is a U/E
ratio of 1.18. The unaware were slightly more disposed in 1993 than the
elite to regard concern for Russians in the former USSR as an important
goal of Russian foreign policy. In both cases, the attentive public responses
are higher than would be expected by extrapolation. There were two other
instances in 1993 where the elite majority position met little resistance
among the unaware—propositions that the United States was not a threat

Table 3.12.

Knowledge and Mass Public Support for Elite Foreign Policy Preferences

	1993				
	Unaware	*Aware*	*Attentive*	*Elite*	*U/E Ratio*
Not send army outside	72%	73%	74%	61%	1.18
former Soviet Union	(72)	(68)	(65)	(61)	
Aid Russians in former	71%	77%	79%	69%	1.03
Soviet Union	(71)	(72)	(70)	(69)	
U.S. is not a threat	61%	65%	74%	71%	.82
	(61)	(64)	(67)	(71)	
Reduce foreign aid	61%	73%	80%	83%	.74
	(61)	(69)	(76)	(83)	
Not aid Russians elsewhere	39%	45%	52%	62%	.63
	(39)	(46)	(55)	(62)	
National interest broad	39%	54%	57%	75%	.52
	(39)	(52).3	(64)	(75)	
Send army within former	26%	33%	38%	53%	.49
Soviet Union	(26)	(36)	(44)	(53)	
Need West's economic help	22%	27%	36%	53%	.42
	(22)	(32)	(43)	(53)	
Reduce military spending	24%	35%	47%	58%	.41
	(24)	(36)	(47)	(58)	
Not send army outside	78%	74%	64%	42%	1.86
former Soviet Union	(78)	(66)	(54)	(42)	
Reduce foreign aid	82%	86%	87%	66%	1.24
	(82)	(76)	(71)	(66)	

to Russian security and that spending on foreign aid should be decreased. The acceptance scores were high but less than 1. For both those items the attentive public's position was higher than expected by mere extrapolation and closer to that of the majority among the elites. There is one item (of nine) for 1993 that doesn't conform to the hypothesis: the attentive public is located exactly where one would expect if one were simply extrapolating. This is in response to the majority elite judgment that defense expenditures should be reduced—a position that shifted sharply in 1995.

For 1995, attentive public responses mesh with that hypothesized in all ten cases. If the U/E ratio is 0.82 or greater in 1995, attentive publics were closer to the elite majority assessment than would be expected by

Table 3.12. (*cont'd*)
Knowledge and Mass Public Support for Elite Foreign Policy Preferences

	1995				
	Unaware	*Aware*	*Attentive*	*Elite*	*U/E Ratio*
Keep or increase military spending	74% (74)	76% (74)	76% (74)	74% (74)	1.00
Not aid Russians elsewhere	50% (50)	57% (51)	61% (51)	52% (52)	.90
Aid Russians in former Soviet Union	59% (59)	72% (63)	75% (68)	72% (72)	.82
U.S. is a threat	37% (37)	34% (41)	42% (46)	51% (51)	.73
National interest broad	37% (37)	51% (51)	56% (66)	80% (80)	.46
Send army within former Soviet Union	25% 25	34% (41)	32% (56)	72% (72)	.35
Western help not needed	17% (17)	30% (29)	35% (41)	53% (53)	. 32
Send army outside former Soviet Union	10% (10)	15% (22)	27% (35)	47% (47)	.21

Sources: See table 3.10.

Note: As indicated in the text, the first row in each instance refers to the actual percentages and the second the extrapolated percentages. U = unaware; E = elite.

Question wording:

For exact wording of questions, see tables 3.1–3.3.

simple extrapolation. Less than that they were all below the expected extrapolated value. (There was no majority view among the elite in response to a question that asked whether Russia should send its troops if asked to aid a country outside the former Soviet Union. Consequently, both minority views are included.) Similarly, for 1995 for all the items with scores below 0.81, attentive publics were less like elites and more like their confrères in the mass public. Attentive publics were disproportionately less prone to characterize the United States as a threat; they were less disposed to view Russia's national interest as extending beyond its borders; they did not follow the elite's lead in asserting that Russia should send troops if asked to aid a country within the former Soviet Union—both the broad conception of Russia's national interest and the view that Russia should intervene within the former Soviet Union receiving substantial support among elites; and relatively few among the attentive public thought Russia's forces should be sent outside the former Soviet Union, if asked (table 3.12).

Implications

Several inferences flow from these results. Most narrowly, knowledge turns out to have predictive consequences for assessing likely responses to propositions that are normative or have rather explicit policy implications as well as for what were largely factual judgments. When even those who were most unaware were relatively more inclined to endorse propositions favored by a majority among elites, the attentive public was proportionately more likely to endorse the views of the majority in the elite than in other circumstances. Analogously, when the value judgments and predispositions of the unware were least challenged by the orientations of elites, the unaware were least likely to evidence conflict between prior dispositions and new orientations. In such circumstances they were far less likely to plead ignorance or refuse to answer questions than under other conditions.

Moreover, while the relation between knowledge and acceptance seems to obtain across a wide range of topics, both normative and factual, widespread differences exist in the propensity of mass publics to accept elite preferences. Assuming this result continues to obtain in a new century, Russian policy makers would ignore these differences at their peril and Western policy makers would be well served not to affect surprise when and if Russian policy makers act in a way that is responsive to domestic constituencies. Scholars, too, may wish to exercise care in generalizing about patterns of acceptance or resistance across political systems when the variation in such ratios is so discrepant for items in surveys conducted in a single country.

On a broader note, there would seem to be the usual blend of good news and bad news in these findings. A major component of the bad news surely concerns the implications for Russian society of enormous inequalities in levels of knowledge, inequalities that overlap with the much commented upon income inequalities characteristic of post-Soviet Russia. Winners are likely to know that the country and they are better off; losers will know just enough to know that things are worse for them and the country. The inherent conflict between haves and have-nots in a society undergoing rapid transformation will be exacerbated by parallel conflict between the knows and know-nots.

The good news perhaps consists in the finding that despite a diverse and contentious Russian media it was the attentive public who was most likely to share elite predispositions toward the domestic political economy. (Writing in 2001, the prospects that such diversity will persist seem problematic.) In the 1970s and 1980s in a Soviet Union where access to information critical of the regime was constricted, it was the political leaders and high-level professionals whose behavior was least congruent with regime values.[22] With all the requisite qualifications about the media taken into account, the diverse information in the media during the 1990s may thus have contributed to the existence in post-Soviet Russia of one of the minimal conditions identified by Almond a half century ago for a democratic policy process in which public opinion plays an important role, namely, an informed audience to whom elites can make their case.[23]

Over time, moreover, one would expect the numbers who constitute the attentive public to increase. Secular changes in Russia such as urbanization and the increase in the university educated across age cohorts should have an effect, as should longer-term experiences with a diverse press, should it persist. Like elites everywhere, elites in Russia will not reach the unaware. But what they do might be another factor affecting the size and sophistication of the attentive public. As we have seen, persons in the attentive public were particularly likely to be the allies of elites when elites advocated policies that found some resonance across the society. Russian elites may gradually be becoming aware of the wisdom for which Lloyd George is usually given initial credit, "I have to follow them. I'm their leader."

This circumstance gives the role of mass publics a Janus-like quality and creates a need for the elites to bring policies, domestic and foreign, in line with those of the public, the scorn among elites for the influence of public opinion noted previously notwithstanding. These two faces of public attitudes relate to militant internationalism and cooperative internationalism. While mass publics in Russia do show some interest in symbolic support for the United Nations and for the defense of human rights elsewhere, they—the unaware, the aware, and the attentive public—have thus far been a drag on Russian use of force while determinedly resistant to economic interdependence and to the thought that Russia needs Western help in rebuilding its economy. The importance of this for specific Russian foreign policy acts is of course problematic. We do not have a good sense of how great the impact of Russian mass attitudes has been on Russia's international behavior, though knowing the attitudes of Russian mass publics facilitates an understanding of the posturing by the members of the Duma and other political leaders throughout the decade of the 1990s.

[22] Millar, ed., *Politics, Work, and Daily Life*, especially the chapters by Bahry, Silver, and Zimmerman.
[23] Almond, *The American People*, p. 139.

Where we have the greatest reason to suspect mass publics play a major role in a partly free country is in their opportunity to select leaders, which can in turn shape the main direction of a country's foreign policy. Do mass publics have enough awareness of their own preferences about Russia's relation to the international system and those of its leaders so that a meaningful dialogue between leaders and citizens can occur? Or as it was often said about American political candidates in the first decades after World War II, do leaders "waltz before a blind audience"?[24]

[24] Aldrich, Sullivan, and Borgida, "Foreign Affairs and Issue Voting."

4

Orientations to the International System and Electoral Behavior in Russia

FOR YEARS, the consensus among political scientists was that foreign policy played little role in electoral outcomes in democratic systems. This generalization was almost entirely based on an analysis of American elections and was part of a broader belief that public opinion had a very limited impact on foreign policy. The consensus about elections rested on two key propositions. The first was that, especially with respect to foreign policy, "public opinion lacks structure and coherence."[1] Second, mass publics were not interested or knowledgeable about foreign policy because of its limited relevance to their daily lives.

Beginning roughly in the late 1980s, however, as part of the reconsideration of the overall consensus about the role of the public in foreign policy formation,[2] the role of foreign policy in explaining electoral outcomes has come in for major reexamination.[3] Aldrich and his colleagues concluded that the reason why presidential candidates often talk so much about foreign policy is that they are not waltzing before a blind audience but rather that the audience 'is reasonably alert,' "appreciates their grace," and "given a choice . . . votes for the candidate who waltzes best."[4]

This chapter examines whether issues concerning Russia's relations with the outside world—foreign policy in the broadest sense—were strong predictors of the 1996 and 2000 presidential elections in Russia. The 1996 election resulted in the July runoff victory of Boris Yeltsin over Gennadii Ziuganov; the March 2000 election essentially ratified the selection of Vladimir Putin as president after Yeltsin had resigned on New Year's Eve 1999. I discuss the two elections in succession.

The evidence that emerges from the 1996 presidential election may be summarized briefly. First, Russian publics were reasonably well informed about the major candidates and those candidates' broad-gauge policy ori-

---

[1] Holsti, "Public Opinion," p. 443.

[2] Graham, "The Politics of Failure"; Holsti, "Public Opinion."

[3] Aldrich, Sullivan, and Borgida, "Foreign Affairs and Issue Voting"; Hurwitz and Peffley, "How Are Foreign Policy Attitudes."

[4] Aldrich, Sullivan, and Borgida, "Foreign Affairs and Issue Voting," p. 136.

entations—including general issues of foreign policy, notably concerning the basic tenor of Russian-American relations and the links between the international economy and the evolving Russian political economy.

Second, in broad terms Russian citizens manifested reasonably coherent notions about the 1996 presidential candidates, their priorities, and the matters they would most effectively address as president. The views of Russian mass publics about these core issues were relatively consistent both among themselves and when assessed against the preferences of Russian mass publics concerning the political system they considered appropriate for contemporary Russia. As others have noted,[5] the 1996 presidential election in Russia was first and foremost a referendum on Russian citizens' views about whether they preferred, on the one hand, the traditional, pre-*perestroika* Soviet system or, on the other, the Russian political system at the time of the 1996 election or Western democracy. In assessing Yeltsin and Ziuganov, Russian publics—with considerable help from the media—defined the choice in their minds as one between the Soviet system on the one hand and the current situation or Western democracy on the other.

Third, that choice, however, was inextricably linked with Russian citizens' core dispositions concerning Russia's relations with the outside world, though not, it should be stressed, concerning foreign policy issues narrowly construed. Russian citizens manifested strong and divergent prior beliefs about East-West security relations and the relation of Russia to the global economy in particular. In voting for Yeltsin or Ziuganov they were giving voice to those feelings. Russian publics knew and made that choice in part on assessments of the nature of the external threat from the United States and their preferences with regard to the links between actors in the international system and the Russian political economy. Knowing a Russian's core dispositions toward the outside world contributed substantially to knowing that person's preferences with respect to the political system. That preference, in turn, constituted a robust predictor of the results of the July 1996 runoff between Yeltsin and Ziuganov.

In short, Russian mass publics in 1996 were an audience. They were not blind. They made a clear choice about whom they thought would waltz best. Although the overwhelming theme of the medley of tunes on which they based their choice concerned the equation of the candidates with a particular political system, issues about Russia's orientation to the international system were also incorporated in their selection of the "best dancer."

---

[5] Michael McFaul, "Russia's 1996 Presidential Election: Institutions, Strategy and Revolutionary Votes" (paper presented at the annual meeting of the AAASS, Boston, 1996).

Assessing the Candidates, Their Policies, and
Their Potential Performance

Recent American foreign policy scholarship has argued that, in the aggregate, American mass publics somehow make judgments consistent with their preferences[6]—without challenging for a moment the legendary ignorance of mass publics in the United States about politics and international politics noted by Almond and, before him, Walter Lippmann. Both the ignorance about politics and international relations and the retroactive plausibility of their aggregate judgments about leaders and policies characterize the bulk of the Russian mass public as well. The ignorance is illustrated by the pattern of responses used in constructing the international knowledge scale to which reference has already been. Those respondents—a third from the 1993 survey of European Russia and slightly less than half of the 1995 survey of Russia—were coded as completely unaware or unaware because *at best* they had typically been able to associate three or four of five Western leaders with their respective country but had not known that Crimea was part of Ukraine or that Russia was a member of the IMF. This lack of awareness was manifest notwithstanding the fact that Crimea was arguably the most salient issue in Russia's relations with the other former Soviet republics in the first half of the 1990s and the prominence of issues concerning Russia's ties to the IMF throughout the decade. (As mentioned above, it was logically possible but a rarity in reality for respondents to identify Crimea with Ukraine or answer that Russia was a member of IMF and only be able to link two or fewer Western leaders with their country and be coded as unaware. In practice respondents did much better with individual leaders.) Ignorance of the world outside one's country is not an American monopoly.

But despite Russians' level of factual knowledge, it turns out that in 1995/96 respondents could link their leaders to broad concepts and in a rough fashion scale their preferences having to do with Russia's relations to the outside world. After the July 1996 election, Russians were asked to associate the presidential candidates with several key concepts: was the candidate, they were asked, a communist, a democrat, a centrist, a patriot, or a socialist? Multiple answers were permitted, though as is typical in surveys, few gave more than a single answer. Table 4.1 presents these results for the five leading vote getters in the first round of the election: Boris Yeltsin, Grigorii Iavlinskii, General Aleksandr Lebed, Vladimir Zhirinovskii, and Gennadii Ziuganov.

[6] Page and Shapiro, *The Rational Public.*

Table 4.1.
Core Attributes of Presidential Candidates, 1995–96

	Communist	Democrat	Centrist	Patriot	Reformer	Socialist	Total
Yeltsin	6%	72%	3%	3%	16%	1%	2087
	(124)	(1506)	(63)	(59)	(324)	(11)	
Iavlinskii	4%	61%	5%	5%	21%	4%	1673
	(69)	(1027)	(78)	(92)	(347)	(60)	
Lebed	3%	36%	6%	48%	5%	1%	1968
	(77)	(700)	(119)	(949)	(104)	(19)	
Zhirinovskii	5%	28%	22%	19%	16%	10%	1346
	(73)	(374)	(290)	(254)	(218)	(133)	
Ziuganov	96%	1%	0%	1%	0%	1%	2223
	(2138)	(15)	(8)	(29)	(8)	(25)	

Source: 1995/96 national survey of Russian citizens conducted by Demoscope.

Note: Percentages indicate proportion giving one of the above answers. The differences in the totals column result from divergent proportions of respondents categorizing particular candidates. Actual number of respondents for particular cells shown in parentheses.

Question wording:

Let's talk a bit about each of the candidates. Written on the card are various words with which one might describe the candidates for president of Russia in the past election. With which of these would you describe . . . ?

Mostly, Russian respondents had it right or right enough to make choices corresponding to their preferences. Overwhelmingly, they selected "democrat" as their preferred designation for Yeltsin, with a sizable fraction characterizing him as a "reformer." More than 80 percent labeled Iavlinskii either a democrat or a reformer. Almost half of those interviewed termed Lebed a "patriot" and, interestingly, roughly three out of eight selected "democrat" as the term of choice. Virtually everyone labeled Ziuganov a "communist." Only Vladimir Zhirinovskii, leader of the putative Liberal-Democratic Party, stumped the respondents. More than 800 fewer respondents of a sample of approximately 2800 said they did not know or refused to answer with respect to Zhirinovskii than with regard to Ziuganov. Moreover, the responses of those who did characterize him were widely dispersed. To some, Zhirinovskii was a communist, to others a democrat, to still others a patriot, and even a reformer, a socialist, or a centrist to some. (It was a commentary on the polarized state of politics in Russia that more respondents categorized Zhirinovskii as a centrist in 1996 than they did the remaining four key vote getters combined.) It was not just the West that did not know what to make of Zhirinovskii.

Table 4.2.

Assessments of Issue-Specific Effectiveness of the Five Leading Presidential Candidates, 1996

	Improvement in Economy	Deal with Unemployment	Deal with Crime and Corruption	Deal with Chechnya[a]	Handle Foreign Policy	Develop Democracy	Ensure Stability
Yeltsin	25%	17%	5%	6%	39%	51%	21%
	(425)	(263)	(104)	(88)	(499)	(615)	(322)
Iavlinskii	26%	10%	1%	2%	9%	15%	5%
	(444)	(155)	(12)	(28)	(111)	(184)	(78)
Lebed	9%	13%	74%	71%	12%	7%	37%
	(160)	(200)	(1457)	(1096)	(155)	(90)	(564)
Zhirinovskii	4%	7%	8%	8%	5%	3%	4%
	(61)	(114)	(148)	(130)	(58)	(34)	(58)
Ziuganov	31%	47%	12%	12%	25%	17%	31%
	(527)	(714)	(233)	(187)	(320)	(206)	(483)
Total	(1697)	(1535)	(1959)	(1538)	(1276)	(1210)	(1534)

Source: 1996 post-presidential survey conducted by Demoscope.

Note: Percentages do not total 100% due to rounding and because the five minor candidates are not included. Actual number of respondents for particular cells shown in parentheses.

[a] Given Lebed's designated role in negotiating with Chechnya, only those interviewed in July 1996 are included, and those interviewed subsequently were excluded. The joint statement ending hostilities was signed August 31, 1996.

Question wording:

Let's talk a bit about each of the candidates. Written on the card are various words with which one might describe the candidates for president of Russia in the past election. With which of these would you describe. . . ?

Those interviewed after the July 1996 election also generally had consensual—and plausible—evaluations of the effectiveness that each major candidate might demonstrate along several substantively important domains were he elected. In many instances, doubtless, the respondents were attributing effectiveness to candidates they preferred. In general, though, when asked which of the candidates for the presidency, in their opinion, could best handle several pressing policy issues, their aggregate responses were largely congruent with the probable factual situation or with what the candidates emphasized.

Table 4.2 reports how the Russian respondents rated the five main vote getters in their capacity to address several key issues. The table percentages are the proportions of respondents, among those saying someone would matter, identifying a candidate as most effective. (Respondents were given the option of stating that there would be no basic difference in the manner the candidates handled an issue. A handful volunteered answers such as "anyone but Yeltsin." Readers can approximate the proportion saying that the outcome made no difference for a particular issue by comparing the total responses per issue in table 4.2.) General Lebed was the overwhelming choice of those who thought one candidate could cope with "crime and corruption" better than any of the others, and he was similarly viewed as the candidate "to decide the problem of Chechnya." Lebed, Ziuganov, and Yeltsin were judged most likely to "guarantee stability [and] calm in society." Yeltsin, the economist Iavlinskii, and Ziuganov were identified as the candidates most likely to address the problem of "enhancing the economy," with Ziuganov seen by almost half the respondents as the candidate most able to cope with unemployment.

By contrast, Yeltsin was viewed as the candidate most likely to further the development of democracy, with Ziuganov and Iavlinskii a distant second and third, respectively. With regard to foreign policy, respondents gave judgments about the candidates' effectiveness in proportions roughly comparable to the distribution of votes among the five preferred candidates in the first round: Yeltsin was termed the candidate most able to handle foreign policy effectively, with Ziuganov rated second of the five leading candidates and Lebed, Iavlinskii, and Zhirinovskii lagging behind. Indeed, the respondents were to large measure reflecting their preferences among the five candidates; a simple bivariate correlation reveals a strong association between how the respondents reported voting in the first round and their assessment of the candidates' putative foreign policy competence ($r = .78$).

But only partly. For one thing, more than a hundred respondents (8 percent) said that Mikhail Gorbachev, otherwise as invisible in the 1995/96 survey as he was in the 1996 election, would handle foreign policy most effectively. Tables 4.3 and 4.4 add to the sense that the respondents may not have simply been telling us whom they voted for in responding to a probe about the foreign policy effectiveness of the presidential candidates. In these tables, I report bivariate correlations between several foreign policy items selected because of their relevance to Russian notions about security in the post–cold war environment or because of the way they are indicative of the interrelation between the Russian economy and the international economy.[7] Table 4.3 shows the bivariate relationship between respondents' answers to six questions concerning orientation to the international system that were asked before the December 1995 parliamentary elections and their thermometer score assessment of what turned out to be the five leading vote getters.[8] Table 4.4 provides the same infor-

---

[7] It should be stressed that many other foreign policy items—for example, aid to Russians abroad, security as a priority, use of force in the near abroad and elsewhere—either were not related in a statistically significant way or were only weakly related to candidate preferences.

[8] In doing the cross-tabulations, I collapsed the 101-point scale into five categories: scores of zero, 1–24, 25–49, 50–74, and 75–100.

Table 4.3.

Foreign Policy Dispositions (December 1995) and Respondent Ratings of the Five Leading Presidential Candidates

Item	Candidate (Tau$_c$ =)				
	Ziuganov	Zhirinovskii	Lebed	Iavlinskii	Yeltsin
U.S. a threat?[a]	−.28	−.06	−.09	.17	.21
Expanded NATO a threat?	−.13	.00	−.04	.01	.09
Western help not needed	−.18	−.06	−.05	.17	.19
Make Russia colony	−.13	−.04	−.09	.06	.12
Foreign firms seek to seize Russian market	−.18	−.04	−.09	.16	.17
Attract foreign capital?	−.19	−.02	−.02	.12	.13

Source: As in table 4.1.

[a] In doing the cross-tabulations, I recoded the items so that when pro-Western responses were positively associated with high scores for the presidential aspirant, the coefficients would be positive. In all cases high scores for Yeltsin, for instance, were associated with relatively pro-Western responses concerning the question asked.

Question wording:

Do you think the United States is a threat to Russian security?

"The expansion of NATO to include countries of Eastern Europe" is a great threat or the greatest threat to Russia.

Russia can resolve its economic problems without the help of the West.

The West is trying to turn Russia into an economic colony whose role is limited to supplying raw materials and energy sources to the world economy.

It is necessary to defend our industry from foreign firms that wish to seize Russian markets.

Russia should attract foreign funds into the economy.

mation concerning selected foreign policy items (including several repeats from the December 1995 surveys) asked in a survey after the July 1996 second round in the presidential election.

What these relationships mean in concrete terms may be enhanced by an example. Of those who viewed the United States as a threat at the time of the 1995 parliamentary election surveys, two-thirds gave Ziuganov a thermometer rating between 75 and 100 and 31 percent rated him a zero. By contrast, 36 percent of those in 1995 who regarded the United States as a threat to Russian security gave Yeltsin a thermometer rating of 75 or higher, whereas 56 percent [*sic*] accorded him a zero.

In both the parliamentary election and the post-presidential election surveys, people were asked whether the United States was "a threat to Russian security," whether Russia should "seek to attract foreign funds into its economy," whether "it was necessary to defend our industry from

Table 4.4.
Foreign Policy Dispositions (Summer 1996) and Respondent Ratings of the Five
Leading Vote Getters in the First Round of the 1996 Russian Presidential Election

Item	Candidate ($Tau_c = $)				
	Ziuganov	*Zhirinovskii*	*Lebed*	*Iavlinskii*	*Yeltsin*
U.S. a threat?	−.29	.04	.02	.09	.29
No NATO in Eastern Europe	−.15	−.01	−.00	−.08	.09
Western help not needed	−.30	−.02	.04	.09	.24
Foreign firms seek to seize Russian market	−.25	−.01	−.02	.04	.14
Attract foreign capital?	−.20	.03	.00	.08	.15
Not end USSR	−.33	−.04	−.01	.06	.21

Source: As in table 4.2.
Note: See the footnote to table 4.3.

Question wording:

Do you think the United States is a threat to Russian security?
"The expansion of NATO to include countries of Eastern Europe" is a threat or the greatest threat to Russia.
Russia can resolve its economic problems without the help of the West.
It is necessary to defend our industry from foreign firms that wish to seize Russian markets.
Russia should attract foreign funds into the economy.
Under no circumstances should the Soviet Union have been broken up.

foreign firms that wish to seize the Russian market," and whether "Russia could rebuild its economy without the help of the West."

At the time of the parliamentary elections, Russians were asked whether whether "NATO expansion into Eastern Europe" was a threat to Russian security and if "the West is attempting to transform Russia into an economic colony, the role of which is limited to the supply of raw materials and energy resources to the world market." (As Michael McFaul notes, "Several of Zyuganov's top deputies, including Chairman of the Duma Security Committee, Viktor Ilyukhin, spoke frequently of an American plot to destroy the territorial integrity and industrial base of Russia.")[9]

In the survey after the July 1996 second round of the presidential election, respondents were also asked whether they thought "the Soviet

[9] McFaul, "Russia's Presidential," pp. 29–30. See also Jerry Hough, "Sociology, the State, and Language Politics," *Post-Soviet Affairs* 12 (1996): 95–227 at p. 113, where he reports that in 1993 Russians asserted "by a 2-to-1 margin, with 23 percent undecided, that America was trying to weaken Russia with its economic advice. This margin increased to 3-to-1 in 1995, with 21 percent undecided."

Union should not have been destroyed under any circumstances" and if "Russia should do everything possible not to allow the formerly socialist countries of Eastern Europe to enter NATO."

There are no surprises in either table 4.3 or table 4.4. Those who thought highly of Ziuganov were those who considered the United States a threat, were fearful of foreign economic penetration, had no interest in attracting foreign capital, lamented the demise of the Soviet Union, and were strongly opposed to NATO expansion. Those who did not consider the United States a threat, who were not fearful about foreign firms in Russia and indeed sought to increase foreign capital, who were not distressed about the demise of the Soviet Union, and who were not especially agitated by the prospect of NATO expansion were likely to regard Yeltsin and to a lesser degree Iavlinskii with more favorable eyes. Similarly, the enthusiasm for Iavlinskii and Yeltsin was less among those who responded affirmatively to the question whether Russian industry should be protected against foreign firms wishing to seize the Russian market. Foreign policy issues did not in the aggregate represent a strong component of the basis for the assessment of Zhirinovskii or Lebed, unless Chechnya is treated as a foreign policy matter. Overall, though, Russian voters in July 1996 were able to link their foreign policy preferences about core issues concerning East-West security issues and Russia's links to the international economy to identifiable presidential candidates.

Why was this so? Perhaps the most plausible explanation is one that links orientations to the domestic political economy and orientations to the international system. It is worth remembering there really was a Soviet system, which had domestic and international ramifications well beyond the political system narrowly conceived. Likewise, liberal democracy involves orientations toward other democratic systems—as the voluminous international relations literature on the democratic peace bears witness—and toward the market.[10] Markets, capital, foreign investment, and assessment of the United States and NATO are part of a package. At the cognitive level, Russians responded to survey questions in 1995–96 as though the Russian political system were part of a larger whole, one component of which constituted international-national linkages.

Determining the 1996 Presidential Vote

The vote in the second round of the 1996 presidential election was a referendum on the political system.[11] Social scientists are never going to be more sure of a finding than about this. Of respondents who chose from

---

[10] Lindblom, *Politics and Markets*; Kullberg and Zimmerman, "Liberal Elites"; and chapter 2.
[11] McFaul, "Russia's Presidential," p. 7.

among the options they were presented concerning the political system most suitable for Russia—the Soviet system before *perestroika*, the present system, or Western democracy[12]—and who reported having voted for either of the two candidates in the second round, a slim majority (51 percent versus 49 percent) of those interviewed after the 1996 presidential election expressed a preference either for the current political system or for democracy of a Western type for Russia. Of those who reported having voted in the second round and having voted for one of the candidates, nearly 85 percent voted for Ziuganov among those who said they thought the Soviet system before *perestroika* the most appropriate political system for Russia. An even higher proportion (93 percent) who told interviewers that they preferred the then current situation or Western-style democracy to the Soviet model answered that they had voted for Yeltsin. (Voters had the opportunity to vote "against both" candidates.)

If, moreover, we include in our analysis whether respondents thought their family's economic prospects were going to improve in the next year, we have almost the entire story. Fully 98 percent of the respondents who both responded that they regarded the current political situation or Western-style democracy as appropriate for Russia *and* expressed optimism about their family's material situation (*material'noe polozhenie*) in the coming year voted for Yeltsin. Similarly, 88 percent of those who identified the Soviet political system before *perestroika* as the system suitable for Russia *and* thought their family situation was going to worsen in the coming year voted for Ziuganov.)[13] Table 4.5 reveals the parsimonious relationship between orientation to the political system and vote for the president in July 1996. Put in simplest terms, Yeltsin and Ziuganov served as tangible icons, the human embodiment of abstract choices labeled "the Soviet system before *perestroika*," "the current political system," or "Western-style democracy."

Explaining the Choice of Political System

There is, therefore, no puzzle as to why Russians voted for Yeltsin or Ziuganov in the summer of 1996. Those regarding the Soviet model as the system most appropriate for Russia voted for Ziuganov. Those favoring

---

[12] Quite a few respondents took the opportunity proffered them by the question to offer an alternative to the three choices presented them. These covered a wide range. Many were of the form "the Soviet system but with features taken from the West" or "specifically Russian democracy." Respondents in the 1999 surveys were asked this question twice, once with the three answers, a second time with four options, including "the Soviet system, but in another, more democratic form." Most of those who volunteered an option when given only three choices elected "the Soviet system, but in another, more democratic form" when presented with four choices.

[13] Including those who voted against both Yeltsin and Ziuganov reduces the proportion of those who voted for Yeltsin among those who expressed preference for the current system

Table 4.5.
The Soviet System, Democratic Alternatives, and the 1966 Russian Presidential Vote

	For Whom Did You Vote?		
Preferred Political System	*Yeltsin*	*Ziuganov*	*Total*
Current system or Western democracy	92.6%	7.4%	52.5%
	(664)	(53)	(717)
Soviet system	15.2%	84.8%	47.5%
	(99)	(551)	(650)
Column total	55.8%	43.8%	100.0%
	(763)	(604)	(1367)

Source: As in table 4.2.
Note: Actual number of respondents for particular cells shown in parentheses.
$Tau_b - .78, p < .0001.$

Question wording:
What political system, in your opinion, is most suitable for Russia?

the changes since *perestroika* and the prospects that Russia might actually be a democratizing state voted for Yeltsin. The puzzle is in explaining the factors that predict support for which political system.

To make the case that Russia's relations to the world outside it were an important consideration in assessing Russians' assessments of the suitability of a particular political system for thier country, I drew once more on the insight that both the Soviet model and liberal democracy constitute a broader package than usually implied by the concept "political system." With that assumption, variables exemplifying aspects of this broader package should have independent effects in a multivariate analysis. Table 4.6 constitutes a logistic regression, the outcome of which is a dichotomous variable dividing the respondents into those who responded that they regarded the current situation or Western democracy, on the one hand, most suitable for Russia and those who said they preferred the pre-*perestroika* Soviet system, on the other.

In bivariate analysis, a long list of demographic variables can be identified that correlate with orientation to the political system, just as it is possible to construct a fairly long list of foreign policy items that are statistically significant in a large sample and correlate weakly with choice of political system. Many of the demographic and foreign policy variables did not prove

---

or Western-style democracy and expressed optimism for the coming year economically to 96 percent. Including those who voted against both candidates results in 83 percent voting for Ziuganov of those saying that the Soviet system was preferable and expecting their personal situation to worsen.

Table 4.6.
Predictors of Political System Most Suitable for Russia, 1996

Variable	Coefficient (B)	S.E.	Probability (P)
Prospective personal economic situation	.786	.13	.000
Prospective Russian economy	.508	.18	.006
University attendance	−.628	.34	.065
CPSU membership	.896	.37	.015
Market versus plan	−.606	.26	.018
Russia follow own path	−.662	.27	.015
Restore economy without West	1.220	.31	.000
Soviet Union not destroyed	−1.572	.28	.000
Attract foreign investment?	−.422	.13	.001
Constant	6.406	1.26	.000

Source: As in table 4.2.
Total: N = 2452. Cases in analysis: 582.
Initial log likelihood function: −2 log likelihood 794.07.
Improvement: 371.04. Goodness of fit: 533.44. Cases correctly predicted: 83.9%.

Note: There are no surprises in the coefficients. In all instances the signs are consistent with what one would expect—thus, given the order of the values for the question about the prospective personal economic situation, it correlates negatively with preferred political system and is to be read as indicating that persons who are optimistic about their personal economic situation are less likely to favor the Soviet system before *perestroika* and more prone to endorse the present system or democracy of a Western type.

Wording of nondemographic items in model:

"Market versus plan" dichotomizes those from the typology described above in chapter 2 who are market democrats and market authoritarians, on the one hand, and those who are social democrats and socialist authoritarians, on the other.

Russia's own path: Should Russia use the experience of the West or should it seek its own path of development? Which of the answers that I will read to you are closest to your view?
The foreign policy items are:
Russia should attract foreign funds into the economy.
Russia can resolve its economic problems without the help of the West.
Under no circumstances should the Soviet Union have been broken up.

statistically significant in multivariate analysis. Size of city lived in, region, even age and sex of respondent, for instance, all failed to be statistically significant in multivariate analysis that included respondents' assessments of their past and prospective economic situations. (These, of course, were affected by respondents' age and sex.) Similarly, many foreign policy variables—for example, NATO expansion, defending against Western firms' efforts to seize the Russian market—did not manifest stable effects. What does prove relevant to the argument developed here is that, along with unsurprising demographic (education) and retrospective and prospective economic opportunity variables, variables that address respondents' preferences for a largely market-based or largely state-dominated planned economy [14] and variables bearing on Russian citizens' views about the outside world prove to have stable and statistically significant effects on their views about the preferred political system. Also included was a variable that ascertained whether "Russia should use the experience of the West or whether it should seek its own path of development."[15] This question nicely got at a late twentieth-century variant of the old Slavophil-Westerner divide and proved a robust predictor of orientation to the political system.[16]

Specifically, those who did *not* agree with the proposition advanced in a survey after the July 1996 elections to the effect that "the Soviet Union should not under any circumstances have been destroyed" were much more likely than other respondents to endorse the present system or Western democracy. Not surprisingly, support for the Soviet Union went hand in glove with support for the Soviet political system. Similarly, there were independent and statistically significant effects for agreeing that Russia should try "to attract foreign funds" for the Russian economy and for having disagreed with the assertion that Russia could "resolve [its] economic problems without the help of the West." Again, the fact that views evocative of autarky covary with favoring the Soviet political system should be readily recognized by observers used to thinking of the Soviet model as something much broader than a "mere" political system. Both the Soviet model and market or liberal democracy imply important propositions about a state's political economy and its relations to the external world.

What is perhaps most interesting, though, is the association between responding that the United States is a threat in the survey and disposition toward the political system. Table 4.7 shows quite clearly the relationship in practice between these two concepts. It reports findings for those who answered the United States was a threat both in December 1995 and after

[14] To construct a composite variable, I used the four items in constructing the economic dimension of the political economy typology discussed in chapter 2: should heavy industry be state owned, is economic competition beneficial, is it normal for someone to become richer using the labor of other people, and if it makes no sense to begin a business since it might fail. The exact wording of the questions is found in table 2.3.

[15] The question was asked in both the pre-parliamentary and post-presidential surveys for 1995 and 1996, respectively. The variable used here is an amalgam of those questions. Thanks go to Benjamin Goldsmith who first brought my attention to the ongoing dialogue in Russia about alternative developmental paths.

[16] I worried, though, that the Slavophil-Westerner distinction was too closely linked to the concept of preferred political system. As a result, the logistic regression was run with and without the variable. The variables relating to Russia's relations to its outside world remained statistically significant in both instances.

Table 4.7.
Assessments of U.S. Threat, 1995–96 and Political System Most Suitable for Russia

	Is the United States a Threat?			
System Most Suitable	*Yes* '95 and '96	*No* '95, *Yes* '96	*Yes* '95, *No* '96	*No* '95 and '96
Soviet system before	73%	68%	45%	25%
perestroika	(228)	(98)	(115)	(145)
Present system or	27%	32%	55%	75%
Western democracy	(84)	(47)	(141)	(428)

Source: As in tables 4.1 and 4.2.
Note: Actual number of respondents for particular cells shown in parentheses.
$\text{Tau}_c = .44, p < .001.$

the presidential election in July 1996, those who said the United States was not a threat in December 1995 and answered in the affirmative after the presidential election, those who answered that the United States was a threat in December 1995 and not after the presidential election, and those who said the United States was not a threat on both occasions. Three-quarters of those who categorized the United States as a threat on both occasions also said they preferred the Soviet system before *perestroika* for Russia, and three-quarters of those who said the United States was not a threat opted for the then current Russian system or Western-style democracy as the political system most suitable for Russia. Again, the point is not to ascribe unidirectional causality to the respondents' threat perception: the view of the United States as a threat for many doubtless flowed from their preference for the old Soviet system. Rather, it is to reassert that orientation to the Soviet system and orientation to democracy were part of a package that included overall judgments about U.S.-Russian relations and Russia's participation or lack thereof in the global economy.

It is also to make a policy observation, namely that perceptions of the American threat or anxiety about foreign market domination are relatively manipulable variables. Efforts by the Russian government, the Russian media, and the West during the half year separating the Duma election and the presidential election primarily directed at affecting the presidential vote[17] simultaneously ameliorated public assessments of the United States.

[17] Boris Yeltsin, in *Midnight Diaries* (New York: Public Affairs Press, 2000), asserts that "in some matters—for example, in our extensive use of demographic polling—we were more advanced than the French. Our pollsters would conduct surveys in a region both before and after I visited there. They measured the reaction of listeners after a presidential radio address and so on" (p. 33).

Timothy Colton[18] and Dimitri Simes[19] have described the efforts of the government and the media to shape voters' attitudes in the 1996 elections. ("Relatively" in this context should be emphasized as much as "manipulable." Colton also demonstrates how savvy viewers—long accustomed to Soviet *agitprop*—were about that manipulation.) According to Colton, the 9:00 P.M. news broadcast on the state channel ORT, for instance, mentioned Yeltsin far more frequently than Ziuganov, and the latter was often mentioned in a negative light. Perhaps the most vivid illustration of the media's role came on the final day before the first round of the presidential election. Russian law ostensibly forbids campaigning on the eve of the election. ORT, consequently, conformed to a narrow construction of the law but brought viewers a documentary "that showed the Berlin wall coming down, a Chinese man facing down tanks before the Tiananmen Square massacre, and Mr. Yeltsin defying the Communist coup-backers in August 1991."[20] The West played a similar role, most notably by providing Russia with another round of funds from the IMF. The $10.2 billion grant was specifically targeted at increased social spending and the payment of wage arrears. As Reuters observed, "The move is expected to be helpful to President Boris N. Yeltsin in the presidential election in June."[21] All these efforts had a direct impact on the presidential outcome. They also, though, appear to have had a separate impact on Russians' response patterns concerning the American threat to Russia as well.

Students of American politics will likely react here and assert that respondents' evaluations of the presidential candidates drove the answers given about foreign policy. I would grant immediately that it is difficult to disentangle the two. It would have been relatively easy to have done so had the December 1995 survey asked which political system was preferable for Russia. In that case, we would have been blessed with responses in December 1995 and after the July 1996 election to questions pertaining to the U.S. threat, respondents' assessment of the political system most suitable for Russia, and their evaluations of Yeltsin. Unfortunately this was not the case.

But the 1995 and 1996 surveys did ask questions calling for respondents to evaluate both Yeltsin and Ziuganov. Employing the evaluations of Ziuganov, rather than of Yeltsin, provides strong evidence that the shift in views concerning the United States was an effect that was in part

---

[18] Colton, *Transitional Citizens*, esp. pp. 60–63.

[19] Dimitri Simes, *After the Collapse: Russia Seeks Its Place as a Great Power* (New York: Simon and Schuster, 1999), pp. 170–76.

[20] *New York Times*, June 16, 1996.

[21] *New York Times*, March 27, 1996.

independent of presidential candidate evaluation. Among those who thought so negatively about Ziuganov as to award him a zero in December 1995 on a thermometer scale, 31 percent regarded the United States as a threat in December 1995 and 21 percent agreed after the July 1996 presidential vote. Among those who regarded Ziuganov highly in December 1995—giving him a 75 or higher—two-thirds (67 percent) regarded the United States a threat while only 56 percent of those who ranked him that highly in the summer of 1996 answered that the United States was a threat. One could readily explain support for Yeltsin producing shifts in the proportion of those giving various scale scores to Ziuganov as being consistent with the hypothesis that the changes in assessments of the American threat was a function of the remarkable change over half a year in Russian assessments of Yeltsin. Where the hypothesis comes a cropper stems from the fact that among *both* those who esteemed and those who despised Ziuganov, respondents were less likely to regard the United States as a threat to Russian security in the summer of 1996 than they had been at the time of the December 1995 Duma elections. This creates the presumption that the shift over the half year in assessments of the U.S. threat had a basis that was to some extent independent of Yeltsin's improved ratings. Consequently, orientations to the international system were relevant to explaining why Russians in 1996 regarded one or another political system as preferable for Russia. The covariance is instructive between the disposition to say the United States was a threat and political system preference as a comment on the way the Soviet model and the perceived threat from the United States were associated in Russian voters' heads, especially in view of the impact of opportunity structures—themselves a function to an appreciable extent of age—in the model. Although views about the nature of the political system and individual assessments of their family's future prospects were paramount in explaining the vote for Yeltsin or Ziuganov, perceptions of threat to Russian security, nostalgia about the Soviet Union, and fears of economic penetration have to be viewed as part of a package contributing to whether Russian citizens prefer the former Soviet political system, the present system, or Western democracy.

The 2000 Presidential Election

The July 1996 presidential election in Russia was followed by another quite different presidential election, one in which the December 1999 Duma elections largely determined the outcome of the March 2000 contest. Whereas after the 1996 election only a slight majority had said that they thought the present system or Western democracy was most suitable for Russia, two-thirds (67 percent) of the Russians who chose among the categories presented to them in 1999 asserted that the Soviet system before *perestroika* was most appropriate for Russia. That notwithstanding, Vladimir Putin defeated his main challenger, Gennadii Ziuganov, and the other candidates in the first round.[22]

In 1996 Russian citizens had relatively coherent views about the links between the economy and, especially, Russia's place in the world, on the one hand, and their views about the political system, on the other. They also had a relatively clear fix on the nation's most likely candidates for president. Their dispositions about foreign policy in the broadest sense connected in important ways to how they chose between Yeltsin and Ziuganov.

These are among the essential requisites of an effective working democracy. For democracy to function well, voters must have reasonably consistent or constrained beliefs about issues, and they need to be able in the broadest sense to determine the preferences of leaders accurately. The Russian electorate in 1996 did just that. They were sufficiently plugged into stimuli from elites through the media to make a more or less considered judgment about their preferred political system. That determination, plus voting their pocketbook prospects, parsimoniously predicted the outcome of the July 1996 presidential election. The Russian voters played the role they should play in a democracy. They constituted an audience that could be reached by Russian elites and other actors. They voted for what they liked.

One component part to their judgment about the preferred political system involved their assessment of Russia's relation to its external environment. Russian elites and other leading actors played these tunes. Russians who in 1995/96 preferred the old, planned economy with its characteristic under- rather than unemployment, who bemoaned the passing of the Soviet Union, who feared the intrusion of Western capital and Western capitalists in the Russian economy, and who considered the United States a threat to Russian security favored the traditional Soviet system for Russia. Those who took the opposite stance about each of these items were more disposed to favor the current system or Western democracy. These were independent effects aside from the predictive power of age, region, television attentiveness, and attitudes that constituted the acceptance or rejection of a late twentieth-century version of Slavophilism.

These dispositions were not cast in stone. As we have seen, when interviewed in July 1996 respondents were less alarmed by threats, economic and political, from the outside world than they had been before the De-

---

[22] Among those interviewed in December 1999 who said they intended to vote, Putin was strongly favored in a pair-wise comparison with Ziuganov, 76 to 24 percent.

cember 1995 parliamentary elections. After the July 1996 presidential election, the same respondents interviewed before the 1995 parliamentary elections showed that, as with respect to questions about whether the United States was a threat, they were less prone to agree with the statement that it is necessary "to defend our industry against foreign firms which wish to seize the Russian market," and more favorably inclined to the assertion that "Russia should attract foreign funds into the economy" than they had been at the time of the parliamentary election.

Russian citizens in the aggregate viewed the world outside Russia with less hostility in July 1996 than they did at the time of the parliamentary elections in December 1995. This apparently had consequences for the presidential election; dispositions to the outside world had an independent effect on orientations toward the political system, thus increasing Yeltsin's chances for election. In this instance, as in Aldrich's study of American presidential elections, leaders did not waltz before a blind audience. Some appreciable part of the music played, moreover, concerned Russia's relations, broadly conceived, with the outside world.

What about the election of Vladimir Putin in March 2000? That election left much to be desired in terms of democratic theory. The timing of President Yeltsin's resignation combined with all the advantages of incumbency and state television gave the election for many a sense of *fait accompli* and was reminiscent of Mexican elections before 2000. That being said, it must be recognized that Putin had enormous approval ratings, something not achieved by others in the sequence of prime ministers during 1998 and 1999. Moreover, citizens clearly had preferences that were reflected in whom they supported for president. After a draft of this book had been written I received the data from the Russian mass survey that Timothy Colton and Michael McFaul conducted after the March 2000 election. These data, in combination with the preferences expressed by respondents surveyed in December 1999 who declared their intention to vote in the presidential election and how they intended to vote at that juncture, help us to assess the links between orientations to the world outside Russia and Russian decisions to vote for Putin rather than Ziuganov in the first round. (All the other candidates finished far behind Ziuganov.)

In the surveys prior to and subsequent to the 1999 Duma election, respondents were not asked questions about the effectiveness of potential presidential candidates in handling specific issues but, logically, about the ability of parties to address such matters. In the 1995 Duma elections forty-three parties competed and in 1999, twenty-eight parties took part. Only six really mattered in 1999: Iabloko, led by Iavlinskii; Edinstvo (Unity), to which Putin affiliated himself quite late in the fall; Otechestvo Rossii (Fatherland of All Russia), in which Evgenii Primakov and Alexander Luzhkov, the mayor of Moscow, were the most prominent figures; the Communist Party of the Russian Federation (KPRF), led by Gennadii Ziuganov; the Zhirnovskii bloc, and the Soiuz Pravikh Sil (Union of Right Forces) headed by former prime minister Sergei Kirienko. Table 4.8 shows the proportion of respondents, of those identifying a specific party, asserting that the various leading parties would be most effective in addressing a particular issue. Overwhelmingly the table reports the respondents' preferences for particular parties.

Closer inspection, though, suggests some ability in the aggregate to sort out the parties or their leaders with respect to particular issues. Putin's association (for the better, at that juncture) with the war in Chechnya was clear, and respondents were considerably more certain of Edinstvo's ability to deal with it than with anything else, though it was also seen as being relatively more able to address the problems of crime and corruption as well. The economist Iavlinskii's Iabloko got higher marks for being able to address the economy than for anything else. The KPRF received its best score for its ability to deal with the tasks of "securing social guarantees for people." Fatherland of All Russia (read: former minister of foreign affairs and former prime minister Evgenii Primakov) was seen as best able, relatively, to handle the task of "supporting Russia's international interests," and the weakly backed Union of Right Forces obtained relatively more support for its ability to build the economy and "to defend human rights and democratic freedoms" than in other domains. The ability of mass publics in December 1999 to differentiate leaders and parties with respect to the domains in which they would most likely be effective seems impressive, especially in view of the fact that, with the exception of the KPRF, parties are notoriously weakly developed in Russia.[23]

The second part of table 4.8 shows how effectively Russians judged the various candidates would address these same issues after the 2000 presidential elections. Once again, the responses overwhelmingly reflect respondents' preferences for individual candidates. Putin dominates all the other candidates on each issue. Once again, also, there were differences across issues that suggested an aggregate judgment that particular Russian leaders would handle certain dimensions of Russia's problems relatively better than others. Ziuganov is seen as being relatively more able to ensure social stability. Iavlinskii, the politically liberal economist, is viewed as being relatively more able to improve the economy and to defend human rights and freedoms. As Edinstvo had done in December 1999, where Putin does particularly well pertains to judgments about his ability to address the problem of Chechnya—scarcely a surprise—and in dealing with crime and corruption. With the former minister of foreign affairs

---

[23] On Russia's political parties, see in particular Colton, *Transitional Citizens*.

Table 4.8.
Assessments of Issue—Specific Effectiveness, 1999/2000

	Six Leading Parties, December, 1999					
Party (Leader)	Improve Economy	Ensure Social Stability	Defense of Rights and Freedoms	Deal with Problem of Chechnya	Support Russia's International Interests	Deal with Crime and Corruption
Iabloko (Iavlinski)	12% (138)	7% (78)	10% (107)	3% (35)	5% (53)	5% (54)
Edinstvo (Putin)	25% (301)	27% (297)	28% (285)	52% (612)	28% (295)	39% (439)
Zhirinovskii bloc	3% (37)	4% (39)	5% (52)	8% (86)	4% (46)	9% (102)
Otechestvo (Primakov)	14% (164)	12% (137)	12% (121)	7% (79)	20% (273)	10% (115)
KPRF (Ziuganov)	35% (414)	43% (467)	36% (370)	25% (280)	31% (317)	33% (309)
Union of Right Forces (Kirienko)	12% (141)	7% (76)	10% (101)	2% (25)	5% (54)	3% (35)

Source: 1999/2000 panel survey conducted by Demoscope.
Note: Percentages shown are proportions party received as fraction of total the six leading parties received. Actual number of respondents in particular cells shown in parentheses.

Question wording:

There are various problems that are necessary to be resolved in our country. I am going to read several of them. Tell me, please, which party or bloc in your view would best deal with these problems. Which party or bloc would best deal with . . . or is there no difference among the parties?

Evgenii Primakov no longer in the picture—and three months of serving as acting president behind him—Putin also does especially well in Russian citizens' estimate of his probable effectiveness in foreign policy.

In 1996 Russians had been able to link their foreign policy preferences with the policy orientations of presidential candidates, especially with those of the two candidates who ended up in the second round, Ziuganov and Yeltsin. Given that the 1996 election was a referendum on democracy and the linkage between orientation to the domestic political economy and to the international system, it was in some ways not surprising.

Neither at the time of the Duma election in December 1999 nor in March 2000 when the presidential election occurred, by contrast, did Russians have extensive information about Vladimir Putin's views. Putin, a classic front-runner in this respect, refused to discuss the details of his

Table 4.8. (*cont'd*)
Assessments of Issue—Specific Effectiveness, 1999/2000

Party (Leader)		*Five Leading Vote Getters, March 2000 Presidential Election*				
	Improve Economy	*Ensure Social Stability*	*Defense of Rights and Freedoms*	*Deal with Problem of Chechnya*	*Support Russia's International Interests*	*Deal with Crime and Corruption*
Zhirinovskii	2% (21)	2% (21)	4% (47)	6% (82)	4% (50)	6% (71)
Ziuganov	23% (293)	29% (345)	26% (286)	14% (185)	20% (240)	19% (245)
Putin	52% (659)	56% (665)	57% (637)	78% (1058)	70% (860)	71% (907)
Tuleyev	7% (89)	8% (90)	4% (39)	1% (12)	1% (14)	2% (27)
Iavlinskii	16% (199)	6% (71)	10% (109)	2% (25)	5% (57)	2% (25)

Source: 1999/2000 panel survey conducted by Demoscope.

Note: Percentages shown are proportions party received as fraction of total the five leading presidential vote getters. Actual number of respondents in particular cells shown in parentheses.

Question wording:

There are various problems that are necessary to be resolved in our country. I am going to read several of them. Tell me, please, who of the candidates for president of Russia in your view would best deal with these problems. Which candidate for president would best deal with . . . or is there no difference among the candidates?

positions or, ostensibly, even to campaign. (He was, of course, in his guise as acting president, highly visible on television acting presidential, doubtless a major reason Russians were disposed to credit him with foreign policy skills.) But they had had ample opportunity to know the views of the leader of the KPRF. Table 4.9 shows the covariance in bivariate correlations between respondents' views on broad foreign policy matters and whether they voted for Ziuganov or Putin in March 2000. The relations are not robust, but they are all in the expected direction and statistically significant. Putin does well regardless of respondent orientations to foreign policy. Between 13 and 21 percent more persons reported having voted for him rather than Ziuganov among those who answered that they did not regard the United States as a threat, if they agreed or agreed strongly that Russia should attract foreign investment, if they did not respond that they agreed or agreed strongly that Russia's firms should be protected against the predatory activities of foreign firms, if they did not agree in some fashion that Russia should sever all ties with NATO if it expanded into the CIS, if they did not agree or agree strongly that Russia and Belarus should be a single country, and if they did not say they agreed or strongly agreed that the Soviet Union should never have broken up.

Table 4.9.
Orientations to Foreign Policy, 1999/2000, and Reported Vote for Putin
(as Opposed to Ziuganov), March 2000 (percentages are those reporting having
voted for Putin)

	Yes	*No*
U.S. is a threat	62%	81%
$Tau_c = -.17, p < .001$	(450)	(290)
	Agree or Strongly Agree	*Other*[a]
Russia should attract foreign investments	75%	62%
$Tau_c = -13, p < .001$	(439)	(346)
Defend market against foreign firms	66%	84%
$Tau_c =.10, p < .001$	(674)	(173)
USSR should not have ever broken up	64%	85%
$Tau_c =.14, p < .001$	(643)	(219)

Source: As in table 4.8.

Note: Actual number of respondents in particular cells shown in parentheses.

[a] Includes those who said they were ambivalent, disagreed, and strongly disagreed.

Question wording:

Defend market: It is necessary to defend our industry from foreign firms that wish to seize
the Russian market.
For the wording of the other questions see table 4.3.

But the voting behavior in the 2000 election differed in significant ways
from that in the 1996 election. Most obviously, Putin was elected in the
first round. Equally important, he received wide support from all categories of people. While assessment of the political system most suitable for
Russia was a robust predictor of how people reported having voted in
March 2000, the congruence between system preference and voting behavior was less than in 1996. Taken in combination with whether respondents believed that Russia's economy would improve in the next year,
however, that assessment is tightly linked with how people reported they
voted. Table 4.10 shows the relationship between how people said they
voted and three things: views about the political system suitable for Russia
taken separately, answers pertaining to the Russian economy in the next
year, and a simple additive scale combining the two.[24]

[24] I combined those who said the economy would improve significantly or improve into
one category and did the same for those who said it would worsen or worsen significantly. I
also collapsed the categories for respondents who viewed the present system and Western

Table 4.10.
Respondents' Assessment of Political System Most Suitable for Russia and the Russian
Economy for Next Year and Reported Vote in March 2000 Presidential Election
(proportion saying they voted for Putin rather than Ziuganov)

	Political System Most Suitable for Russia			
Voted for	Soviet System before Perestroika	Soviet System in a more Democratic Form	Present System	Western Democracy
Putin	34% (112)	67% (319)	96% (258)	94% (79)

	Russian Economy Will				
Voted for	Worsen Significantly	Worsen	Stay the Same	Improve	Improve Significantly
Putin	10% (2)	35% (17)	45% (117)	85% (496)	92% (44)

Additive Scale Combining Responses about the Political System Appropriate for Russia and Assessments of Russian Economy in Coming Year (I: said economy would worsen or worsen significantly and said Soviet system before perestroika was most suitable for Russia; V: economy would improve and present system or Western democracy was most suitable for Russia.)

Voted for	I	II	III	IV	V
Putin	7% (2)	22% (29)	53% (111)	84% (212)	97% (259)

Source: As in table 4.8.

Note: In creating the scale, I trifurcated the question addressing the political system most suitable for Russia by dividing the responses into those who chose the Soviet system before *perestroika*, those who opted for the Soviet system in another, more democratic form, and a third category that combined those who said "the present system" and those who said "Western-type democracy." Similarly, I divided the responses to the item about the Russian economy into those who said it would improve or improve significantly, those who said it would remain the same, and those who said it would worsen or worsen significantly. I added the two scores. Those who said the Soviet system before *perestroika* was the system most suitable for Russia and who thought the economy would worsen received the lowest score. Those who said the present system or Western democracy was most suitable *and* said the economy would improve or improve significantly received the highest. (Actual number of respondents in particular cells shown in parentheses.)

Of those (far fewer in 2000 than in 1996, though somewhat more than in December 1999) who said they thought either the present system or Western democracy preferable for Russia, 95 percent voted for Putin rather than Ziuganov, while almost two-thirds of those who said they preferred the Soviet system before *perestroika* voted for Ziuganov. Respondents'

democracy as the system preferable for Russia. Adding the two recoded variables provides a range of categories from 2 to 6.

read on the Russian economy produced, in classically sociotropic fashion, equally dramatic links with how they said they voted.[25] Combining the two variables yielded even more striking results. Russians who said the economy was going to worsen and who termed the old Soviet system preferable voted virtually unanimously for Ziuganov. By the same token, respondents voted for Putin, if respondents answered that the present system or Western democracy was the preferred system for Russia and they favorably assessed the near-term development of the Russian economy.

Thus in a sense, the 2000 election was also a referendum on the political system for Russia, but in a more complicated manner than had been true of the 1996 election. In 1996, the choice was simple or, many would say, had been made to seem simple as a result of the framing of the issue in the media: for democracy, for Yeltsin; for communism, for Ziuganov. In 2000, choice of political system for Russia and assessment of Russia's economic prospects for the coming year properly classified four-fifths of the votes for Putin and Ziuganov. Judgment about the political system most suitable for Russia combined with "It's the economy, stupid" parsimoniously explained how people voted for president in 2000. Russia's relation to the outside world entered the picture in two ways. First, in regressions directly predicting how people voted, the decade they were born and whether they considered the United States a threat and thought Russia should protect its economy from predatory foreign firms had small but statistically significant (the latter marginally so [$p < .10$]) independent effects in models where the overwhelming explanatory power came from assessment of the political system most suitable for Russia and respondents' judgments about the near-term development of the Russian economy.

Second, how respondents reacted—along with demographic data about education and income, which were not statistically significant direct predictors of how Russians had voted—to assertions about market relations and to broad foreign policy propositions correlated with how they oriented themselves to the Russian political system. Thus assertions that the Soviet Union should never have been broken up, that Russia should pursue its own path of development, and that Russian enterprises needed to be protected against foreign firms that are out to seize the Russian market were significant at the <.05 level, and the assertion that Russia should sever all connections with NATO if the latter expanded into the CIS at the <.10 level, in models explaining respondents' answers to questions about the political system most suitable for Russia. Hence, as in the 1996 election, dispositions to foreign policy orientations broadly defined covaried with beliefs about the political system preferable for Russia, which in turn was a robust predictor of how Russians voted.

[25] Kinder and Kiewiet, "Sociotropic Politics."

Implications

We began this chapter by asking whether Russian leaders waltzed before a blind audience and whether, if its memebers could see, their assessment of how leaders danced was driven in part by judgments about Russia, its leaders, and its orientation to the world outside. Many Russians truly know little about the world outside Russia. But the evidence of this chapter is that in the aggregate—with a large error term, to be sure—they know enough to link their preferences with the policy orientations, including those pertaining to Russia's relations to the United States and to the world economy, of at least the most prominent presidential candidates. This was clearly the case in 1996, though for the 2000 election it may be more correct to say that Russians knew Ziuganov's dispositions. Respondents imputed to Putin views, unspecified, that were not Ziuganov's in sufficiently large numbers as to produce substantial differences in the aggregate in the response patterns pertaining to Russia's orientation to the international system of those who reported voting for Putin and those who reported voting for Ziuganov. In aggregate terms they were able to distinguish among issue domains, including foreign policy in the broadest sense, where leaders would be relatively more and relatively less effective. In neither election did specific foreign policy issues play a major role. Assessments of broader matters having to do with the world outside Russia— the U.S. threat and Russia's orientation to the international economy— did, however, play a role in explaining the 1996 presidential vote. Broad foreign policy orientations, similarly, did play a direct and indirect— through their impact on preference for the political system for Russia— role in understanding the vote in the 2000 presidential election. This was so even though the greatest purchase on how Russians voted in that election was obtained by knowing their assessments of the near-term prospects for the Russian economy and their judgments as to the proper political system for Russia.

It is easy to be cynical about mass publics and their impact on foreign policy orientations. With respect to American democracy that cynicism has given way to a more benign view of the electorate's role. Western democracies, including the United States, and at the beginning of the twenty-first century, most East European states, typically receive 1's and 2's on Freedom House's seven-point civil liberties and political freedom scales. There are good reasons why Freedom House consistently gave Russia 3's and 4's in the 1990s and a 4 and a 5 in 1999–2000 (just as it was not appropriate, it bears repeating, to give to it the 6's or 7's the Soviet Union consistently received). It is easy to enumerate the conditions conducive to democracy in which Russia is most lacking. It lacks a well-defined and institutionalized party system, it has a super-presidential system that permits the top-down manipulation of a potential heir apparent, it lacks a truly effective and independent court system, and tolerance for dissent is relatively low for a system professing to be democratic. One area, though, in which Russia satisfies a minimalist construction of the prerequisites for democracy concerns the links between mass preferences and mass judgments about elite preferences and performance.[26] In the aggregate, Russian mass publics know enough to make a choice that links their preferences with the views of leaders—and Yeltsin, for one, monitored these links carefully in the 1996 election, as we saw above—and enough to differentiate among leaders and the domains in which they are likely to prove effective. This generalization must obviously be qualified with the proviso that these publics must have a choice on the one occasion all recognize they are most likely to have such an impact, an election. That is important as a minimal prerequisite for the effective functioning of foreign policy in a partly free political system. Subsequent chapters assess how preferences for the political system bear on elite and mass orientations to foreign policy matters and how specifically a key post–cold war era matter—NATO expansion—has been influenced by elite and mass preferences.

---

[26] It should also be the case that individual preferences can be aggregated so that the sum of those individual choices is collectively rational. The likelihood that this will occur increases substantially when large numbers of people rank politicians along a single continuum and when these preferences are "single peaked"—that is, there is some point along that continuum that the voter thinks is best and there is a decline in both directions from that point. The textbook example is a left-right continuum. A large majority of the Russian respondents in the 2000 postpresidential survey (up from 1995/96) were able to locate themselves along such a continuum in some way. Moreover, the aggregate distribution of preferences for Putin and Ziuganov was single peaked.

5

Elite Political-Economic Orientations and Foreign Policy

SOME PARTS of an answer to the question, "How do Soviet and post-Soviet Russian foreign policies differ?" do not require exploration of the differences in the dispositions of those who play central roles in the determination of policy or in the political processes of the two systems. These stem primarily from the differences in the basic capabilities of the two states and require only a brief enumeration. Regardless of the players and the nature of the post-Soviet Russian policy process, Russia will not again be a superpower or aspire to challenge the United States' position as the major power in the international system. The days when a government in Moscow was the leader of a genuine world power are no more.

For a historically brief moment there was a time when the government in Moscow plausibly had some pretensions about transforming the existing international order and some basis for talking seriously about catching up and outstripping the United States in areas that mattered politically. Such a time is gone, presumably forever. With the collapse of the Soviet Union, the area governed by Moscow is currently smaller than it was at the beginning of the nineteenth century. Moscow is more limited in the domain over which it can project power and influence than at any time since the early years after the Bolshevik seizure of power.

Moreover, in the early 1990s, Russia lacked the domestic political capacity to mobilize effectively those resources potentially at its disposal—whether the end was to maximize its influence in foreign policy or to implement policy decisions regarding environmental protection.[1] If ever a political system might be said to suffer from input overload, it was the Russian system in the first decade after the demise of the Soviet Union. Readers will have their own lists of Russia's attendant domestic problems. Most such lists would include high inflation, growth of crime, ecological disasters, intense intra-elite conflicts, and inter-nationality conflicts within Russia itself. In such circumstances, the country's disposable surplus for foreign policy was minimal.

Russia remains, nevertheless, a regional great power, regardless of the features of its domestic political system or who plays a role in its foreign

---

[1] Zimmerman, Nikitina, and Clem, "The Soviet Union and the Russian Federation."

policy process. It inherited from its Soviet predecessor the bulk of an enormous arsenal of thermonuclear weapons and long-range delivery vehicles. Its conventional weaponry and economic resources render it vastly more powerful than Georgia, Lithuania, Uzbekistan, and Ukraine or even all the former Soviet republics put together. There will come a time, perhaps in the Putin administration that commenced June 2000, when the political system will become more stable than it was in the 1990s. When that happens, Russia, once again, by virtue of its enormous natural resources, its highly educated and skilled population, and its military power, will play a significant role as a regional player in the power-balancing games of the major powers.

To say more, though, requires exploring the connections between opening the domestic political system and foreign policy. Opening a political system has two important consequences for foreign policy making. One of these pertains to the role of mass publics. Mass publics constrain elite choices, and they serve ultimately as the selectorate that chooses among candidates selected by and drawn from segments of the elite. In previous chapters, we have seen that in the 1990s Russian mass publics were markedly less prone than were elites to favor the use of force abroad and more reluctant to open the economy to global penetration. I also have argued that mass public dispositions concerning Russia's connections to the international system played a significant part in the public's preference for Yeltsin over Ziuganov in the 1996 presidential election and some part in defining how they voted in choosing, basically, between Putin and Ziuganov in the March 2000 election as well.

But opening a political system has a second key impact on foreign policy making. Changing the composition of the participants in what is largely an elite dialogue changes the balance of considerations among elites. Whether and to what extent they have consequences for foreign policy outcomes is the subject of this chapter.

The chapter is to some extent a thought experiment. It asks what difference did it make for Russian foreign policy that market democrats predominated among foreign policy elites in the 1990s. There are several variants to this question. The first is the most straightforward: that is, to consider whether those elites who are attitudinally liberal democrats have distinctive orientations to foreign policy questions. A corollary would be to ask, "How would it have mattered if in the 1990s it had been the socialist authoritarians or only members of the former CPSU among the elites who had called the shots?" One could imagine that consensus about external threats, goals, and Russia's capabilities would yield minimal differences in foreign policy views, despite differences in domestic orientation. If not an "objective" national interest, there might be an intersubjective national interest.[2] But assuming major differences in orientation to foreign policy across groups defined by political economy stance, what are they and have they changed over time? Would others have moved even further away by century's end from the views expressed in the honeymoon period in East-West or U.S.-Russian relations of the early 1990s?

Market Democratic Elites and Foreign Policy Orientations

Do Russian foreign policy elites with views that are recognizably liberal or market democratic give different answers than others to key foreign policy questions? The vapid but correct answer is "It depends," but the more important exercise is to specify the "On what," the "About what," and the "Compared with whom." With a couple of exceptions, knowing someone's orientation to the domestic political economy contributes little to an understanding of elite attitudes toward Russia's regional goals, its regional security perceptions, or the use of force on Russia's periphery. With qualifications to be incorporated in later parts of this chapter, differences in orientation to the domestic political economy are associated with important differences in answers to questions about foreign policy largely in the following domains: U.S.-Russian security issues (including NATO expansion) and aggregate defense spending, Russian unification with Ukraine and Belarus, and, less certainly and less thoroughly, global economic integration and the penetration of the Russian economy.

Questions dealing with regional security goals, perceptions of risk, and the use of force on Russian borders by and large are not matters about which market democrats and other elites divide sharply. In part this is because in many of these instances there exists near unanimity among the elite. In these cases, the absence of differences among elite *groupings* is largely a function of the absence of differences among elites. Table 5.1 utilizes a somewhat arbitrary cutoff point of 80 percent[3] to identify items about which there is, or seems to be, elite consensus. Using that as a cutoff leaves as a marginal consensus call the question whether "for the most part" Russia's national interests "should be limited to its current territory" or whether they are "broader." In 1993 slightly more than 20 percent of those interviewed said that Russia's national interests should be limited to its present territory. Overall and in 1995 and 1999, though, 80 percent

[2] On national security as an ambiguous symbol, Arnold Wolfers, *Discord and Collaboration: Essays in International Politics* (Baltimore: Johns Hopkins Press, 1962), pp. 147–66, remains worth reading.

[3] But see Graham, "The Politics of Failure," p. 57, where he too defines 80 percent as the threshold for "virtual unanimity" among American foreign policy attitudes.

Table 5.1.
Foreign Policy Elite Consensus 1993, 1995, 1999

	1993	1995	1999
Responded national interest broader	77% (149)	80% (144)	83% (168)
	Goals: Less Important or Very Important		
Less Important Goal			
Aiding Russia's friends abroad	—	86% (151)	88% (180)
Defend human rights elsewhere	—	80% (142)	80% (165)
Settlement of conflicts outside former Soviet Union	84% (168)	—	—
Very Important			
Defense of Russian state	—	92% (165)	94% (197)
Extricate Russia from its current crisis	98% (194)	94% (170)	94% (195)
Develop relations with "near abroad"	89% (177)	83% (149)	80% (163)
Defense of Russia's economic interests	97% (194)	97% (174)	99% (207)
National security	90% (178)	96% (172)	96% (200)
Defense of territorial integrity	86% (172)	93% (167)	97% (203)
Shouldn't forget global problems	97% (191)	95% (170)	94% (196)
	Use of Force Legitimate?		
Yes			
Defense of territorial integrity	—	91% (161)	99% (207)
Defense of Russian state	—	86% (144)	85% (164)

or more of those elites interviewed opted for a broader conception of the national interest—noticeably more than the proportion responding in that fashion in either the 1993 or the 1995 mass samples.

Respondents were asked which of several possible goals were very important and which were less important. These included "protecting the interests of Russians (Rossiian) in the countries of the former republics of the USSR"; "protecting the interests of citizens of Russia in other countries"; "protecting the territorial integrity" of the Russian Federation; "protecting the interests of the Russian state"; "obtaining the security of our friends abroad"; "obtaining conditions favorable for extricating Russia from its current crisis"; and "developing relations with the 'near abroad.'" Those that Russian elites considered very important included defense of the Russian state, obtaining conditions favorable to extricating Russia from its present crisis, developing relations with the "near abroad" (the former Soviet republics), defense of Russia's economic interests,"

Table 5.1. (*cont'd*)
Foreign Policy Elite Consensus 1993, 1995, 1999

	Use of Force Legitimate?		
	1993	*1995*	*1999*
No			
Extricate Russia from its current crisis	—	90% (161)	82% (159)
Protect Russia's friends abroad	—	84% (146)	90% (177)
Protect Russian citizens living outside former USSR	—	82% (143)	92% (182)

Source: ROMIR surveys for the respective years.

Note: Actual number of respondents in particular cells shown in parentheses. Dash indicates question not asked.

Question wording:

Which of the statements below is closer to your opinion?

The national interests of Russia for the most part should be limited to its present territory.

The national interests of Russia for the most part should extend further than its present territory.

Which goals of Russian foreign policy, in your opinion, are very important and which less important?

Obtaining the security of countries friendly to Russia.

Support and defense of human rights in other countries.

Settlement of conflicts of other conflicts [outside the former Soviet Union].

Defense of the interests of the Russian state.

Obtaining favorable circumstances for getting Russia out of its present crisis.

Development of relations with the near abroad.

Defense of Russia's economic interests.

Achievement of national security.

Defense of the territorial integrity of the Russian Federation.

In determining the tasks of a new Russian foreign policy, one must not forget such global problems as hunger, the preservation of the environment and the like.

Do you think it is legitimate in your view to use military force in order to:

Defend the territorial integrity of the Russian Federation.

Defend the interests of the Russian state.

Achieve conditions which would give Russia the possibility of exiting from its current crisis.

Obtain the security of countries friendly to Russia.

Defend the interests of Russian citizens living in other countries [than those part of the former USSR].

"defense of Russia's national security," and defense of Russia's territorial integrity. They were also in broad agreement that in pursuing "the new tasks of Russian foreign policy, [they] should not forget such global problems as hunger and the environment" (table 5.1). The last piety having been endorsed, Russian elites were also in broad agreement that the "security of our friends abroad" and the "defense of human rights elsewhere" were "less important."

In the 1995 and 1999 surveys, elites were offered the opportunity to say whether a number of goals, including several in the previous two paragraphs, were ones for which they would spill blood and treasure—whether it was "legitimate to use military force" to achieve these ends. The consensus among elites was that defending the interests of the Russian state and defending Russia's territorial integrity warranted the use of force. There was equally broad agreement that extricating Russia from its current crisis, protecting friends abroad, and protecting Russian citizens outside the former Soviet Union (about those within the former Soviet Union there was less agreement) were not goals that warranted the use of force (table 5.1).

This tendency for consensus among elites concerning many of Russia's goals on its periphery was largely paralleled by the absence of significant differences between the responses of market democrats and others. Moreover, this consensus also extended to the use of force there and the threat to Russia's security posed by border conflicts. Whereas elites and mass publics often differ on these matters, statistically significant differences among elite groups defined by orientation to the political economy were rare concerning Russia's regional goals, its use of force on its periphery, and the dangers of border conflicts.

We have already noted that elites overwhelmingly elected to answer that the national interests of Russia for the most part should be broader than Russia's current territorial borders. Market democrats and others were not of different minds in this connection. Bivariate correlations for 1993, 1995, and 1999 comparing liberal democratic and other foreign policy elites proved not significant. Several of these items are ones that, with hindsight at least, might not be expected to result in any variance in the answers.[4] In the event, in bivariate analysis there were no statistically significant differences between liberal democratic and other elites collectively, much less between the former and other political-economic groups considered separately, in responses to questions about Russians outside the former Soviet Union, or the protection of the Russian state, or developing relations with the near abroad, or whether extricating Russia from its current crisis is a very important goal of Russia's foreign policy. On a few occasions, we observe statistically significant but quite nonrobust relationships—for the protection of Russian territorial integrity and protecting

[4] Of course "all" of the elites would say national security is a very important foreign policy goal. But in 1993 "only" 88 percent of the liberal democratic elites chose to call it a very important goal, and 14 percent of the elite respondents overall regarded Russia's territorial integrity as a lesser goal. I think these responses bespeak a weak tendency in 1993, especially among the most liberal politically, to write off parts of Russia, a tendency that had been fairly thoroughly quashed by 1995 and especially by 1999.

Table 5.2.
Foreign Policy Elites Saying that Ensuring the Security of Russia's Friends Abroad Is a Very Important Goal

	1995	1999
Liberal democrats	11% (14)	6% (8)
Others	21% (10)	24% (17)
	n.s.	$Tau_c = .16, p \leq .001$

Source: As in table 5.1.
Note: Actual number of respondents in particular cells shown in parentheses.

Question wording:
See table 5.1.

Russians within the former USSR—as table 5.2 indicates. In general, though, liberal democratic orientation among elites provided little or no purchase with respect to most goals related to Russia and its periphery.

There was one regionally relevant goal among those enumerated above wherein 1999 liberal democrats and others taken as a whole and socialist authoritarians in particular diverged in their responses. This concerned protecting the security of Russia's foreign friends. Russian elites in general do not think such protection is a very important goal, as table 5.1 indicates. Nevertheless, it is noteworthy that in both 1995 and 1999 (the question was not asked in 1993) far fewer liberal democrats were disposed to regard the security of Russia's friends abroad as a very important goal than were others, socialist authoritarians in particular (table 5.2). In 1995 liberal democrats were less likely to say that the use of force to ensure the security of Russia's friends abroad was "legitimate."

The quite restricted ability to differentiate among goals relevant to Russia's periphery among Russia's foreign policy elites on the basis of group orientation to the political economy extended to the use of force abroad. In none of the three surveys did we detect statistically significant differences in bivariate analysis between orientation to the political economy and responses to the question whether "Russia should send its armed forces if asked to aid countries part of the former USSR." In only one, the 1999 survey, did we detect a weak but significant congruence between willingness to respond to a request for aid "from other countries" and whether the respondents were categorized as liberal democrats or not, with the liberal democrats in 1999 being somewhat less disposed to answer that they thought Russia should respond favorably.[5]

[5] Mass publics, as we have seen, are much less disposed to favor the use of force than are elites. Among mass publics, though, there was a weak but significant disposition of those

The generalization that orientations to the political economy provide little purchase on Russian orientations to views about Russia's policies vis-à-vis its periphery needs to be qualified somewhat by the fact that liberal democratic elites were less likely than other elites to view border conflicts as a danger or the greatest danger to Russian security. In all three years for which we have survey data (1993, 1995, and 1999), liberal democrats were modestly less inclined to say that they considered border conflicts with states members of the CIS or elsewhere as posing a threat or the greatest threat to Russian security. Their relative tranquility in comparison with other elites was most obvious in 1999, when their differences were statistically significant and when they were different from the socialist authoritarians as a group in particular. Overall, though, not much insight into Russian elite orientations to Russia's periphery, whether with respect to goals, perceptions of threat, or proneness to resort to the use of military power, can be provided by knowing elite orientations to the political economy.

By the same token, inferences back to the preferences of Russian elites about the desired political system for Russia—say, by Western policy makers or publics—on the basis of behavior or goals relating to Russia's periphery would be inappropriate and might have consequences for other domains—East-West relations, for instance, or the importance attached to reunification with former Soviet republics—where orientation to the political-economic system is a robust discriminator of elite foreign policy dispositions. It is in these domains that market liberals most evidently differed from other elites during the 1990s.

This difference is brought out vividly by tables 5.3 through 5.5 Each of these tables is set up in the following manner. The column percentages are the proportion, respectively, of market democrats and "others" endorsing a particular item.[6] The presence of superscripts in the first column indicates that, when the elites are aggregated for the three years 1993, 1995, and 1999, liberal democrats,[7] differed statistically from another group identified in the political economy typology to which we have re-

coded as liberal democrats to be *more* favorable than others to the use of force if requested by states outside the former Soviet Union.

[6] In the case of items that had five possible responses, the figure shown is the number answering 4 or 5. These questions all concern whether something constituted a threat to Russia's security, with 1 being labeled "absence of threat" and 5 "the greatest threat." Items asked of elites dealing with dispositions toward the unification of Ukraine and Belarus with Russia had seven possible responses, ranging from 1, "Russia and Ukraine [Belarus] should be entirely separate countries," to 7, they "should become united into a single country." In these cases the percentages shown are the number electing 6 or 7 on the scale.

[7] I employed analysis of variance in discriminating among the categories and employed the so-called Bonferroni test, which is comparable to employing multiple t tests, which permit discriminating among group means at the .05 level.

ferred on several occasions. This provides a way of indicating when the group means of the small number of socialist authoritarians, inter alia, differed from that of the liberal democrats. The superscripts stand for the three other substantive groups in the typology in the order listed in table 2.3: (^{2}), market authoritarians; (^{3}), social democrats; and (^{4}), socialist authoritarians. These constitute the "others." The few ambivalent or unmobilized among the elites were excluded from the analysis.[8] The use of superscripts for the columns indicating the year of the survey similarly indicates a statistically significant difference for that particular year between means for liberal democrats and another group from the political economy typology.

The use of superscripts to reflect differences of means between liberal democrats and other specific groups is my way of statistically having my cake and eating it too. I have grouped market authoritarians, social democrats, and socialist authoritarians under the umbrella rubric "other" to increase numbers. This facilitates bivariate analysis but comes at the expense of information. The superscripts flag those instances where, despite the small number of individuals coded as market authoritarians, social democrats, or socialist authoritarians, I detected a statistically significant difference in group means for liberal democratic elites and that particular constructed elite group.

Table 5.3, for instance, emphasizes the shift during the decade of the 1990s in Russian elites' responses to questions concerning East-West security matters. Thus expressions of concern about the projection of American power rose considerably in the decade. In 1999 far more elites, liberal democratic or otherwise, were disposed than in 1993 to agree that the United States was a threat to Russian security, to regard the growth of American military might as a great danger (4) or the greatest (5) danger, to respond that it was a very important goal of Russian foreign policy "to balance Western military might," and to keep or increase military spending. In every instance, though, fewer liberal democrats viewed American behavior as threatening than did the remaining foreign policy elites.

In 1993 more than half of those elites not liberal democrats—to reiterate, a disparate bevy of respondents in terms of their attitudes to the political economy—responded that the United States was a threat to Russian security. Fewer than a fifth of those coded here as liberal democrats an-

---

[8] In reporting the aggregated responses of elites when a question was asked in all three surveys, the sizable number (43) of respondents interviewed in 1993 and interviewed again in 1995, out of a total of 200 in 1993 and 180 in 1995, were counted only once. The same rule was employed for the 11 interviewed in 1995 and re-interviewed in 1999. For those instances where a question was not asked in 1993 but asked in 1995 I computed the aggregate scores using all the 1995 respondents.

Table 5.3.
Liberal Democrat and Other Elite Assessment of East-West Relations: U.S.-Russian
Security Issues

	1993	1995	1999
Agreed: U.S. threat to Russian security			
Liberal democrats[3,4]	17%[3,4] (24)	46% (58)	52%[4] (65)
Others	56% (28)	70% (33)	79% (54)
Tau_c	−.30	−.19	−.25
$p <$	.001	.005	.001
Very important goal:			
balancing power of the West			
Liberal democrats[3,4]	—	37% (48)	58%[4] (76)
Others	—	70% (33)	81% (61)
Tau_c		−.26	−.22
$p <$		.001	.001
Great(4) or greatest (5) threats to Russian security:			
Growth of U.S. military power			
Liberal democrats[2,3,4]	10%[2,3,4] (15)	40%[3] (51)	49%[4] (66)
Others	48% (25)	78% (38)	82% (61)
Tau_c	−.40	−.33	−.34
$p <$	.001	.001	.001
NATO expansion in Eastern Europe	1993	1995	1999
Liberal democrats[4]	—	58% (76)	52%[4] (70)
Others	—	80% (39)	70% (52)
Tau_c		−.17	−.17
$p <$		.005	.01

swered that the United States was a threat. Liberal democrats were statistically distinguishable from both social democrats and socialist authoritarians. In 1995 and 1999 about three-quarters (70 percent in 1995; 79
percent in 1999) of those not identified as liberal democrats answered that
the United States was a threat. By contrast, as table 5.3 shows, about half
of the liberal democrats interviewed in 1995 and 1999 answered that the
United States was a threat, a sharp increase from 1993, to be sure, but
modest in comparison with the responses of those who were not market
democrats. While the differences between the liberal democratic responses
and those of others in 1995 were insufficient to generate statistically significant differences, given the size of the sample, they and the socialist
authoritarians were statistically distinguishable in 1999.

Table 5.3. (*cont'd*)
Liberal Democrat and Other Elite Assessment of East-West Relations: U.S.-Russian Security Issues

	1993	1995	1999
NATO intervention in internal conflicts in European countries	1993	1995	1999
Liberal democrats	—	—	56% (74)[4]
Others	—	—	77% (57)
Tau$_c$			−.20
			p = .001
Military spending: increase or keep same			
Liberal democrats[3,4]	35%[3,4] (50)	73%[3] (93)	94%[4] (125)
Others	57% (29)	87% (41)	96% (71)
Tau$_c$	.20	.16	.14
p <	.005	.05	.05

Source: As in table 5.1.

Note: As explained in the text, the superscripts refer to respondents' orientation to the political economy depicted in chapter 2: [2] refers to the market democrats, [3] to the social democrats, and [4] to social authoritarians. Actual number of respondents for particular cells shown in parentheses. Dashes indicate question not asked.

Question wording: Do you think that U.S. policy is a threat to Russian security?

Which goals of Russian foreign policy, in your opinion, are very important and which less important?

. . .

Achieving a balance of military power with the West.

Which of the below represent the greatest threat to the security of Russia and which do not threaten it at all? Evaluate, please, the level of danger of each item listed on a five-point scale, where 1 indicates absence of threat and 5 the greatest danger.

Growth of U.S. military power in comparison with that of Russia.

The expansion of NATO to include countries of Eastern Europe.

Military intervention by NATO in inter-nationality conflicts among European states.

Much the same story is contained in the other items reported in table 5.3. In the aggregate, liberal democrats differed statistically from market authoritarians, social democrats, *and* socialist authoritarians in the level of threat they perceived in the growth of U.S. military power. Only 10 percent said in 1993 that the growth of U.S. power was a threat or the greatest threat to Russian security, whereas almost half the others had responded in that fashion. Again the proportion of liberal democrats saying that the growth of U.S. power was a threat or the greatest threat jumped in 1995 and 1999. It remained, however, far less than for the others and statistically distinguishable in 1995 from the responses by social demo-

crats and in 1999 from the socialist authoritarians. In 1995 only 37 percent of the liberal democrats considered balancing the West's military
power very important in comparison with 70 percent of the other elite
respondents. Even in 1999, when almost three in five of the liberal democrats interviewed characterized balancing the power of the West as very
important, that proportion was still markedly less than the response patterns of the other elites surveyed and statistically distinguishable from the
pattern of responses by the socialist authoritarians.

Fewer liberal democrats have considered NATO expansion in Eastern
Europe to be a great or the greatest danger than have other elites. While
more than half (58 percent in 1995 and 52 percent in 1999) the liberal
democrats considered NATO expansion a great or the greatest threat to
Russian security, roughly three-quarters (80 percent in 1995 and 70 percent in 1999) of the remaining foreign policy elites termed it such. Likewise, asking about the security threat to Russia of "NATO involvement
in inter-nationality conflicts within European countries," in 1999 in the
aftermath of the NATO intervention in Kosovo, as table 5.3 shows, produced approximately the same distribution of responses on the part of
market democrats and the remaining respondents as did the question
about NATO expansion. For both questions, liberal democrats were statistically distinguishable from the socialist authoritarians as a group and
from those among the elite respondents who were socialist authoritarians,
market authoritarians, or social democrats taken together.

Finally, table 5.3 considers Russian defense spending. Again, the shift
over time was substantial. In 1993 almost two-thirds of those coded as
liberal democrats favored reducing the Russian defense budget in contrast
to 6 percent in 1999. (Table 5.3 shows those who responded to increase
or keep military spending levels the same.) Throughout, though, liberal
democrats were more resistant to increased military spending than were
others, and their response pattern was distinguishable from that of both
the social democrats (overall and in 1995) and the socialist authoritarians
(overall and in 1999).

Liberal democratic elites also differed in some respects from other elites
in their assessment of East-West relations and economic interdependence.
Table 5.4 speaks to this matter by considering whether Russia can rebuild
its economy without the help of the West and whether having "key sectors
of the Russian economy owned by foreign companies," or "the increase in
the gap between rich and poor countries" constituted a threat to Russian
security. As we saw in considering Russia's overall security orientation, Russian elites of all stripes in 1999 were more disposed to assert that Russia
could rebuild its economy without Western help, more prone to consider
the gap between rich and poor countries a threat, and more disposed to
worry about foreign companies controlling sectors of the Russian economy
than they had been earlier in the decade. Liberal democrats were least dis-

Table 5.4.

Liberal Democrats and Other Elite Assessments of East-West Relations

Economic Interdependence	1993	1995	1999
Rebuild economy without Western help			
Liberal democrats[3,4]	35% (49)	45%[2,3] (57)	64% (85)
Others	70% (32)	79% (37)	83% (58)
Tau$_c$	−.26	−.27	−.17
$p <$	.001	.001	.005

Great (4) or Greatest (5) Threat to Russian Security:	1993	1995	1999
Having "key economic sectors in foreign hands"			
Liberal democrats	—	42% (55)	50% (67)
Others	—	49% (24)	64% (47)
Tau$_c$		.05	.19
$p <$		n.s.	.01

	1993	1995	1999
Gap between rich and poor countries			
Liberal democrats[3,4]	10%[4] (15)	24% (31)	30%[4] (40)
Others	35% (18)	29% (14)	48% (35)
Tau$_c$	−.19	−.04	.−26
$p \leq$	.001	n.s.	.001

Source: As in table 5.1.

Note: For an explanation of the superscripts, see note to table 5.3. Actual number of respondents for particular cells shown in parentheses. Dashes indicate question not asked.

Question wording:

Do you agree or not with the following assertions:

We can solve our economic problems without the help of the West.

Which of the below represent the greatest threat to the security of Russia and which do not at all threaten it. Evaluate, please, the level of danger of each item listed on a five-point scale, where 1 indicates absence of threat and 5 the greatest danger.

The transfer of basic parts of the Russian economy into the hands of foreign companies.

The increasing gap between rich and poor countries.

tinguishable in this regard with respect to the worry about foreign companies. In 1995 the difference between liberal democratic and other elites was insignificant statistically and in 1999 the difference, while statistically significant, was not especially robust. In neither instance, nor overall, were liberal democrats statistically separable from other individual groups.

Their responses to the issues of the danger inherent in the growth in the gap between rich and poor countries and of the value of Western help in rebuilding the Russian economy were more distinctive. By and large liberal democrats were less exercised than were other foreign policy elites about the increase in the gap between rich and poor countries, though once again we see that the proportion regarding the growth in the gap as dangerous to Russian security was considerably higher for both liberal democratic and other respondents in 1999 than in 1993. Russian socialists in general were more inclined than others to view the increase with alarm, with the result that liberal democrats as a group were usually statistically distinguishable from both social democrats (overall and in 1993 and 1999) and socialist authoritarians (overall and in 1993 and 1999).

Liberal democrats were also far more inclined than others, especially those categorized as social democrats or socialist authoritarians, to disagree with the proposition that Russia can rebuild its economy "without the help of the West" (table 5.4). Even so, almost two-thirds of the liberal democratic foreign policy elites answered in 1999 that Russia could rebuild its economy without the help of the West; barely a third had given that response in 1993. Others throughout the decade were consistently dismissive of the need for Western help; more than two-thirds of those lumped here as "others" in 1993 had maintained that Russia could restore its economy on its own and five in six asserted the same in 1999.

A third domain in which those coded here as liberal democrats differed from other Russian elites pertains to the enthusiasm with which the former value the reunification of Russia with Ukraine and Belarus, as table 5.5 shows. Liberal democrats have far less nostalgia for the old Soviet Union and for Slavic unity than do others. Not only do they differ from other elites taken as a whole but also they are distinguishable statistically from socialist authoritarians as a group. (With respect to Ukraine, it is socialist authoritarians that should be said to be distinguishable from other groups, since their mean scores in 1999 were statistically separable from those of social democrats, market authoritarians, and market democrats.) As the new century began, fewer than a third of the market democrats said Russia and Ukraine should definitely be united into a single country, and half answered that Belarus and Russia should be a single country. Considerably more than half of the other foreign policy elites answered that Russia and Ukraine should be a single country, and three-quarters responded that Belarus and Russia should be a single country (table 5.5).

Tables 5.3 through 5.5 also permit an answer to an additional variant on the question with which we have been seized in this chapter, namely, do those, regardless of whether they were members of the CPSU or are members of the KPRF, who are ideologically socialist authoritarian differ significantly from other groups in their foreign policy orientations. I should repeat that the number of persons among the elite coded as socialist

Table 5.5.

Liberal Democrats and Other Elite Orientations to Reunification of Parts of the Former Soviet Union

	Ukraine and Russia Should Definitely (6 or 7 of 7) Be One State		
	1993	*1995*	*1999*
Liberal democrats[4]	—	46% (60)	30%[4*] (40)
Others	—	71% (34)	59% (43)
Tau$_c$		.19	.27
p <		.005	.001
	Belarus and Russia Should Definitely (6 or 7 of 7) Be One State		
	1993	*1995*	*1999*
Liberal democrats[4]	—	—	49%[4] (66)
Others	—	—	77% (56)
Tau$_c$			.25
p <			.001

Source: As in table 5.1.

Note: For an explanation of the superscripts, see the note to table 5.3. Actual number of respondents in particular cells shown in parentheses. Dashes indicate question not asked.

* Socialist authoritarians differ statistically from all three other orientations to the political economy—liberal democrats, market authoritarians, and social democrats.

Question wording:

There are different views about the relations Russia should have with Ukraine. Some assert that Russia and Ukraine should be completely independent countries. This corresponds to 1 on a seven-point scale. Others think that Russia and Ukraine should be united into one country—that corresponds to 7. What position [on the scale] corresponds to your point of view?

There are different views about the relations Russia should have with Belarus. Some assert that Russia and Belarus should be completely independent countries. This corresponds to 1 on a seven-point scale. Others think that Russia and Belarus should be united into one country—that corresponds to 7. What position corresponds to your point of view?

authoritarian is small; this limits my ability to sort out differences. At the same time, it is also worth remembering that statistically significant differences, when detected under these circumstances, are generally quite robust and often have substantive implications for the course of Russian foreign policy. We can quickly conclude two points from examining tables 5.2 through 5.5.

First, the finding that there is little statistically significant difference to be detected when comparing the views of the liberal democratic and other, undifferentiated elites' responses to questions about Russia's regional goals, the use of force, or the prospects for conflict extends to comparing group means of the liberal democrats and socialist authoritarians in particular (see table 5.2). What differences there were concerned the greater propensity of socialist authoritarians—likely with states such as Milosevic's Serbia, Iran, or Iraq in mind—to answer that support for Russia's friends abroad ought to be a very important foreign policy goal and, for socialist authoritarians as a group (both in the aggregate and in 1999 taken alone), to be more disposed to consider border conflicts in the region a danger or the greatest danger to Russian security.

The second is that in other domains, by contrast, the key cleavage is between the market democrats and the socialist authoritarians or on some occasions between liberal democrats and socialists, whether they be democratic or authoritarian politically. Thus, aggregating the three surveys, we find that socialist authoritarians differed statistically from liberal democrats in their answers to all the questions concerning overall U.S.-Russian relations. They were more likely to regard the United States as a threat to Russian security, to be concerned about the growth of U.S. power, to consider balancing the power of the West a very important goal, to worry about NATO expansion and involvement in Eastern Europe, and to favor increased military spending. This divide was apparent in 1993 in almost all instances, not clear-cut in 1995, and evident with regard to all the items in table 5.3 again in 1999.

With regard to Russia's orientation to the international economy and the involvement of foreign firms and institutions in Russia's economy, the three items addressed in table 5.4 suggest that the key cleavage may be a socialism–market divide rather than socialist authoritarians versus liberal democrats per se. Overall, social democrats and socialist authoritarians were separable statistically from market democrats in their responses to questions about rebuilding the Russian economy with the help of the West and the threat to Russian security of the gap between rich and poor countries. Socialist authoritarians and market democrats were distinguishable in 1993 and 1999 with regard to the perceived danger to Russia's security inherent in the increasing gap between rich and poor countries.

One area of policy where the socialist authoritarians were highly distinctive pertains to their orientation to the reunification of Russia with Ukraine or Russia and Belarus. Here the division between liberal democrats, who are least likely to say they think Russia and Ukraine or Belarus should be a single country, and socialist authoritarians is apparent from table 5.5, but it should be emphasized that on this dimension the socialist authoritarian means were distinguishable not only from market democrats but from democratic socialists and market authoritarians as well. Liberal democrats and socialist authoritarians constituted statistically separable groups in addressing the issue of Russian-Ukrainian reintegration in the aggregate and in assessing the pattern of interviews specifically for 1999. The item concerning Belarus was only asked once, in 1999, but here too the key divide was between socialist authoritarians and liberal democrats.

Civilian Market Democrats and Other Elites

Thus far, we have spoken about liberal democrats as a group and contrasted them with other elites, knowing full well that the "other" category includes people with a wide range of views, and have augmented that analysis with comparisons of the mean scores of liberal democrats, market authoritarians, social democrats, and socialist authoritarians. In this analysis we did not differentiate between civilians and members of the armed forces. As we saw in chapter 2, however, failing to make that differentiation can produce distortions.

In 1993 and 1995 elite respondents in the armed forces were only modestly less prone to support market democracy than were their civilian counterparts. Consequently, estimates of those among the foreign policy elites who were liberal democrats for those years differed only slightly with the military included and excluded. In 1999, by contrast, those interviewed from the military were strikingly less supportive of market democracy than were civilian foreign policy elites. Assertions about elite support for market democracy in 1999 required qualification as to whether we were speaking of civilian elites or of civilian and military elites.

How does differentiating between civilian and military elites affect our sense of the difference in foreign policy dispositions by liberal democratic and other elites? With respect to goals relevant to Russia's periphery, the use of force, or concerns about the danger of border conflicts, parsing the elites into civilian liberal democrats, other civilians, and the military produces much the same null findings as we found in comparing market democrats, including the military, with other elites. Divided this way respondents did not differ in their propensity to endorse a broad versus a narrow conception of national interest or in their view of how important Russians outside the former Soviet Union were for Russian foreign policy, of the importance of developing Russia's relations with the near abroad, or of the protection of the Russian state as a very important goal of Russian foreign policy. In 1993 and 1999 there were weak but statistically significant differences[9] as to whether defense of Russia's territorial integrity was

[9] Tau_c=.13, $p \leq .001$ and tau_c=.05, $p \leq .01$, respectively.

a very important goal. The difference in 1999 was between the civilian market democrats, who were nearly unanimous (95 percent) in terming it a very important goal, and the remaining elites, who were completely unanimous in their view. Russian elites throughout the decade were largely disposed to consider the security of Russians within the former Soviet Union a very important goal. Only in 1995 did these proportions differ. At that juncture, the other civilians and the military elites were more inclined than the market democrats to say that the protection of Russians within the former Soviet Union was a very important goal. Likewise, in 1999 we observe a weak but statistically significant difference[10] between civilians of all political stripes and the military in their tendency to regard "creating favorable conditions for extricating Russia out of its current crisis" as a very important goal of Russian foreign policy. On this, the civilians were virtually unanimous in considering it a very important goal, while a third of the military respondents did not. By contrast, when compared with other civilian elites and with the military, civilian market democratic elites were distinctly less disposed to regard the security of Russia's "friends abroad" as a very important foreign policy goal—even though, it bears repeating that Russia's friends abroad should not count on more than a small fraction of persons among the Russian foreign policy elite considering their security as very important to Russian foreign policy, regardless of whom they have in mind.

By the same token, we observe no statistically significant difference among the three groups in the propensity to say that Russia should send its troops if asked, either within the former Soviet Union or elsewhere, and a stable but modest tendency for civilian liberal democrats to be less inclined to state that border conflicts, especially those with states not part of the Commonwealth of Independent States, represent a threat to Russian security.

Tables 5.6 through 5.8 parallel tables 5.3 through 5.5 except that the superscripts refer to statistically significant differences between civilian liberal democrats and the armed forces elite group means (^{2}) and between civilian liberal democrats and other civilian elites (^{3}).

Liberal democratic civilian elites in the 1990s oriented themselves to the general international system differently than did other elites, civilian or military. There existed a sizable gap in any particular year between the proportions of civilian liberal democrats who expressed great concern about American power and the proportions of other elites. Elites generally were more inclined at the end of the decade to regard the United States as a threat and to view the growth in U.S. power with alarm than they

---

[10] $Tau_c = .08$, $p < .01$.

were in 1993. In 1993 these were matters of almost no concern to civilian market democratic elites (table 5.6), but of concern to roughly half the others. In 1999, civilian market democrats were divided more or less evenly as to whether the United States was a threat to Russian security, whether the growth in U.S. power was a threat, and whether NATO expansion was a threat. By contrast, the reaction of other civilian elites and the military (regardless of attitudes to the domestic political economy) was overwhelmingly adverse. (The seven officers coded as liberal democrats in 1999 answered that the United States was a threat to Russian security, as did 90 percent of the others.) While I emphasize the important shifts in responses over time, it is equally important to note that the gap between civilian liberal democrats and other elites persists for each of the items in the various surveys.

The virtually unanimous opposition in 1999 to reducing spending on defense—which contrasts sharply with the strong support for reduced spending in 1993—constitutes a bit of an exception to the overall generalization. There is much the same progression as in the other items concerning East-West security. In 1993 more than two-thirds of the civilian market democrats endorsed reducing military spending in comparison with fewer than half among the military or the other civilians advocating reduced spending—but almost no one advocated increased expenditures for defense. In 1995 the number favoring reductions in defense had decreased to less than a third among the civilian market democrats, one in seven among other civilian elites, and a single respondent in the military (out of thirty). In 1995 a third of the civilian market democrats, nearly half the other civilian elites, and 87 percent of the military, including (but not noted in table 5.5) all eighteen officers coded as market democrats, endorsed increasing military spending. By 1999 practically no one associated themselves with reduced spending for defense. By then, three-fifths of the civilian market democrats, close to three-quarters of the other civilian elites, and the same 87 percent of the military as in 1995 elected "increased military spending" when asked. The civilian liberal democrats continued to be statistically separable from the military, though not from the other civilian elites. With this one exception, on matters of international security civilian liberal democratic elites differed both from other civilian elites and from the officers on each occasion they were interviewed (1993, 1995, and 1999)—and in the aggregate.

They also differed from both other civilian elites and the military concerning the rebuilding of the Russian economy. When the three interviews are combined, there is a statistically significant difference in the mean scores of the civilian market democrats and both the other civilian elites and the military (table 5.7). Those relationships were observed in the

Table 5.6.
Civilian Liberal Democrat, Armed Forces, and Other Civilian Elite Assessments of East/West Issues

	Agreed U.S. Threat		
	1993	*1995*	*1999*
Civilian liberal democrats[2,3]	12%[2,3] (14)	42%[2,3] (45)	49%[2,3] (58)
Military	51% (20)	75% (21)	93% (26)
Other civilians	53% (18)	69% (25)	74% (35)
Tau$_c$	−.38	−.28	−.28
p <	.001	.001	.001

	Security Threat: Growth of U.S. Power		
	1993	*1995*	*1999*
Civilian liberal democrats[2,3]	7%[2,3] (9)	35%[2,3] (38)	45%[2,3] (58)
Military	38% (15)	77% (23)	97% (29)
Other civilians	46% (16)	76% (28)	77% (40)
Tau$_c$	.33	.39	.29
p <	.001	.001	.001

	Security Threat: NATO Expansion in Eastern Europe		
	1993	*1995*	*1999*
Civilian liberal democrats[2,3]	—	54%[2,3] (60)	50%[2,3] (63)
Military	—	90% (27)	77% (23)
Other civilians	—	76% (28)	69% (36)
Tau$_c$	—	−.25	−.20
p <	—	.001	.005

	Security Threat: NATO Intervention in Internal Conflicts in Europe		
	1993	*1995*	*1999*
Civilian liberal democrats	—	—	54%[2,3] (67)
Military	—	—	83% (25)
Other civilians	—	—	75% (39)
Tau$_c$	—	—	−.22
p <	—	—	.001

Table 5.6. (*cont'd*)
Civilian Liberal Democrat, Armed Forces, and Other Civilian Elite Assessments
of East/West Issues

	"Very Important Goal": Balance Western Power		
	1993	1995	1999
Civilian liberal democrats[2,3]	—	31%[2,3] (35)	56%[2,3] (69)
Military	—	80% (24)	87% (26)
Other civilians	—	63% (22)	79% (41)
Tau$_c$	—	−.34	−.24
$p <$	—	.001	.001

	Not Reduce ("increase" or "keep the same") Military Spending		
	1993	1995	1999
Civilian liberal democrats[2,3]	32% [2%][2,3] (38)	68% [33%][2,3] (75)	94% [60%][2] (117)
Military	58% [10%] (23)	97% [87%] (29)	100% [87%] (30)
Other civilians	53% [12%] (18)	86% [51%] (30)	94% [73%] (49)
Tau$_c$	.18	.24	.11
$p \leq$	.001	.001	.05

Source: As in table 5.1.

Note: Number in brackets indicate percentage favoring increase. Actual number of respondents for particular cells shown in parentheses. Dashes indicate question not asked.

The superscript [2] indicates that civilian liberal democrats differed statistically from the military and [3] indicates that they differed from other civilian elites.

Question wording:

For wording of questions, see table 5.3.

1993 survey as well, whereas the difference in means was only statistically significant between the civilian market democrats and the other civilian elites in 1995 and with the military in 1999. Across the three surveys the pattern was basically the same one we observed with respect to issues about international security. The overall proportion of those saying that Russia could do without the help of the West in rebuilding its economy increased from 1993 to 1995 to 1999, as did the number of market democrats among the elites—from a third to a little less than two-thirds—who

Table 5.7.
Civilian Liberal Democrats, Armed Forces, and Other Civilian Elite Assessments
of East-West Relations and Economic Interdependence

	Agreed: Rebuild Economy without Western Help		
	1993	*1995*	*1999*
Civilian liberal democrats[2,3]	33%[2,3] (39)	42%[3] (46)	62%[2] (78)
Military	55% (21)	66% (19)	90% (27)
Other civilian	68% (21)	81% (29)	79% (38)
Tau_c	−.27	−.32	−.18
$p <$	.001	.001	.005

	Security Threat: Gap between Rich and Poor Countries		
	1993	*1995*	*1999*
Civilian liberal democrats[3]	8%[2,3] (10)	27% (30)	29%[3] (37)
Military	30% (12)	14% (4)	34% (10)
Other civilian	31% (11)	30% (11)	54% (28)
Tau_c	.26	.05	.23
$p \leq$	.001	n.s.	.001

	Security Threat: Key Economic Sectors in Foreign Hands		
	1993	*1995*	*1999*
Civilian liberal democrats[3]	—	39% (44)	50% (63)
Military	—	57% (17)	37% (11)
Other civilian	—	49% (18)	77% (40)
Tau_c	—	.12	.20
$p \leq$	—	.05	.001

Source: As in table 5.1.
Note: Actual number of respondents for particular cells shown in parentheses. Dashes indicate question not asked.

For an explaination of the superscripts, see the note to table 5.6.

Question wording:

For wording of these questions, see table 5.4.

agreed that the rebuilding could be done without the help of the West.
At the same time, the proportion of those civilian market democrats responding that the rebuilding of Russia could be done without the help of
the West was less than the responses by other civilian elites or the military
in each of the three surveys.

In 1993 the mean scores for civilian market democratic elites and both other civilians and the military concerning the "increase in the gap between rich and poor countries" differed statistically. While for Russian elites generally that increase was not a matter of great concern in 1993, civilian liberal democrats were particularly disposed at that juncture not to consider it a major danger. By century's end, though, the proportion of Russian market democratic elites expressing alarm about the gap between rich and poor countries was about the same as had been the case for officers throughout the decade and for other civilians in 1993 and 1995. Military responses in 1993 and 1999 were essentially the same. But the civilian elites who were not categorized as market democrats gave answers indicating they had become increasingly concerned, with the result that, as in 1993, the means of two civilian groups were again statistically distinguishable. Unlike 1993, those between the military and either civilian group were not.

The story seems similar with regard to worries about foreign companies gaining control "over key sectors of the Russian economy." This question was only asked in the 1995 and 1999 surveys, and with two data points we can scarcely speak of a trend. We do, however, again detect an increase in the proportion of both civilian groups (but not among the military) in 1999, as opposed to 1995, giving an answer indicating that they regarded this to be a great danger or the greatest danger to Russian security. We also observe in the aggregate and in 1999 a statistically significant difference between civilian market democrats and other civilian elites, but in neither instance between the civilian market democrats and the military respondents.

This is not so with respect to unification with Ukraine and Belarus. Here differentiating among civilian and military elites as well as between liberal democratic and other elites brings home the point that it was civilian market democrats, not market democrats generally, who were least committed to the unification of Russia with Ukraine or Belarus (table 5.8). Elites drawn from the military strongly supported reunification with Ukraine in both 1995 and 1999 and in 1999 with Belarus. At the same time, enthusiasm among civilian elites, though not among the military, for reunification with Ukraine apparently waned between 1995 and 1999. As with East-West security and less clearly with Russia and the international economy, civilian liberal democrats differed substantially from other civilian elites and from the military in their enthusiasm for Russian unification with Ukraine or Belarus. As a result, it was more appropriate to speak of the differences between civilian liberal democrats on the one hand and other civilian elites *and* the military on the other, rather than simply dichotomizing market democratic and other elites.

Table 5.8.
Liberal Democrats, Armed Forces, and Other Civilian Elite Assessments of
Reunification with Parts of the Former Soviet Union

	Russia and Ukraine Should Be One Country		
	1993	1995	1999
Civilian liberal democrats[2,3]	—	43%[3] (48)	29%[2,3] (36)
Military	—	67% (20)	77% (23)
Other civilians	—	72% (26)	47% (24)
Tau$_c$	—	.26	.24
$p \le$	—	.001	.001
	Russia and Belarus Should Be One Country		
	1993	1996	1999
Civilian liberal democrats	—	—	48%[2] (61)
Military	—	—	83% (25)
Other civilians	—	—	71% (36)
Tau$_c$			.18
$pp \le$			.005

Source: As in table 5.1.
Note: Actual number of respondents for particular cells shown in parentheses. Dashes indicate question not asked.
For an explaination of the superscripts, see note to table 5.6.

Question wording:

For wording of these questions, see table 5.5.

Age and Elite Attitudes

Let us consider three other possible ways that speaking of "market democrats" versus "others" may obscure analysis. Given the tumultuous changes that have occurred in Russia in the years 1985–2000, changes of the magnitude that often engender substantial elite replacement, we might be distinguishing people from different generations and labeling them liberal democrats and others when we should more appropriately be referring to older and younger cohorts. Certainly, among mass publics, age provides a robust correlate with fear of the United States, regret for the passing of the Soviet Union, and resistance to opening Russia's borders to economic penetration.

Among civilian elites in 1993, being categorized as liberal democrats or others was not helpful in anticipating how a foreign policy elite respondent would answer whether Russia should send troops, if asked, to a country in the former Soviet Union. Instead, age in this instance provided some differentiation where orientation to the political economy did not. Those who were born before 1950 and those born in 1950 and after differed in their responses as to whether Russia should send its armed forces, if asked, to aid a former republic of the Soviet Union. Moreover, liberal democrats born before 1950 were more inclined to send in the troops than were other civilian elites born 1950 and after. Specifically, among elites born 1950 and after, 43 percent of the liberal democrats and three (30 percent) of the other elites agreed that Russia should send its armed forces, if asked, to aid a country of the former Soviet Union. More than half (59 percent) of the liberal democrats and almost three-quarters (73 percent) of the other civilian elites born before 1950 agreed.[11]

Age was statistically insignificant in assessing the response patterns in 1993 to other key foreign policy items. Rather, civilian liberal democrats born before 1950 and in 1950 and after are generally distinguishable, usually by large margins, from other elites regardless of when the latter were born. Thus, 10 percent of those born in 1950 and after and 13 percent born before who were coded as liberal democrats considered the United States a threat. Half of the other elites born before 1950 and 60 percent born in 1950 and after from among the other elites characterized the United States as a threat. A similar pattern is observed in the case of the assessment of the threat to Russian security of the growth in U.S. power. Only 10 percent of the liberal democrats born before 1950 and 4 percent (two respondents) born in 1950 and after termed the growth of U.S. power a great or the greatest danger to Russian security. By contrast, among the "others," 40 percent of those born before 1950 and 60 percent born in 1950 and after responded that the growth of U.S. power was a great or the greatest danger. On the questions regarding whether Russia could rebuild its economy without the help of the West and the implications for Russia's security of the gap between rich and poor countries, liberal democrats, regardless of age cohort, were quite distinguishable from other elites.

A similar generalization applies to a variety of questions asked in 1999. Age has only limited relevance for distinguishing among liberal democrats. Nor does it compound fundamentally the distinction between lib-

---

[11] Tau$_c$ = 16, $p < .10$ for the comparison between liberal democrats and others born in 1950 and after and those born before 1950; tau$_c$ = .37, $p < .05$ for the comparison between other civilian elites.

eral democrats and other elites. There is, to be sure, near consensus, regardless of age or orientation to the political economy, concerning the use of force in response to a request by a former Soviet republic. Age does differentiate the responses by liberal democrats to questions concerning the growth of U.S. power and NATO expansion, and perhaps concerning whether the United States is a threat. Nevertheless, liberal democrats, both those born before 1950 and in 1950 and after, were consistently less prone to consider the United States a threat, to regard the growth of U.S. power or NATO expansion as a great or the greatest danger, to assert that Russia could rebuild its economy without the help of the West, to consider the gap between rich and poor countries a threat, or to favor strongly reunification with Belarus or Ukraine. Even in those instances where the age differences among liberal democrats are statistically significant, there generally remains a gap, usually quite large, between liberal democrats and other elites.

The case of the assessment of the danger to Russia of NATO intervention in an ethnic dispute within a European country is an exception. In this instance, there is an overlap between those liberal democrats born before 1950 and other elites born in 1950 and after. Liberal democrats born in 1950 and after differ from liberal democrats born before 1950 and all other elites. But those liberal democrats born before 1950 are indistinguishable from other elites born in 1950 and after, while both are noticeably less agitated by NATO intervention in interethnic conflicts than are other civilian elites born before 1950.

The more typical pattern is represented by Russian responses in 1999 to the perceived growth in American military power. There the distinction between civilian liberal democrats born before 1950 and those born subsequently is a substantial one: more than half (54 percent) of the liberal democratic elites born before 1950 regarded the growth of U.S. power as a threat, whereas only a third (34 percent) of those born in 1950 or subsequently termed the growth of U.S. power a great or the greatest danger. Even in this instance, though, liberal democrats in both age categories were much less likely than other civilian elites to regard the growth of U.S. military might as constituting a danger: three-quarters or more of the other elites, regardless of date of birth, regarded the growth of U.S. power a threat. On matters where the differences in response rates between liberal democrats born before 1950 and subsequently are small—reunification with Ukraine, rebuilding the Russian economy with or without Western help, and whether the gap between rich and poor countries represents a threat to Russian security, for instance—the contrast in 1999 between market democrats and other elites, controlling for age, was of course even sharper.

Aren't They All Communists?

Most of the foreign policy elites interviewed in 1993, 1995, and 1999 said they had in fact been members of the CPSU. Indeed, of those who answered the question—most, but not all, of the respondents—a sizable majority (73 percent of the total interviewed) and virtually all (93 percent) the military officers reported having been members of the CPSU. Given the experience of the cold war, and pervasive notions in the social science literature about prior socialization, we need to explore whether CPSU members had substantially different orientations to foreign policy in the 1990s than did other Russian elites and whether that cleavage was sufficiently great as to constitute a challenge to the "liberal democratic" versus "other" divide central to this chapter.

Once again we find that the linkage between orientation to the political economy and responses about Russia's goals and behavior on its periphery is tenuous. For 1993, among liberal democrats, those who had been members of the CPSU were considerably more inclined to use force if asked, both within the former Soviet Union and elsewhere, than were other civilian elites, liberal democratic or not. Indeed, the distribution of the responses suggests that in this regard former Communist Party members classified as liberal democrats shared more in common with other former members of the CPSU than with noncommunist liberal democrats. Regardless of their orientation to the politial economy, three-eighths of those who had not been members of the CPSU agreed that Russia should send military assistance, if asked, to former republics of the Soviet Union. Almost two-thirds of those who had been members of the CPSU agreed.

Former members of the CPSU were also more disposed to regard the United States as being a threat in 1993 than were other liberal democrats. But in this case all civilian liberal democrats, including former members of the CPSU, were much less inclined to say that the United States was a threat than were other civilians, whether the latter had or had not been members of the CPSU. Specifically, 96 percent of the market democrats saying they had not been members of the Party, and 84 percent who said they were, answered that the United States was not a threat. By comparison, 38 percent of the other civilians who had been members of the CPSU and three-quarters of the small number of those foreign policy elites who were neither liberal democrats nor former members of the Party termed the United States not a threat in 1993.

In other respects, past CPSU membership does not seem to have strongly colored the foreign policy responses of elites in 1993. Market democrats, former CPSU members or no, were much less likely to see as a great danger or the greatest danger the expansion of U.S. power or the

Table 5.9.
Comparing the Foreign Policy Orientations of Those among Civilian Liberal
Democratic Elites Who Were and Were Not Formerly CPSU Members, 1999

		Member CPSU?	
Very Important Goal		*Yes*	*No*
Achieve balance with West	Liberal democrats	60% (53)	44% (16)
	n.s.		
	Other civilians	73% (26)	94% (15)
	$Tau_c = -.18, p \le .05$		
Perceived Dangers			
U.S. threat	Liberal democrats	55% (47)	33% (11)
	$Tau_c = .18, p = .05$		
	Other civilians	82% (28)	54% (7)
	$Tau_c = .23, p < .10$		
Great or Greatest Threat			
Growth U.S. power	Liberal democrats	54% (50)	22% (8)
	$Tau_c = -.26, p < .001$		
	Other civilians	81% (29)	69% (11)
	n.s		
NATO expansion	Liberal democrats	61% (55)	22% (8)
	$Tau_c = .32, p < .001$		
	Other civilians	75% (27)	56% (9)
	n.s.		
Border conflict with CIS members	Liberal democrats	51% (46)	46% (16)
	n.s		
	Other civilians	61% (22)	56% (9)
	n.s.		
Growing gap between rich and poor countries	Liberal democrats	34% (31)	17% (6)
	$Tau_c = -.25, p \le .005$		
	Other civilians	56% (20)	50% (8)
	n.s.		

growth in the gap between rich and poor countries. They disagreed more
with the assertion that Russia could rebuild its economy without the help
of the West than did other civilians, regardless of past CPSU membership.

In 1995, similarly, only with respect to the fear of the growth of American military might did having been a member of the CPSU make for significant differences among liberal democrats, though once again liberal

Table 5.9. (*cont'd*)
Comparing the Foreign Policy Orientations of Those among Civilian Liberal
Democratic Elites Who Were and Were Not Formerly CPSU Members, 1999

		Member CPSU?	
Very Important Goal		*Yes*	*No*
Foreign control key economic sectors	Liberal democrats Tau$_c$ = −.18, $p \le$ .05	55% (50)	37% (13)
	Other civilians n.s.	75% (28)	75% (12)
Agreed: Solve economic problems without Western help	Liberal democrats n.s.	66% (59)	53% (19)
	Other civilians n.s	86% (30)	62% (8)
Unification strongly desirable with Ukraine	Liberal democrats n.s.	32% (29)	19% (7)
	Other civilians n.s.	51% (18)	38% (6)
. . . with Belarus	Liberal democrats Tau$_c$ = .17, p <.05	54% (49)	33% (12)
	Other civilians n.s.	74% (26)	63% (10)

Source: As in table 5.1.

Note: Actual number of respondents in particular cells shown in parentheses.

Question wording:

For wording of the questions, see tables 5.3–5.5.

democrats, including former CPSU members and those who had not been
Party members, were substantially less inclined to term the United States
a threat than were the other civilian elites or the military.

When we turn to the data for 1999, though, there is some evidence
that CPSU membership, almost a decade after the collapse of the Party,
differentiates among liberal democrats more than it did in the early years
of the Russian Federation—but not much among other civilians or, of
course, among the military, since they were virtually all CPSU members—
along several dimensions (table 5.9). (See also chapter 6.) For liberal democrats in 1999, membership in the CPSU did not distinguish respondents
with questions concerning Russia's periphery—resort to armed forces,
when asked, within the former Soviet Union or elsewhere, or concerns
about border conflicts, within the CIS or elsewhere.

But in the domains where, as we have seen, orientation to the political economy usually mattered, having been a member of the CPSU often distinguished erstwhile CPSU members who were market democrats from other market democrats. Thus they were more likely to view the United States as a threat than other market democrats and to view the growth of U.S. power as a danger. Similarly, they were noticeably more concerned about the dangers posed for Russia by the growing gap between rich and poor countries and by foreign control over key economic sectors, and perhaps more inclined to assert that Russia was able to restore its economy without the help of the West (the latter relationship was not, however, statistically significant). They were more enthusiastic about reunification of Russia and Belarus and possibly Russia and Ukraine (though again the latter covariance was not significant) than were other liberals. They were dramatically more willing (61 percent versus 22 percent) to term NATO expansion a great danger or the greatest danger to Russia's security. Their responses to questions about international security matters, the international economy, and reunification with Belarus and Ukraine generally placed them between those who had never been in the CPSU among the liberal democrats, on the one hand, and other civilian elites who were not market democrats, on the other, but who had also not been members of the CPSU. These responses included those items dealing with the growth of U.S. power, the gap between rich and poor countries, and reunification with Belarus or Ukraine. In other instances (whether the United States is a threat, the NATO expansion danger, rebuilding the economy without the West's help), the response patterns of former CPSU members coded as liberal democrats were essentially indistinguishable from those of other civilian elites who were neither liberal democrats nor former members of the CPSU. At the same time, their response patterns clearly differed from those of elites who were both former CPSU members and not liberal democrats.

Slavophils and Westernizers Redux

A final cleavage that must be considered concerning Russian elite views at the onset of a new century is an old one indeed, one that long predates the divide between former members of the CPSU and others. I have in mind of course the recrudescence of the Slavophil-Westerner debate of the middle of the nineteenth century. Elite surveys in 1995 and 1999 asked respondents whether they more identified with the statement that "owing to Russia's history and its geographical position at the crossroads of Europe and Asia, it should follow its own unique path" or the proposition that Russia should "take the path of other developed countries . . . familiarizing itself with the achievements of Western civilization." As table

Table 5.10.

Orientation to Political Economy, Assessment of Political System Most Suitable for Russia, and Preferred Developmental Path, 1999

	Market Democrats	*Market Authoritarians*	*Social Democrats*	*Socialist Authoritarians*
Pursue unique Russian path	46% (57)	58% (7)	68% (13)	86% (18)

Tau$_c$ = .24, $p < .001$

	Soviet System before Perestroika	*Present System*	*Western Democracy*
Pursue unique Russian path	93% (27)	67% (14)	28% (21)

Tau$_c$ = .54, $p < .001$

Source: As in table 5.1.

Note: Actual number of respondents in particular cells shown in parentheses.

Question wording:

Should Russia use the experience of the West or should it seek its own path of development? Which of the answers that I will read to you are closest to your view?

5.10 indicates, the overlap between responses to this question and either the constructed political economy typology or respondents' answers to a question concerning the political system most suitable for Russia was very large. Those coded as socialist authoritarians or who answered that the Soviet system before *perestroika* is the political system most suited for Russia were overwhelmingly inclined to assert that Russia should follow its own path. Those oriented to the market, notably liberal democrats but also market authoritarians, or those who answered that Western-type democracy is the political system most suitable for Russia were in like fashion far more likely to be late twentieth-century Westernizers.

The socialist authoritarians almost uniformly answered that Russia should take its own path. Those coded as liberal democrats divided evenly between those who answered that Russia should follow its own path and those who responded that their views were closer to the statement that Russia should "take the path of other developed countries." These responses raise two obvious questions. Were the foreign policy orientations of "Russian-path" liberal democrats on the eve of the twenty-first century more like Westernizing liberal democrats or more like those of other foreign policy elites? Can the distinction between the foreign policy orientations of liberal democrats and other elites be sustained?

Consistent with a theme that has permeated this chapter, orientation to the political economy plays little role in defining Russian elite orientations to the use of force or in concerns about the outbreak of hostilities on

Russia's border. There was a modest and statistically significant distinction among the liberal democrats between the modern-day Westernizers and modern-day Slavophils with respect to the use of force within the former Soviet Union.[12] There was none, however, with regard to whether they considered Russia's national interests to be broader than its current territorial boundaries or whether conflicts on Russia's borders represented a danger or the greatest danger to Russia's security.

In contrast, as reference to table 5.11 reveals, on matters of reunification with Belarus (but not Ukraine), economic interdependence, and, most notably, in regard to U.S.-Russian security relations, the differences *among* the liberal democrats between the Western emulators and those who said Russia should follow its own path were generally substantial.

With regard to reunification with Ukraine, the cleavage was between liberal democrats, regardless of whether they answered that Russia should follow its own path or whether they identified with borrowing from Western experience, and other elites (table 5.11). In the case of reunification of Russia and Belarus, liberal democrats who answered that Russia should benefit from Western experience were distinguishable from all other elites, including both liberal democrats who answered that Russia should follow its own path and others.

As for whether the gap between rich and poor countries represented a threat to Russia, the difference between Westernizing and "Russian-path" liberal democrats was statistically significant. Both, though, were less likely to assert that the gap represented a major threat than were other elites. On foreign ownership of key industries, the cleavage was between liberal democrat Westernizers and others, including both those who favored a Russian path and the handful of respondents who have been classified as others but who answered that Russia should follow the West. Likewise, on the question of Russia's addressing the rebuilding of its economy without help from the West, Westernizing liberal democrats differed from all other elites, including the "Russian-path" liberal democrats and others.

Similarly, those in 1999 who were liberal democrats and Westernizers were sharply set off both from "Russian-path" liberal democrats and from other elites as to whether balancing against Western power was a very important goal. They were also far less likely to favor increased spending for defense. Slightly less than half (49 percent) of the liberal democrats who favored emulating the West said in 1999 that Russia should increase its military expenditures. Almost two-thirds (65 percent) of those who were not liberal democrats but favored following a Western path, almost three-quarters (73 percent) of the liberal democrats who favored Russia's following a separate path, and more than four-fifths (81 percent) of those

---

[12] Tau$_c$ = $-.15$, $p < .10$ and tau$_c$ = $-.17$, $p < .10$, respectively.

Table 5.11.

Foreign Policy Preferences among Civilian Elites, Controlling for Developmental Path and Orientation to Political Economy, 1999

		Follow Russian Path	*Follow West*
U.S. threat	Liberal democrats	71% (35)	30% (17)
	Tau$_c$ = −.41, p < .001		
	Others	86% (31)	36% (4)
	Tau$_c$ = −.36, p < .01		
Balance West very important	Liberal democrats	79% (42)	36% (21)
	Tau$_c$ = .44, p < .001		
	Others	87% (33)	57% (8)
	Tau$_c$=.23, p < .05		
Perceived dangers:			
NATO expansion	Liberal democrats	68% (36)	37% (22)
	Tau$_c$ = −.31, p < .001		
	Others	79% (30)	43% (6)
	Tau$_c$ = −.28, p < .05		
NATO intervention	Liberal democrats	69% (37)	44% (26)
	Tau$_c$ = −.24, p < .01		
	Others	84% (32)	50% (7)
	Tau$_c$ = −.27, p < .05		
Growth U.S. power	Liberal democrats	65% (35)	31% (19)
	Tau$_c$ = −.42, p < .001		
	Others	87% (33)	50% (7)
	Tau$_c$ = −.41, p < .005		
Foreign control of "key economic sectors"	Liberal democrats	65% (35)	35% (21)
	Tau$_c$ =.33, p ≤.001		
	Others	84% (32)	57% (8)
	Tau$_c$ =.29, p < .05		
Gap between rich and poor countries	Liberal democrats	41% (22)	23% (14)
	Tau$_c$ = −.30, p < .005		
	Others	53% (20)	57% (8)
	n.s.		
Solve economic problems without Western help	Liberal democrats	76% (40)	54% (33)
	Tau$_c$ = −.21, p ≤ .01		
	Others	83% (29)	69% (9)
	n.s.		
Strongly favor reunification: with Belarus	Liberal democrats	65% (35)	38% (23)
	Tau$_c$ = −.26, p < .005		
	Others	76% (29)	54% (7)
	n.s.		
. . . with Ukraine	Liberal democrats	31% (17)	25% (15)
	n.s.		
	Others	50% (19)	38% (5)
	n.s.		

Source: As in table 5.1.

Note: Actual number of respondents in particular cells shown in parentheses.

Question wording:

For question wording, see tables 5.3–5.5.

who were not market democrats and asserted that Russia should follow a
separate path favored a policy of balancing against Western power.

In general, it was with regard to U.S.-Russian security relations that
distinguishing between civilian democrats who found the assertion that
Russia should follow its own path congenial and those who were favorably
disposed to emulating the West produced the clearest pattern. On the
questions whether the United States was a threat or the growth of U.S.
power was a great danger or the greatest danger to Russian security,
whether NATO expansion was a great or the greatest threat to Russian
security, or whether NATO intervention in a European country to mute
ethnic conflict represented a great or the greatest threat, the major divide
was between those who responded more favorably to the statement that
Russia should follow its own path and those who associated themselves
with emulating the experience of "other developed" states, not between
liberal democrats and other elites (table 5.11).

The Continued Relevance of Distinguishing among
Orientations to the Political Economy

The increased role for former membership in the CPSU and the importance of the modern-dress version of the Slavophil-Westernizer dispute
by century's end calls into question whether for elites the importance of
distinguishing orientation to the political economy in assessing foreign
policy dispositions no longer matters. To test that proposition I ran a series
of logistic regressions in which all the factors discussed in the past few
pages—age, membership in the former CPSU, pattern of political development, and orientation to the political economy—were treated as dummy
variables in predicting civilian elite foreign policy orientations.

Table 5.12 summarizes the relevant aspect of those analyses by reporting the significance levels of distinguishing between (a) those fifty
and over in 1999 and younger respondents, (b) those who had been CPSU
members and others, (c) those who were more attracted to the proposition
that Russia should follow its own path and those attracted to borrowing
from the West, and (d) market democrats as opposed to foreign policy
elites categorized as market authoritarians, social democrats, or socialist
authoritarians. (Significance levels were used because logistic regression
coefficients are not readily interpretable in the way that ordinary least-
squares coefficients are.)

Inspection of this table reveals that of the four predictors, age (especially) and CPSU membership were the variables that least frequently
played an independent role in multivariate analysis. The distinction be-

Table 5.12.

Age, CPSU Membership, Developmental Path, and Orientation to Political Economy as Predictors of Foreign Policy Preferences among Civilian Elites, 1999 (p)

	Age 50 or Over	CPSU Membership?	Russian Path	Market Democrats
U.S. threat	.594	.196	.000	.101
Balance West very important?	.779	.349	.001	.073
Perceived dangers:				
NATO expansion	.899	.018	.001	.146
NATO intervention in internal affairs	.252	.098	.005	.073
Growth in U.S. power	.687	.150	.000	.005
Foreign ownership of key economic sectors	.003	.306	.001	.011
Gap between rich and poor countries	.921	.289	.232	.016
Increase military expenditures	.201	.668	.007	.258
Rebuild economy without Western help	.009	.015	.021	.138
Strongly favor reunification: with Belarus	.681	.201	.005	.090
. . . with Ukraine	.449	.370	.509	.032

Source: As in table 5.1.

Question wording:

For wording of questions, see tables 5.3–5.5.

tween those drawn to the Russian path and the late twentieth-century Westernizers had such a status most frequently, especially as regards security matters. In the multivariate analysis, nevertheless, there remained an independent and statistically significant role for distinguishing between liberal democrats and others with regard to several variables of considerable importance to Russian foreign policy behavior. Controlling for CPSU status, developmental path preferred, and age, distinguishing liberal democrats from other civilian elites proved an independent and stable, though not robust, predictor[13] of items pertaining to the growth of U.S. military

---

[13] Omitting age, as the least robust variable in the model, did not affect the stability of the coefficients for distinguishing liberal democrats and others.

might and what should be done about it, reunification with former parts of the Soviet Union, and participation in the global economy. Even on security items where the Westernizer/Russian path divide was a powerful predictor, distinguishing liberal democrats from others remained important. At the dawn of a new century, the former were less likely than other Russian elites to regard the growth of U.S. military power as constituting a threat to Russia and less inclined to say that balancing the power of the West was a very important goal. Distinguishing orientation to the political economy contributed to understanding Russian elite dispositions to the possibility of NATO's use of force within a European state even when controlling for the independent effects of age, former CPSU membership, and orientation to the long-term development of Russia, and probably did the same in the case of Russian elite assessments of the U.S. threat to Russian security. Likewise, the distinction had a modest independent role in explaining some elite dispositions to Russia's interaction with the international economy. Similarly, the role ascribed to differentiating market democrats from other civilian elites with regard to orientation to reunification with Ukraine and Belarus in the bivariate analysis is sustained in the multivariate analysis.

Implications

Qualifications need to be made to propositions about the links between elite orientations to the domestic political economy and their foreign policy dispositions. Although the proportion of liberal democrats among civilian elites remained relatively constant in the 1990s, we find that having been a member of the CPSU seemed to play a greater role at century's end in distinguishing among liberal democrats than it did in the first post-Soviet years. This finding is somewhat puzzling; we might expect such effects to be weaker over time. What I suspect is at work here is that over the course of the decade those who were never CPSU members remained relatively optimistic about East-West relations. At the same time, events like the expansion of NATO and NATO actions in Yugoslavia probably rekindled cold war dispositions among former CPSU members. The overlap between opting for the Russian path and being a socialist authoritarian by the criteria employed in this book was virtually complete at the beginning of the twenty-first century; half the liberal democrats had opted for a distinctive Russian developmental path as well. Those Russian elites, generally liberal democrats who did not accept the proposition that Russia should follow its own distinctive path, differed in major ways from other elites in their orientation to foreign policy along several key dimensions.

Nevertheless, even when controls for CPSU membership and developmental path preference (as well as age) were entered in multiple regressions, there remained an independent role for orientation to the political economy in understanding Russian elite assessments of East-West security and economic relations and in explaining differences in Russian elite views about the desirability of Russian reunification with Ukraine and Belarus.

Major shifts have occurred in the median responses of Russian elites to a wide range of foreign policy questions from 1993 to 1995 and 1999. The distribution of responses among all Russian elites in 1999 was markedly different from the pattern of responses in 1993. What goes on in the world outside a country, in this instance the Russian Federation, shapes and constrains responses that elites give to foreign policy questions. The impact of events—NATO expansion, the intervention in Kosovo—has taken a considerable toll, as did the economic crisis within the country, a crisis that many Russians, both mass and elites, blamed in large measure on the West.

Changing the domestic coalition mattered substantially as well. A more open elite structure in Russia in the 1990s has ensured a broader range of views than would have been possible in the absence of the profound changes in the political system in the last decade of the twentieth century. Those, such as the military, who had a role-reinforced propensity to view the external world in hostile terms were relatively quick to assert that U.S. behavior represented a threat to Russian security. Those whose views about politics were an amalgam of statist authoritarianism and Russian uniqueness were primed to view the world in adversarial terms. Logical concomitants to this were stronger sentiments for reunification with Belarus and Ukraine and greater resistance to economic interdependence and penetration of the economy by foreigners. Others were more cross-pressured. The former members of the CPSU who were market democrats in 1999 expressed views with regard to the international system and the international economy as well as about Russian reunification with Ukraine or Belarus that often fell between those expressed by market democrats who had not been CPSU members and those typically expressed by the military or by civilian elites who were not market democrats. By contrast, those (overwhelmingly market democrats) civilian elites who advocated borrowing from the West's experience were noticeably less likely to view the world in adversarial terms, more favorably disposed to global interdependence, and less enthusiastic about Russian reunification with Ukraine or Belarus. The shift in response patterns across time by all Russian elites requires emphasis. So, too, does another major constant, to wit: market democrats, especially the Westernizers, remained throughout the decade more inclined than other elites to relatively benign assessments of American behavior, including NATO expansion, relatively more disposed to view Russia's growing international economic linkages favorably, and relatively less enthusiastic about reunifying Russia with either Ukraine or Belarus.

In the next chapter, we explore in greater detail elite and mass assessments in the 1990s of an aspect of post-Soviet Russian foreign policy that is key to making judgments about Russian foreign policy in the first decade of the new millennium: the Russian response to NATO expansion.

6

NATO Expansion Past and Future: A Closer Look

THE EXPANSION of the North Atlantic Treaty Organization to include three former members of the Warsaw Treaty Organization (Poland, the Czech Republic, and Hungary)—formal acceptance of which took place in March 1999—was one of the most significant changes in European politics in the post–cold war period. Opposition came from many quarters. The most vocal were members of the Russian Federation officialdom. The notes various public officials struck differed in intensity, but the consistent theme was that NATO expansion constituted a threat to Russian security. The Russian president, Boris Yeltsin, while asserting that compromises were possible, raised the danger of the emergence of a "cold peace." Vladimir Lukin, in 1995 the chairman of the Duma's Committee on International Affairs, asserted that "if NATO's expansion eastward assumes real forms, Russia may come to the conclusion that previous bilateral or multilateral accords are losing all meaning." "A reliable source" at the General Staff was reported as having recognized that Russia "did not now have the capability to prevent . . . [NATO] expansion to Poland" but that the armed forces of the Russian Federation would "immediately be sent into Estonia, Latvia, and Lithuania" "if NATO decides to admit the Baltic republics as members."[1]

Opposition to NATO expansion also came from Russian specialists (scholars and diplomats) in the West and from Western international relations theorists. To those who favored expansion,[2] it was seen as enhancing the prospects for democratic development in the former Soviet bloc and increasing the chances of peace by deterring or containing a revisionist Russia from using force to reasserts its place in Eastern Europe at some time in the future. To those, East and West, who opposed expansion,[3] it

---

[1] The reference to Yeltsin comes from *Rossiiskaia gazeta*, December 5, 1994, as translated by the *Current Digest of the Post-Soviet Press* [*CDSP*] 46, no. 49 (1995): 6; Lukin's statement appeared in *Izvestiia*, May 12, 1995 (*CDSP*, 47, no. 20 [1995]: 8–9 at p. 9); the "reliable source" was quoted by *Komsomol'skaia pravda*, September 29, 1995, as cited in *CDSP* 47, no. 40 (1995): 9.

[2] See, for instance, Condoleezza Rice, "Now, NATO Should Grow," *New York Times*, July 8, 1996.

[3] Perhaps the strongest assertion in this vein is that of George Kennan, "A Fateful Error: NATO Expansion Would Be a Rebuff to Russian Democracy," *New York Times*, February 5, 1997.

was seen as undermining Western efforts to reassure Russia about the benign nature of Western intentions and the position of pro-Western elements in Russia.[4] The issue of NATO expansion was in this respect a replay of the argument about deterrence versus reassurance that persisted throughout the cold war, notwithstanding the fact that the Soviet Union no longer existed and that in cold war terms, Russia has experienced rollback of a magnitude unimaginable to the harshest Western hawk in the 1950s.[5]

The impact of NATO expansion on Russia is central to the question of the desirability of NATO expansion. The policy dialogue has been rife with assertions, many extravagant, about the consequences for Russia and for Russia's behavior internationally. These assertions have often been largely bereft of evidence. This chapter seeks to extend the analysis of previous chapters by showing how, with respect to a particular policy issue, survey data coupled with insights about foreign policy orientations in relatively open systems can provide valuable indicators of probable policy choices, both retrospectively, in regard to the first phase of NATO expansion, and prospectively, especially in the aftermath of the NATO intervention in Kosovo, in regard to the scope of NATO's mission or to a further increase in NATO membership.

In this chapter I make four assertions. The first concerns the salience of NATO-related issues to elites and mass publics. NATO expansion (conceived here in terms of both expanding numbers and expanding roles, for example, humanitarian interventions within states in Europe) is an issue

[4] As readers will have noted throughout there is ample evidence that sizable fractions of the Russian public do not view Western motives benignly, especially as regards Western interests in the Russian economy. See also Jerry Hough, "The Russian Election of 1993: Public Attitudes toward Economic Reform and Democratization," *Post-Soviet Affairs* 10, no. 1 (1994). At the same time, survey data from foreign policy elites and mass publics in 1993 (chapter 3; Zimmerman, "Markets, Democracy, and Russian Foreign Policy," pp. 103–126), and the entire tenor of Russian foreign policy in the first two to three years of the post-Soviet era reflected an assumption that in security terms the United States was not a threat. The point here is that opponents of NATO expansion, West and East, often asserted that expansion would undermine the belief in a benign West and reinforce the claims by Russian hawks that the West constituted a security threat to Russia.

[5] The fullest argument for reassurance is contained in Richard Ned Lebow and Janice Gross Stein, *We All Lost the Cold War* (Princeton: Princeton University Press, 1994). The literature on deterrence and the Soviet Union is, of course, enormous. The theoretical debate over deterrence and reassurance is best entered by LeBow and Stein, on the one hand, and Paul Huth and Bruce Russett, on the other. For LeBow and Stein, see in addition to *We All Lost the Cold War*, "Rational Deterrence Theory: I Think, Therefore I Deter," *World Politics* 41, no. 2 (January 1989): 208–224; LeBow and Stein, "Deterrence: The Elusive Dependent Variable," *World Politics* 42, no. 3 (April 1990): 336–69. For Huth and/or Huth and Russett, see Huth and Russett, "What Makes Deterrence Work? Cases from 1900 to 1980," *World Politics* 36, no. 3 (July 1984): 496–526; Huth, *Extended Deterrence and the Prevention of War* (New Haven: Yale University Press, 1988); Huth and Russett, "Testing Deterrence Theory: Rigor Makes a Difference," *World Politics* 42, no. 4 (July 1990): 466–501.

about which Russian elites were exercised early on. It only became a policy issue for mass publics that approached in salience and concern many other foreign policy issues in 1999 in the aftermath of the NATO intervention in Kosovo. Moreover, the evidence suggests that the level of awareness at that juncture may have receded a year later.

The second proposition is that the impulse to take strong action in response to NATO expansion converged with the perception of an American threat and, often, an orientation to the domestic political economy, but not directly with the perception of Russia's relative power position. Russian advocacy of countervailing NATO expansion flowed from the perceived need to balance threat, not from an assessment of the distribution of power between the United States and Russia.

Third, when asked about what Russia should do in response to NATO expansion, Russian publics revealed that they too, like American mass publics, were "pretty prudent." They were not readily available for the kind of mobilization for adventurism Jack Snyder and Edward Mansfield have found to be historically characteristic of countries undergoing democratization.[6] The first wave of NATO expansion did not produce the adverse policy reaction Western critics of expansion had considered probable; indeed, there was about as much support among mass publics for joining NATO in response as there was for, for instance, canceling various key arms control agreements. Even the sharp response to NATO intervention in Kosovo muted noticeably after a period of months, though the overall perception of the United States as a threat to Russian security remained higher at the end of the 1990s than it had been in the early 1990s (though less than during the cold war).

Fourth, concern at the beginning of the new century about further NATO expansion increases as we move from Eastern Europe to the Baltic states to states that are members of the CIS. Here, too, for both mass publics and foreign policy elites, perception of the U.S. threat and orientations to further NATO expansion were tightly connected. Orientation to the domestic political economy was frequently an important discriminator in dispositions toward further NATO expansion geographically and in regard to the response appropriate should NATO expand to include one or more members of the CIS.

The Matter of Salience

Table 6.1 presents the mean responses to a battery of questions asked of foreign policy elites and a national sample of ordinary Russians in late fall

---

[6] Snyder, "Democratization, War"; Snyder, *From Voting to Violence*; Mansfield and Snyder, "Democratization and the Danger."

Table 6.1.
Elite and Mass Public Assessment of Threats to Russian Security, 1995 and 1999
(1 = absence of danger; 5 = greatest danger)

	Mass Publics: Mean (S.E.)	
	1995	1999
"Uncontrolled growth in global population"	2.28 (.03) (2078)	—
"Increase in the gap between rich and poor countries"	3.14 (.03) (2186)	3.49 (.03) (1565)
"Spread of NATO to Eastern Europe"	3.48 (.03) (1877)	—
"Growth of U.S. military power"	3.74 (.03) (2375)	4.01 (.03) (1680)
"NATO intervention" in internal affairs of European countries	—	4.03 (.03) (1571)
"Border conflicts within the Commonwealth of Independent States"	3.91 (.02) (2330)	3.90 (.03) (1644)
"Involvement in conflicts" which don't concern Russia	3.96 (.02) (2331)	4.15 (.02) (1673)
Non-CIS conflicts	3.99 (.02) (2296)	4.11 (03) (1645)
Having "key economic sectors in foreign hands"	4.02 (.03) (2215)	—
"Inability . . . to resolve domestic conflicts"	4.13 (.02) (2371)	4.20 (.02) (1695)
	Elites: Mean (S.E.)	
	1995	1999
"Uncontrolled growth in global population"	2.46 (.09) (175)	2.50 (.07) (206)
"Increase in the gap between rich and poor countries"	2.79 (.09) (178)	3.13 (.07) (207)
"Spread of NATO to Eastern Europe"	3.73 (.09) (179)	3.63 (.09) (208)
"Growth of U.S. military power"	3.38 (.10) (177)	3.65 (.09) (210)
"NATO intervention" in internal affairs of European countries	—	3.67 (.09) (207)
Border conflicts within the Commonwealth of Independent States	3.43 (.10) (180)	3.52 (.08) (207)

Table 6.1. (*cont'd*)
Elite and Mass Public Assessment of Threats to Russian Security, 1995 and 1999
(1 = absence of danger; 5 = greatest danger)

	Mass Publics: Mean (S.E.)	
	1995	1999
"Involvement in conflicts" which don't concern Russia	3.15 (.10) (176)	2.99 (.08) (209
Non-CIS conflicts	2.99 (.10) (179)	3.03 (.08) (208)
Having "key economic sectors in foreign hands"	3.20 (.11) (179)	3.41 (.09) (208)
"Inability . . . to resolve domestic conflicts"	4.31 (.07) (179)	4.31 (.06) (208)

Sources: Demoscope conducted the 1995 and 1999 nationwide mass surveys. ROMIR conducted the elite surveys.

Note: Second number in parentheses indicate actual number of respondents. Dashes indicate question not asked.

Question wording:
(In the order they are listed for mass publics, above [not as they appeared in the surveys]).

The increase in the gap between rich and poor countries.
The uncontrolled growth in global population.
The enlargement of NATO by including countries of Eastern Europe.
The growth of U.S. military power relative to that of Russia.
Armed intervention by NATO into inter-nationality conflicts in the countries of Europe.
Russian border conflicts with countries of the CIS, that is, the former republics of the USSR.
Russian involvement in conflicts that are not its concern.
Russian border conflicts with other foreign countries.
The transfer of basic branches of the Russian economy into the property of foreign companies.
The inability of Russia to resolve its internal problems.

1995 and again in the fall of 1999 concerning perceived security threats to Russia. As the table reveals, NATO expansion was both far more salient and a greater source of concern for Russian elites than it was for mass publics in 1995. In 1995, all foreign policy issues were of less concern to both elites and mass publics than their misgivings about "the inability of Russia to resolve its internal problems." The gap between domestic and foreign policy concerns and the handling of domestic problems was greater for elites than for those in the mass public who expressed views. Of the foreign policy concerns mentioned, for elites in the late fall of 1995, NATO enlargement was easily the most pressing.

The issue figured far less at that juncture for the mass publics. Among those who expressed an opinion, only concerns about the global population explosion and the gap between rich and poor countries were rated lower dangers to Russian security. (This point, it should be emphasized, holds when we control for respondents' level of knowledge of the world outside Russia. Contrary to Alexei Arbatov,[7] those among the mass public in 1995 who were highly knowledgeable about foreign affairs did not differ from other mass respondents in the ranking of NATO expansion among threats to Russian security.) Moreover, as table 6.1 also shows, many fewer respondents expressed an opinion about NATO expansion in 1995 than about the other items. Interpreting "don't knows" is always problematic, but they almost certainly constitute an indicator of salience or, in this instance, lack thereof. (This is especially so when respondents were offered five options ranging from strongly agree and agree on the one hand to disagree and disagree strongly on the other, with an intermediate response, "I'm ambivalent" [*koleblius'*] a possibility.)

The evidence that NATO expansion as an issue had not penetrated the mass public very deeply in the 1995–96 period is striking.[8] Those with little education, who knew little about the outside world, and or who devoted little attention to newspapers, radio, or television or did not talk about politics with their friends, were quite disengaged from the debate. Of those who knew practically nothing about the outside world, more than half (58 percent) declined to express an opinion about the danger inherent in NATO expansion. Of the internationally attentive public—defined by their factual knowledge of the outside world—7 percent did not express an opinion. After the 1996 presidential election, respondents were asked whether "Russia should do everything possible not to allow the entry into NATO of the former socialist countries of Eastern Europe. "To this question, again more than half (56 percent) among the completely unaware declined to express an opinion. Even the attentive public was reticent to express a view; in their case a quarter (24 percent) failed to answer.

The question of the measures to take to thwart NATO expansion produced more bafflement by respondents than most foreign policy questions. Table 6.2 illustrates this point by comparing the lack of willingness of respondents in the 1995/96 mass survey to express views about it and two other issues relevant to foreign policy. One of the two was whether Russia should try to balance the West's military power, a rather broad and abstract issue, the other the specific and tangible issue whether the level of military spending should be "increased, decreased, or kept the same." Even in relative terms, the extent to which mass publics were unable to

---

[7] *New York Times*, August 27, 1997.

[8] For similar findings from two other Russian polling groups, see *New York Times*, May 27, 1997. See, too, Simes, *After the Collapse*, p. 219.

Table 6.2.
"Don't Knows" or "Refuses to Answer" for Three Foreign Policy Questions by Mass Publics, 1995

	Completely Unaware	Unaware	Moderately Aware	Attentive
Resist NATO expansion	56% (291)	37% (232)	28% (283)	24% (63)
Balance West very important	39% (232)	16% (114)	10% (117)	7% (20)
Military spending: increase, stay same, decrease	14% (81)	6% (40)	4% (43)	2% (6)

Source: same as in table 6.1.
Note: Actual number of respondents in particular cells shown in parentheses.

Question wording:
Items used to indicate knowledge of world outside Russia:
Now, I'll read you the names of several political figures. Tell me, please, which country do they represent?

> François Mitterrand [Jacques Chirac]
> John Major
> Juan Carlos II
> George Bush [Bill Clinton]
> William Zimmerman [not included in measure]
> Helmut Kohl

Have you heard of the International Monetary Fund [IMF]?
> [If yes] Is Russia a member of the IMF?
> [If yes] In what year did Russia become a member of the IMF?

Of which state is the Crimea a part at this moment? Is it part of Russia, part of Ukraine, or neither?
> [If Ukraine] Do you know, even approximately, in what year Crimea became part of Ukraine?

Russia should do everything possible not to allow the entry of the formerly socialist countries of Eastern Europe into NATO.
Which goals of Russian foreign policy, in your opinion, are very important and which less important?

> . . .
> Achieving a balance of military power with the West.

assess a response to NATO expansion is noteworthy. Among the unaware, half again as many declined to express views about the policy response to NATO expansion as refused to express a view on whether Russia should balance against the West. Among the internationally attentive public, 2 percent of the respondents declined to answer the question about military spending, 7 percent refused to answer the military balancing question, and as we have just seen, a quarter of the respondents declined to express a view about what was to be done to prevent East European states from becoming members of NATO. Regardless of respondents' knowledge about the world outside Russia, they were far more likely to express a view

Table 6.3.
Are You Aware of the Plans for NATO Expansion to the East?

Yes	32% (477)
More yes than no	16% (244)
More no than yes	9% (134)
No	43% (645)
Total	(1500)

Source: January 1997 ROMIR Omnibus survey.
Note: Actual number of respondents in particular cells shown in parentheses.

about defense spending than whether to balance militarily against the West. They were more willing to give some answer to a question about defense spending or about balancing against the West than an answer about policy choices regarding NATO expansion. For all the claims by elites, Russian and American, of the significance of NATO expansion for the future evolution of Europe and for Russia's place in the new Europe, a very sizable proportion of the Russian population in 1995–96 either had simply not heard of, or had only the slightest conception of, NATO expansion as an issue.

The lack of awareness extended to at least 1997. In January 1997 the Russian survey firm ROMIR conducted its periodic omnibus survey of a national sample of 1500 respondents. Respondents were given four clumsy but indicative response choices to the question "Are you aware of the plans for NATO expansion to the East?": yes, more yes than no, more no than yes, and no. The responses are reported in table 6.3. Only a third gave an unmodifiedly affirmative answer. More than half the respondents either said flatly they were unaware of such plans or had only a vague awareness of them ("more no than yes"). This about an issue that then president Boris Yeltsin had informed the world was the most vexing issue between the United States and Russia since the Cuban missile crisis.

From the perspective of an aware public, it gets worse. The respondents who indicated some form of awareness of NATO expansion plans were presented with a follow-up question that asked them to name the three states most likely to join NATO first. Table 6.4 reports simple cross-tabulations of the countries mentioned and whether the respondents had answered yes, more yes than no, or more no than yes. (Those who had answered no were obviously not asked the follow-up question.) How plugged into the realities of the issue even those of the Russian public who claimed to be well informed were in 1997 is exceedingly problematic. The countries included in the table are those mentioned most frequently by Russian respondents—the three Baltic republics—and the three countries

Table 6.4.

Key Countries Identified by Russian Mass Publics as among the First to Join NATO, 1997

	Self-Described Awareness of NATO Expansion		
	Yes	*More Yes than No*	*More No than Yes*
Those admitted			
Czech Republic	23% (110)	16% (38)	7% (9)
Hungary	20% (96)	9% (22)	7% (9)
Poland	42% (202)	27% (66)	24% (32)
Those mentioned most often by Russian respondents			
Estonia	47% (225)	34% (83)	16% (22)
Latvia	55% (262)	39% (94)	22% (29)
Lithuania	56% (266)	39% (96)	22% (29)
Poland	42% (202)	27% (66)	24% (32)

Source: January 1997 ROMIR Omnibus survey.

Note: Actual number of respondents in particular cells shown in parentheses.

(Poland, the Czech Republic, and Hungary) that actually joined in the first round.[9] More respondents answered that the three Baltic countries, especially Latvia and Lithuania, would be among the first to join than said Poland, the Czech Republic, or Hungary.

Moreover, those who answered yes were significantly more likely to answer that the Baltic states would be the first to join than were those who acknowledged only the vaguest awareness of NATO expansion; it was those who had said "more no than yes" about NATO expansion who mentioned Poland more than either the Baltic states or Hungary or the Czech Republic. Much of the reason for this anomalous finding is that the responses of those who had only the barest reported awareness of NATO expansion were more randomly dispersed across eighteen possible countries—that is, they were truly guessing—than were those who had confidently but ignorantly affirmed that they were aware of NATO expansion plans. That granted, these data are not those, unlike the more general issues of Russia's orientation to the international system discussed in chap-

[9] A research assistant and I first received the data and then saw the actual question wording. (They had initially been labeled V1, V2, etc.) When we saw the frequencies, our assumption was that the question asked was "Which countries, were they to join NATO, would constitute the greatest threat to Russian interests?"

ter 4, that one would muster to argue against the proposition that in Russia foreign policy elites waltz before a blind audience.

The 1999 data reinforce the sense that the problem of NATO expansion had retained its preeminent place for Russian elites among external threats to Russian security. As reference again to table 6.1 indicates, NATO expansion, the possibility of NATO intervention in interethnic conflicts within European states in the aftermath of NATO action in Kosovo, and the growth of American military power constituted a cluster of the most worrisome external threats. As in 1995, however, the greatest worry for elites remained the ability to cope with domestic issues.

There is evidence that in 1999, in the aftermath of the NATO bombing of Serbia and occupation of Kosovo, the salience of, and concern about, NATO expansion was more evident among mass publics than it had been previously. The mean scores for international threats to Russia were generally up for Russian mass publics in 1999 in comparison with 1995, though the ability of the country to address domestic issues retained pride of place of sorts. Prompted, presumably, by widespread media coverage of NATO intervention in Kosovo, concern about U.S. military might and the possibility of NATO's expanded role had become matters about which mass publics showed response patterns in the range of other foreign policy items.[10]

Moreover, a NATO-related item no longer provided the striking bafflement in 1999 that such items had in 1995–96 (table 6.1). The item still produced more nonresponses than all but one of the foreign policy questions in table 6.1. But it was no longer distinctive. In 1995 NATO had been an issue about which unusually few mass respondents—200 fewer than for any other item in table 6.1 out of a sample of 2452 respondents in the third wave of the survey—expressed a view. Likewise, the distribution of responses across levels of attentiveness was more typical of other foreign policy items related to threats to Russia's security.

The 1999 mass survey did not replicate the questions utilized in 1993 and 1995 to tap respondent knowledge of international affairs, nor did it ask the NATO expansion question asked in 1995. We cannot therefore compare precisely the relative propensity to answer a NATO-related question across international attentiveness for 1995 and 1999. We can, however, make do by utilizing other indicators of attentiveness. Table 6.5 reports the number of persons who failed to answer the question concerning the danger to Russian security prompted by the possibility of NATO intervention into interethnic disputes of European states, controlling for attentiveness. In the absence of questions about knowledge of international events, attentiveness here is defined in two ways: the attention to politics

---

[10] J. L. Black, *Russia Faces NATO Expansion: Bearing Gifts or Bearing Arms* (Lanham, Md.: Rowman and Littlefield, 2000).

Table 6.5.
Failure to Respond and Attentiveness to NATO Intervention in Ethnic
Disputes in European Countries, Mass Survey 1999

Attention Devoted to Reading about Politics			
Very Attentive	*Somewhat Attentive*	*Only Glances at Articles about Politics*	*Reads Nothing about Politics*
4% (6)	9% (34)	11% (52)	24% (31)
Reported Level of Political Interest			
Constantly	*Sometimes*	*Very Rarely*	*Don't Follow*
8% (60)	14% (97)	23% (53)	40% (61)

Source: 1999 Demoscope national survey.
Note: Actual number of respondents in particular cells shown in parentheses.

Question wording:

When you read the newspaper, how much attention do you devote to articles about politics?
Some people constantly follow politics, others are not interested in it.
What would you say about yourself—that you follow political events constantly, sometimes, very rarely, or generally don't follow them?

respondents reported they showed in reading newspapers and their self-reported interest in politics. With regard to the respondents' propensity to give some answer, the pattern seems to be more like that noted in table 6.2 concerning the importance of balancing U.S. power than like the responses in 1995 to the proposition that everything possible should be done to prevent NATO expansion. The very attentive declined to answer less than 5 percent of the time; those who read nothing about politics did not answer about a quarter of the time. With all the elite utterances, the outpouring of media about Kosovo, demonstrations at the American embassy in Moscow, and the like, a case could be made that NATO expansion had achieved by 1999 a level of mass public awareness that brought it in line with other major foreign policy concerns.

But when we examine other items in the 1999/2000 survey, we find evidence suggesting that such was not the case. If we again use respondents' reported diligence with which they attended to the reading of political matters in newspapers as a surrogate for international attentiveness, we find that in answering questions concerning how they viewed the prospects of NATO expansion, those who said they paid no attention to politics when reading the newspaper refused to answer or said they did not know in very large numbers. When asked in December 1999 about Russia's response to NATO expansion in Eastern Europe, the Baltic states, and the Commonwealth of Independent States, about 40 percent of those interviewed said they did not know or refused to answer. Nearly the same number refused to answer the item pertaining to NATO expansion to include Russia. After the March 2000 election, fully 56 percent refused to express a view or said they did not know in response to the proposition that "Russia should break off all relations with NATO if its leaders try to expand NATO to include any former republics of the Soviet Union that are now members of the CIS."

Of those who said they read about politics very attentively, 7 to 9 percent responded "don't know" or refused to answer questions concerning NATO expansion to other states in Eastern Europe, to the Baltics, and to the CIS. Fourteen percent gave such answers to an item concerning NATO membership for Russia itself (an issue about which even the most attentive respondents had few cues in December 1999—this was before Putin's statement early in the year 2000 that under some circumstances Russia would consider joining NATO). After the March 2000 election 15 percent of those who said they read about politics very attentively and more than a fifth (22 percent) of those who described themselves as constantly interested in politics refused to answer or said they did not know to the item pertaining to the appropriate policy response of NATO expansion to include a CIS state. There is some evidence that mass public awareness of issues of NATO expansion increased in response to the NATO incursion in Kosovo. On balance, though, not even an event of that magnitude seems unambiguously to have heightened for long the salience of issues pertaining specifically to NATO expansion to the level of other foreign policy issues narrowly conceived—which remained in turn of far less moment than domestic policy issues.

Differential Assessments of the NATO Threat

Needless to say, some Russians, elites most notably, were more alarmed by NATO expansion than others. They were, as a consequence, more prone to assert that everything should be done to prevent NATO expansion, to characterize it as a great or the greatest threat to Russian security, and to express alarm at the possibility of NATO interference in inter-nationality conflicts within European countries.

One consideration that did not discriminate among Russian foreign policy elites or ordinary citizens in the mass public was their assessment of the distribution of power between Russia and the United States. As we shall see, perception of threat, not perception of power, was a major discriminator in Russian assessments of NATO expansion.[11] Both elites and mass publics in 1995 were asked whether the United States was much stronger, stronger, about equal to, weaker, or much weaker than Russia. There was no statistical relationship between assessments by elites of the United States' relative power vis-à-vis Russia and their assessment of NATO expansion into Eastern Europe as a threat. There was, to be sure, a weak, statistically significant association between assessment of the power relationship between the United States and Russia for mass publics.[12] But it was in the opposite direction from what would be hypothesized were balancing power the respondents' chief concern. Marginally more respondents in the 1995/96 mass sample who did not say the United States was much stronger than Russia termed NATO expansion a danger or the greatest danger than those who did. No relationship at all ($tau_c = .00$) was observed between mass public assessments of the relative power of the United States and Russia and the tendency to say that "everything possible" needed to be done to prevent NATO expansion into Eastern Europe.[13]

Instead, we need to consider again the factors that have been at the center of the discussion in previous chapters. These include orientation to the political economy, the differences among civilian and military elites, respondents' internationalism as identified by a "militant internationalism/cooperative internationalism" scale, whether the respondents considered the United States a threat, and previous membership in the CPSU.

A persistent theme in this book has been the importance of orientation to the domestic political economy in explaining dispositions toward East-West security relations. For the 1995/96 panel survey, less than a third (29 percent) of those coded as liberal democrats, about two-fifths (39 percent) of the market authoritarians and the social democrats (42 percent), and 56 percent of the socialist authoritarians agreed or strongly agreed that "everything possible should be done not to allow the formerly socialist East European countries' to become NATO members. Fewer than half the market oriented, both liberal democrats and market authori-

---

[11] Stephen M. Walt, *The Origins of Alliances* (Ithaca, N.Y.: Cornell University Press, 1987); John A. Vasquez, "The Realist Paradigm and Degenerative versus Progressive Research Programs," pp. 899–912, Kenneth Waltz, "Evaluating Theories," pp. 913–18; Thomas J. Christensen and Jack Snyder, "Progressive Research on Degenerate Alliances," pp. 919–24; Colin Elman and Miriam Fendius Elman, "Lakatos and Neorealism: A Reply to Vasquez," pp. 923–26; Randall L. Schweller, "New Realist Research on Alliances: Refining, not Refuting, Waltz's Balancing Proposition," pp. 927–30;, Walt, "The Progressive Power of Realism," pp. 931–36: all in the *American Political Science Review* 91, no. 4 (1997).

[12] $Tau_c = -.04$, $p < .05$.

[13] Similarly, I ran numerous multivariate analyses in which the outcome variable pertained to NATO expansion using the 1995 data. In none of these was the perceived perception of the United States' relative power position statistically significant.

Table 6.6.
Logistic Regression Predicting 1996 Mass Public Agreement That "Everything Should Be Done" to Prevent NATO Expansion to Eastern Europe

Variable	Coefficient (B)	Standard Error	Probability (p)
Orientation to political economy	−.320	.06	.000
U.S. power assessed	.046	.10	.646
Membership in former CPSU	.450	.19	.017
U.S. a threat (June 1996)	.143	.04	.001
Constant	−.014	.42	.973

Source: Post-presidential survey of Russian national sample conducted by Demoscope.
Note: For the construction of the political economy typology, see chapter 2.
Number of initial cases: 2452. Number in Analysis: 900.
Initial log likelihood function: −2 log likelihood 1206.39.
Improvement: −2 log likelihood 51.97.
  Goodness of fit: 906.11.
  Correct predictions: 61.9%.

Question wording:
Compare, please, the power of these countries in comparison with Russia. Are they much more powerful, somewhat more powerful, equal, somewhat weaker, or much weaker?

    . . .
The USA
Do you think that U.S. policy is a threat to Russian security?

tarians, regarded the spread of NATO to Eastern Europe a great or the greatest danger, whereas three of five among the socialists termed NATO expansion a danger. Orientation to the domestic political economy also had an independent and stable effect in multivariate analysis of NATO expansion.

Table 6.6 is illustrative. The outcome variable in a logistic regression distinguishes those who agreed or strongly agreed that everything possible should be done to prevent NATO expansion from other respondents. The predictors are the domestic political economy minus the ambivalent and unmobilized, perception of U.S. power in comparison with that of Russia, membership in the erstwhile CPSU, and whether respondents thought the United States a threat or not.[14] The same finding results using the same independent variables and predicting to whether or not mass

[14] The item used as the outcome variable in the regression in table 6.6 was one asked after the presidential election in June 1996. Since the U.S. threat question was asked both in December 1995 and after the June 1996 presidential election, I have naturally used the question from 1996 in that regression.

survey respondents in 1995 answered that NATO expansion was a great or the greatest danger.

The participants in the 1999 mass panel survey were asked to evaluate the threat to Russian security of NATO interference in inter-nationality conflicts within European states. In the aftermath of the NATO action in Kosovo and against a background of greater mass public anxiety about the world outside Russia overall (compare the mean scores in table 6.1), the Russian public's level of concern about NATO's expanded mission was somewhat higher than was that of foreign policy elites. In that setting, orientation to the domestic political economy continued to differentiate modestly in bivariate analysis among the proportion of respondents in the mass public who viewed NATO's enlarged role as threatening. A "mere" two-thirds (66 percent) of the market democrats—as opposed to exactly three-quarters of the other respondents with defined political economy postures— regarded NATO interference in interethnic conflicts as a threat to Russian security. This distinction has statistically significant independent and stable effects in multivariate models that do not include assessment of the United States as a threat. In ones in which the U.S. threat is included, the distinction between liberal democrats and others was usually only significant at the $p < .10$ level.

In chapter 3, it will be remembered, we employed a militant internationalist/cooperative internationalist measure to good advantage in ascertaining mass and elite respondents' foreign policy orientations. The MI/CI scale combined questions about the United States as a threat and the willingness to use force abroad if asked, both within the former Soviet Union and elsewhere, with a question concerning respondents' disposition toward economic cooperation internationally.[15] Those who scored high on the militant internationalist dimension and low on economic cooperation were labeled hard-liners. Internationalists were high on both the militant and the cooperative dimensions; accommodationists were low on the militant dimension and high on economic cooperation. Finally, isolationists were low on both the militant and the cooperative dimensions. For the mass public, the measure was of some value in capturing respondents' dispositions concerning NATO expansion, though it was not a robust discriminator. Five out of eight (62 percent) of the hard-liners, slightly more than half of the isolationists (54 percent), and roughly two-fifths of the internationalists and accommodationists (44 and 38 percent,

---

[15] Since we are comparing the 1995 and 1999 mass surveys, I have used the alternative MI/CI scale (see chapter 3) that asked whether respondents thought it necessary to defend Russian firms against the predatory acts of foreign firms. Using the MI/CI scale employed in analyzing the three elite surveys and the 1993 mass survey—which asked whether Russia can restore its economy without Western aid—results in very minor differences in the results for the 1995 survey.

respectively) termed NATO expansion a great or the greatest threat to Russian security in 1995. Likewise, more than half (52 percent) the hard-liners agreed or strongly agreed that "everything should be done to stop NATO expansion," a view shared by two-fifths of the isolationists (43 percent) but only by a bit more than a quarter of the internationalists (32 percent) and the accommodationists (26 percent).

In 1999, similarly, about three-quarters of the hard-liners (77 percent), the internationalists (74 percent), and the isolationists (71 percent) termed "NATO interference in inter-national disputes within European countries" a great or the greatest danger. There was a gap between these constructed types and the accommodationists. But even among the latter, 56 percent of the mass respondents termed NATO interference a great or the greatest danger. Torn between their isolationist impulses—expressed in resistance to the use of use force abroad and to economic penetration—and rekindled fears of the United States as a threat, among those who gave answers, mass publics were quite broadly alarmed in 1999 about the prospect of NATO interference in ethnic disputes in European states.

To get a better sense of the impetus for their concern I undertook a logistic regression (table 6.7) that decomposed the MI/CI variable into its component parts—regarding the United States as a threat, use of force abroad, and defending the economy against foreign predations. The analysis included in the model former membership in the CPSU and a distinction between liberal democrats and other persons with committed positions about the political economy. Of these, concern about the United States as a threat was the most important single predictor of mass misgivings about NATO interference in interethnic conflicts. Importantly, too, the distinction between liberal democrats and others continues to hold even in analysis that includes the United States as a threat. Slightly more than half (53 percent) the 1995 respondents considered NATO expansion to Eastern Europe a great or the greatest threat. Almost three-quarters (72 percent) of the 1999 interviewees considered NATO interference in inter-nationality disputes a major threat. In 1995, 65 percent of those who termed the United States a threat (and 42 percent of those who did not) regarded NATO expansion a great or the greatest threat. In 1999 exactly four out of five respondents who termed the United States a threat also said that NATO interference in interethnic disputes within European countries was a great or the greatest threat in comparison with 56 percent from among those who did not consider the United States a threat.

As for the elites, there were important differences between 1995 and 1999 in the factors that predicted responses pertaining to NATO expansion. If we control for orientation to the political economy, differences among civilian elites in 1995 were small. Among civilians, 54 percent of the liberal democrats answered that NATO expansion was a major threat,

Table 6.7.
Logistic Regression Predicting 1999 Mass Public Assertions That NATO Interference in Inter-Nationality Conflicts within European Countries Constitutes a Threat to Russian Security

Variable	Coefficient (B)	Standard Error	Probability (p)
Use force abroad	.188	.10	.053
U.S. threat	1.157	.16	.000
CPSU	.805	.28	.004
Liberal democrats versus others	−.327	.17	.053
Protect Russian industry against foreign firms	.107	.08	.157
Constant	−4.400	.74	.000

Source: 1999 Demoscope national sample.
Number of initial cases: 1919. Number in analysis: 853.
Initial log likelihood function: −2 log likelihood 1011.88.
Improvement: −2 log likelihood 87.36.
Goodness of fit: 824.63.
Correct predictions: 73.3%.

Question wording:

"Use force abroad" combines two questions: "Should Russia send its troops, if asked, to aid countries of the former USSR?" and "Should Russia send its troops, if asked, to aid other foreign countries?"

Do you think the United States is a threat to Russian security?

Russia can resolve its economic problems without the help of the West.

It is necessary to defend our industry from foreign firms that wish to seize the Russian market.

while 65 percent from the other three committed categories—market authoritarians, social democrats, socialist authoritarians—said that NATO expansion was a great or the greatest danger. By contrast, the military were considerably more concerned about NATO expansion than were civilians in 1995. The militant internationalist/cooperative internationalist measure revealed large differences among civilian hard-liners and others as well. Of the officers interviewed, 93 percent (that is, all but two) stated that NATO expansion represented a great or the greatest threat to Russian security. Likewise, the MI/CI measure revealed that among civilian elites, three-quarters of the hard-liners (76 percent), exactly half of both the internationalists and the isolationists and 44 percent of the accommodationists considered NATO expansion a major threat in 1995.

Table 6.8.

Militant and Cooperative Internationalism and NATO Expansion among Civilian Elites, 1999

Threat	Hard-liners	Internationalists	Accommodationists	Isolationists
NATO expansion Tau$_c$= .33, p < .001	70% (37)	68% (15)	21% (7)	40% (12)
NATO intervention in internal conflicts Tau$_c$= .41, p < .001	77% (40)	68% (15)	39% (7)	33% (10)

Source: ROMIR survey of foreign policy elites.

Question wording:

The items used in constructing the MI/CI for elites were:
Should Russia send its troops, if asked, to aid countries of the former USSR?
Should Russia send its troops, if asked, to aid other foreign countries?
Do you think the United States is a threat to Russian security?
Russia can resolve its economic problems without the help of the West.

Which of the below represent the greatest threat to the security of Russia and which do not at all threaten it? Evaluate, please the level of danger of each item listed on a five-point scale, where 1 indicates absence of threat and 5 the greatest danger.
. . .
The expansion of NATO to include countries of Eastern Europe.
Military intervention by NATO in inter-nationality conflicts among European states.

The 1999 elite response patterns differed from those in 1995 in important respects. Of the civilian elites, exactly half of the liberal democrats viewed NATO expansion as a great or the greatest danger. Two-thirds (68 percent) of the other elites with committed positions categorized NATO expansion as such a threat. Similarly, 54 percent of the civilian market democrats, as opposed to three-fourths of the other civilian respondents (74 percent), said that NATO interference in internal interethnic conflicts was a great or the greatest danger. The gap separating the military from the nonliberal democratic civilian elites was actually narrower than it had been in 1995. Three-quarters (77 percent) of the officers in the 1999 survey (down from 1995) said that NATO expansion was a threat or the greatest threat, and 85 percent termed NATO interference in internal interethnic conflicts a great or the greatest danger. Finally, in this respect, the militant internationalist/cooperative internationalist measure discriminated even more than in 1995 among civilian elites. As table 6.8 shows, among civilians roughly 70 percent of the hard-liners and internationalists said that NATO expansion was a great or the greatest threat in contrast with about a *fifth* of the accommodationists and exactly two-fifths of the isolationists. In like fashion, about the same number of hard-liner and internationalist civilian elites labeled NATO interference in the "international conflicts within European countries" as a major threat, a view maintained by a bit less than two-fifths of the accommodationists and a third of the isolationists (table 6.8).

Three multiple regressions, one for 1995 and two for 1999, largely bear out the relationships suggested by the bivariate descriptive statistics. As in the analysis of the mass publics, I decomposed the MI/CI measure into its component parts: the United States as a threat to Russian security, the use of force, and orientation to economic interdependence. I also included among the predictors the distinction between civilian and military responses, CPSU membership, and whether the respondents were liberal democrats or not. Overwhelmingly for 1995, it was perception of the United States as a threat to Russian security that was the principal discriminator, and the civil-military distinction had an independent and statistically significant role as well (table 6.9).

For 1999, two regressions were performed, one predicting whether respondents regarded NATO expansion as a great or the greatest threat or not, the other distinguishing those who viewed NATO interference in interethnic conflicts within a state as a major threat from those who did not. Once again, considering the United States a threat constituted a significant and stable predictor, other things held constant, in both instances. As we saw in the last chapter, CPSU membership took on an importance in 1999 that it had rarely had in 1993 or 1995. It is significant at the .05 level with regard to whether NATO expansion is a great or the greatest threat and at $p < .10$ in the case of NATO interference in an internal internationality conflict. The same is true for the distinction between liberal democrats and other orientations toward the domestic political economy, as table 6.9 shows. In contrast to 1995, the civilian-military distinction proves statistically insignificant in both models.

The most plausible interpretation of these findings in my judgment is that various elites responded with alarm at NATO expansion differentially. In all cases, the perception of a U.S. threat to Russian security was key. Russian officers, given their role, reacted more rapidly than did civilians. The initial reaction among civilians was rather general, but by 1999 those civilian elites who were market democrats were relatively less alarmed by NATO expansion. At the same time, prior socialization meant that former membership in the CPSU asserted itself as a predictor that had an independent effect when other things were controlled for. Those who had been members of the CPSU, regardless of their orientation to the political economy, were more prone to process information about NATO expansion in a way that interpreted expansion threateningly. Relatively fewer of those who had not been socialized by CPSU experience to expect malign Western motives cast that expansion in strongly adversarial terms. Al-

Table 6.9.
Predictors of Elite Reaction to NATO Expansion, 1995 and 1999

A. 1995 Outcome Variable: NATO Expansion Threat to Russian Security

Variable	Coefficient (B)	Standard Error	Probability (p)
Liberal democrats versus others	−.239	.49	.629
CPSU	.256	.44	.561
U.S. threat[*]	1.454	.41	.000
Use force abroad	.104	.24	.666
Not need West help	.335	.42	.425
Civilian–military	−1.359	.68	.047
Constant	−1.960	1.48	.184

Number of initial cases: 180. Number in analysis: 141. Initial log likelihood function: −2 log likelihood 184.54. Improvement: −2 log likelihood 29.26. Goodness of fit: 151.73. Correct predictions: 75.9%.

B. 1999 Outcome Variable: NATO Expansion Threat to Russian Security

Variable	Coefficient (B)	Standard Error	Probability (p)
Liberal democrats versus others	−1.050	.51	.039
CPSU	1.143	.51	.024
U.S. threat	2.412	.47	.000
Use force abroad	.097	.27	.720
Not need West help	−.434	.50	.386
Civilian–military	.469	.63	.457
Constant	−3.9965	1.44	.006

Number of initial cases: 210. Number in analysis: 151. Initial log likelihood function: −2 log likelihood 203.73. Improvement: −2 log likelihood 57.60. Goodness of fit: 144.98. Correct predictions: 78.2%.

though the latter are a minority among foreign policy elites, their presence meant that the reaction to NATO expansion was not as uniform as it would have been if it were actually the case that Russian foreign policy elites were in their entirety a replication of the Soviet *nomenklatura*. The answer to the old deterrence versus reassurance question for the 1990s appears to have been "both of the above." NATO expansion both in numbers and in role has very likely deterred those Russian elites who from a Western perspective warranted being deterred *and* has disabused Russian elites who would have been likely to respond favorably to policies designed to reassure.

Table 6.9. (*cont'd*)
Predictors of Elite Reaction to NATO Expansion, 1995 and 1999

C. 1999 Outcome Variable: NATO Interference in Inter-Nationality Conflicts within European Countries a Threat to Russian Security			
Variable	Coefficient (B)	Standard Error	Probability (p)
Liberal democrats versus others	−.813	.48	.090
CPSU	.803	.47	.089
U.S. threat	1.512	.43	.000
Use force abroad	.296	.25	.245
Not need West help	−.476	.46	.305
Civilian–military	−.430	.66	.513
Constant	−2.108	1.37	.123

Number of initial cases: 210. Number in analysis: 149. Initial log likelihood function: −2 log likelihood 195.13. Improvement: −2 log likelihood 48.90. Goodness of fit: 155.31. Correct predictions: 73.8%.

Source for A., B. and C.: ROMIR surveys, 1995 and 1999.

Question wording:
See table 6.8.

Possible Policy Responses to the First Round of NATO Expansion

NATO expansion into Eastern Europe, it might well have been argued, would have been the kind of action that would have served as the pretext for the "belligerent foreign behavior" and "exceptionally aggressive" and "strategically excessive wars" that Jack Snyder has found were characteristic of democratizing great powers historically.[16] Given the role of elites in this kind of decision, I regret I am limited in the data I have. Russian elites surveyed in 1995 or 1999 were not asked a battery of questions about what should be done in response to NATO expansion.

The Russian survey group ROMIR did, however, conduct a survey of regional elites in September 1999 in which respondents were asked what Russia's relationship should be with NATO. The regional elites expressed quite jaundiced views about NATO behavior. Overwhelmingly, they thought NATO had become a global force, did not envisage its protecting human rights or serving as "a force for stability and democracy in Europe," and did see it as a threat to "any sovereign nation with internal ethnic conflicts" and as a "tool of United States foreign policy." Never-

[16] Snyder, "Democratization, War," p. 31.

theless, when presented with the options of avoiding all cooperation with NATO, cooperating with but not joining, and joining, NATO, 78 percent of the regional elites said cooperate but don't join, while 11 percent elected to say Russia should avoid all cooperation and 9 percent said Russia should join.

We are more fortunate in the data we have concerning Russian mass publics' response to NATO expansion. In the two 1997 surveys to which reference has been made, the respondents who said they were aware of NATO expansion were presented with a list of eleven possible responses to NATO expansion. In table 6.10, I have listed them in what I construe to be a continuum, ranging from the most hawkish to the most conciliatory responses. (This is not the order in which they appeared in the survey, which was more nearly random.)

Clearly, Russian publics responded favorably to the proposition that "something" had to be done; only 20 percent in January and 26 percent in June 1997 of the respondents chose doing nothing as a preferred option. But it was unclear what that something was. The options presented the respondents ranged enormously: from deploying nuclear weapons in Armenia and Belarus and inserting Russia's army in Belarus to joining NATO.[17] Deploying nuclear weapons in Armenia found no resonance among those interviewed. The greatest support was for the most vapid response, namely, "strengthen European collective security." This was followed by two other largely symbolic responses: form a military alliance within CIS and sign a military treaty with Belarus. (One of the first things Vladimir Putin did after the March 2000 election was to make clear, as Radio Free Europe reported, that "the Belarusian armed forces will only be under the control of their Ministry of Defense . . . and the Russian forces under the command of their [Russian] leadership.")[18] None of the other policies, including bringing troops or nuclear weapons into Belarus, received the support of more than 35 percent of the respondents.

Among other options, joining NATO received as much support as the more provocative moves in 1997. It was marginally preferred in January 1997 over more provocative moves like canceling the SALT treaty, canceling the conventional weapons limitations treaty, or bringing troops or nuclear weapons into Belarus. In June 1997, likewise, joining NATO had essentially the same support as canceling the limitations on conventional weapons, canceling the SALT treaty, and canceling (unspecified) disarma-

---

[17] For an assertion from a putatively "reliable source" at the General Staff that the General Staff "sees the deployment of tactical nuclear weapons in Belorussia" "as the only method of deterring NATO expansion . . . available to us," see *Komsomol'skaia pravda*, September 29, 1995, as cited in *CDSP*, 47, no. 40 (1995): p. 9.

[18] ITAR-TASS as reported by RFE/RL Newsline, May 18, 2000, pp. 9–10.

Table 6.10.
Possible Reactions to NATO Expansion, Russian National Sample in January and June 1997

Russia Should	January 1997[a]	June 1997[b]
1. Deploy nuclear weapons in Belarus	26% (224)	20% (307)
2. Deploy nuclear weapons in Armenia	11% (96)	9% (146)
3. Bring troops into Belarus	28% (241)	30% (470)
4. Sign a military treaty with Belarus	72% (618)	74% (1162)
5. Form a military alliance with the CIS	76% (647)	71% (1118)
6. Cancel disarmament treaties	35% (298)	27% (430)
7. Cancel SALT treaty	28% (240)	26% (408)
8. Cancel limitation of conventional weapons	29% (251)	27% (420)
9. Strengthen European collective security	82% (702)	72% (1129)
10. Take no steps	20% (174)	26% (402)
11. Join NATO	33% (279)	25% (399)

Source: ROMIR Omnibus surveys for 1997.

Note: Actual number of respondents in particular cells shown in parentheses.

January 1997 total: 1500, 645 of whom had not heard of NATO expansion plans.

June 1997 total: 1569, 608 of whom had not heard of NATO expansion plans.

[a] Except for the joining NATO option, the "don't knows": ranged from about 100 to 140 of a total of 1500. Joining NATO produced 189 "don't knows."

[b] The proportion saying "don't know" ranged from 77 (form a military alliance with CIS) to 179 (cancel disarmament treaties).

ment treaties, slightly more support than deploying nuclear weapons in Belarus, and slightly less than bringing Russian troops into Belarus. One person's reasonable response is another's overreaction to external events. But the reactions were, in my view, by and large, not belligerent or excessive. Those Russians who said they had heard of NATO expansion usually supported what were, as Jentleson has put it about the American public, "pretty prudent" policy responses to NATO expansion.[19] These were not the responses of people in a democratizing state who could be readily mobilized for foreign adventures.

---

[19] Jentleson, "The Pretty Prudent Public."

Table 6.11.
Proportion of Mass Public and Elite Respondents Viewing further NATO
Expansion Unfavorably/Very Unfavorably in 1999.

	Mass Publics	Elites
Eastern Europe	64% (906)	68% (142)
Baltic States	72% (1016)	76% (159)
CIS	75% (1097)	80% (167)
Russia	66% (905)	—

Source: Demoscope national survey for 1999, 1999 ROMIR survey of elites.

Note: Actual number of respondents for particular cells shown in parentheses.
Dash indicates question not asked.

Question wording:

As you know, recently the Czech Republic, Hungary, and Poland became members of NATO. How do you react to the expansion of NATO to include these countries: very positively, somewhat positively, equally positively and negatively, somewhat negatively, or very negatively?

And how would you react to a decision to accept the Baltic countries into NATO: very positively, somewhat positively, equally positively and negatively, somewhat negatively, or very negatively?

And how would you react to a decision to include one or more countries from the CIS in NATO: very positively, somewhat positively, equally positively and negatively, somewhat negatively or very negatively?

And, last, how would you react to the entry of Russia into NATO?

Future NATO Expansion

In the event, NATO did expand. Poland, Hungary, and the Czech Republic have become members. Others are likely to join in the future. What do Russians think about this prospect? The proportions of those viewing NATO expansion unfavorably or very unfavorably in 1999 are reported in table 6.11. Needless to say, the bulk of the respondents did not view NATO expansion favorably. Aggregate levels of anxiety increased as one progresses from East European former Soviet allies, to the Baltic republics, to the members of the CIS. Mass publics in 1999 viewed the prospects of NATO expansion to additional East European states less negatively than to the Baltic states. In turn, expansion to the Baltic states was seen less negatively than expansion to include states of the CIS. Importantly, though, among mass publics expansion to involve Russia in NATO was viewed less negatively than an enlargement involving either Baltic or CIS states—presumably because such an expansion would be seen as being less directed against Russia. Not only were mass publics rather moderate in their responses to NATO expansion,[20] but the progression observed speaks to the kind of aggregatively rational public Page and Shapiro have observed in studying American public opinion.

Likewise, the overall pattern of responses among mass publics to the proposition articulated after the March 2000 survey that Russia should have no further dealings with NATO should the latter organization expand to include one or more members of the Commonwealth of Independent States received a generally moderate response. Exactly a quarter of those who gave an answer agreed or strongly agreed that Russia should have no further dealings with NATO in that circumstance, with the remainder divided between those who disagreed or strongly disagreed and those who answered "I hesitate to say" (*koleblius'*).

In an exception to the general pattern, orientation to the political economy does not differentiate among mass respondents as to whether they would react favorably or not to further NATO expansion, whether in Eastern Europe, the Baltic states, or the CIS. Liberal democrats were, however, far less prone after the March 2000 presidential election than others to indicate that Russia should break off all connections with NATO if it expanded to include one of the states in the CIS. Among those coded as liberal democrats, one in seven (14 percent) agreed or agreed fully whereas exactly three out of five disagreed or strongly disagreed with that proposition. By contrast, among others who had adopted committed positions concerning orientation to the political economy, almost a third (32 percent) agreed or agreed strongly that relations with NATO should be broken in response to NATO expansion to states of the CIS while approximately two-fifths (39 percent) disagreed or disagreed strongly.[21]

Elite reaction to projected further NATO expansion observed the same progression, as table 6.11 shows. Two-thirds regarded NATO expansion in Eastern Europe negatively or very negatively. Three-quarters gave negative responses about the prospects for expansion to the Baltic states, and four-fifths reacted adversely to expanding to include states in the CIS. Of the foreign policy elites, moreover, slightly more than 30 percent were very negative about expansion to Eastern Europe, exactly 40 percent would view expansion to the Baltic states very negatively, and exactly half would view expansion to the CIS very negatively. In bivariate analysis, the evaluation of future NATO expansion to the Baltic states and the CIS

[20] Stephen White, Neil Munro, and Richard Rose, "Parties, Voters, and Foreign Policy" (unpublished 2000), report analogous results data by the Russian polling firm VTsIOM.
[21] $\text{Tau}_c = .25$, $p < .001$.

Table 6.12.
Proportions of Foreign Policy Elites Viewing NATO Expansion Unfavorably/Very
Unfavorably by Orientation to the Political Economy, 1999

	Liberal Democrats	Market Authoritarians	Social Democrats	Socialist Authoritarians
Eastern Europe	60% (82)	75% (9)	79% (15)	86% (18)
Tau$_c$ = .17, p < .005				
Baltic states	68% (92)	75% (9)	89% (17)	95% (20)
Tau$_c$ = .18, p < .001				
CIS	73% (99)	75% (9)	95% (18)	95% (20)
Tau$_c$ = .15, p ≤.001				

Source: As in table 6.9.
Note: Actual number of respondents in particular cells shown in parentheses.

Question wording:
See table 6.11.

varies across orientation to the domestic political economy, whether we distinguish between liberal democrats and others, whether we sort out the respondents into the four constructed groups (as in table 6.12), or whether the ambivalent and unmobilized are included.

The results in multivariate analysis fluctuate depending on whether one of the predictor variables is the political economy typology or a simple dichotomizing of liberal democrats and others and whether the "others" include the ambivalent and unmobilized. The distinction between market democrats and others, along with whether respondents had been members of the CPSU, persists consistently in various models that did not include whether respondents regard the United States as a threat to Russian security. The latter was, as we have seen, the central and most stable predictor of dispositions about NATO expansion for foreign policy elites.[22]

How respondents orient themselves to the domestic political economy discriminates even in multivariate analysis distinguishing between those who would view NATO expansion to the Baltic states very negatively and others. But the sense that NATO expansion to encompass CIS states would impinge on Russian interests was apparently sufficiently pervasive among Russian foreign policy elites that orientation to the political econ-

[22] Pearson *r* for the correlation between the United States' being seen as a threat to Russian security and reaction to expansion to the Baltic states and to states that are members of the CIS is, respectively, .58 and .59.

omy was basically irrelevant in a multivariate analysis of NATO expansion to the CIS.

Implications

The expansion of NATO into Eastern Europe and its intervention in Kosovo that followed almost immediately thereafter have been among the most important events in Russia's relations with the West since the collapse of the Soviet Union and the formation of the Russian Federation. Russian reactions to NATO's expansion of territorial domain and conditions of engagement have been instructive. Among sizable portions of the mass public, for a considerable period of time, it was inappropriate even to speak of there being a reaction. As we have long known to be true about American mass publics, Russians in the mid-1990s showed an impressive ability to tune out international events. NATO expansion? "Never heard of it" was the response of many in the years 1995 to 1997. Those who answered yes when asked whether they had heard of NATO expansion were more likely to think that the Baltic republics would be the first to join than the three states—Poland, Hungary, and the Czech Republic—that did. The 1999 NATO incursion in Kosovo seemed briefly to catch the attention of Russian mass publics, but by 2000 issues involving NATO were probably once again not even at the same level as other foreign policy issues.

And yet when respondents among mass publics were asked abstract policy questions about how Russia should respond to NATO expansion, those who answered did so in ways that were both rational and proportionate. The differentiated level of concern pertaining to expansion to Eastern Europe, the Baltic states, and the CIS bespeaks a rational public analogous to Page and Shapiro's view of the American public.[23] Russians did not overreact in the manner that some like the American diplomat George Kennan or the Russian diplomat V. A. Savel'ev have feared might happen in a democracy.[24] Nor did the mass publics give answers, when they gave answers, that suggested they would respond enthusiastically to a call to arms of the sort Jack Snyder has found to be characteristic of democratizing states historically. Whatever the role of mass publics in Russian foreign policy making, it has not been one that increased the likelihood of Russian foreign policy risk-taking in response to NATO actions.

[23] Page and Shapiro, *The Rational Public.*
[24] Kennan, *American Diplomacy;* V. A. Savel'ev, *Diplomaticheskii vestnik,* nos. 9/10 (May 1993), p. 56.

Elite reactions were more immediate and initially more intense. Their hostility to NATO expansion also intensified, as they showed in 1999 when asked to consider a progression of developments from Eastern Europe to the Baltic republics and then to states that were members of the CIS. The response to NATO expansion has varied in intensity and rapidity. In 1995, differences in elite dispositions toward NATO expansion were clearly a function, aside from perception of the U.S. threat to Russia, of whether persons were civilian or military elites. While there were differences in the proportions among civilian elites varying with orientations to the political economy, these were not significant in most multivariate models that included the threat of the United States to Russian security. In 1999, civilians in general and those who were not market democrats particularly had apparently "caught up" with military elites in their level of concern. But the pattern was not uniform. Unlike 1995, among civilians the differences between liberal democratic and other orientations to the political economy were significant in multivariate analysis.

For the study of comparative foreign policy, analysis of Russian mass and elite assessments of NATO expansion enhances the sense conveyed in other chapters that insights about mass publics and their orientation to policies based largely on data from the United States extended to the Russian Federation in its first decade. Fears of overreaction by mass publics have not been borne out by Russian responses to NATO expansion. Worries about the potential susceptibility of the Russian publics to calls for major foreign adventures derived from studies of democratizing states historically are overdrawn.

The elite response also bears on the comparative study of foreign policy. One could easily hypothesize that the responses would be driven by perception of the distribution of power between the United States and Russia. They were not. Overwhelmingly, Russian elites had similar perceptions of that power distribution. What mattered was the sense of threat Russians felt. That was shaped, inter alia, by considerations of role (as in the distinction between military officers and civilians), socialization (the intriguing reemergence at century's end of former CPSU membership, or lack thereof, as an independent predictor of foreign policy orientations), preferences concerning the desired political economy for Russia, and gut judgments about American intentions.

In policy terms, too, NATO expansion has been instructive. In the West's public dialogue on American-Russian relations, the arguments for and against NATO expansion have emphasized old chestnuts from the cold war. Would expansion deter Russia or be seen as being threatening to Russia and thereby undermine efforts to assure it that the West bore it no animus? The answer seems to be that in the context of post-Soviet Russian-American relations, NATO expansion has probably deterred those who many in the West would assert should be deterred, but it has also aggravated East-West relations by raising the level of perceived threat of those whose predispositions are to view Western actions benignly. For better and worse, NATO expansion has both deterred and failed to assure.

7

Conclusion

WE CAN now return to the three questions raised at the outset concerning the impact of the opening of Russia on its foreign policy, how persons who are recognizably liberal democrats orient themselves to foreign policy in ways that distinguish them from others, and the extent to which concepts and generalizations drawn largely from American foreign policy transfer to post-Soviet Russia.

This book has argued that the opening up of the Russian political system in the 1990s had identifiable consequences for Moscow's foreign policy. In comparison with Moscow's foreign policy under Soviet power, the elites were more heterogeneous. That diversity helped enlarge the range of possible policies Russia might adopt. The orientation to the domestic political economy of those who dominated foreign policy decisions throughout the 1990s had profound implications for Russia's relations with the West, albeit very little for its behavior on its periphery. In the 1990s, moreover, Russian mass publics played the minimal role needed in a functioning democracy. On average and in general they were able to sort out the policy preferences of elites and to link those preferences with their own, despite widespread ignorance of the world outside Russia. Although measuring their impact on policy remains for future research agendas, it is evident that mass publics' policy preferences were more isolationist and less activist than were those of elites but that their policy preferences in response to actions taken abroad were proportionate.

These findings have implications both for the comparative study of foreign policy and for Western policy making. As we have noted throughout, for all the exhortations to scholars to engage in truly comparative foreign policy, the literature, especially that not based on aggregate data, remains overwhelmingly American in focus. In particular, the study of elite–mass interactions in foreign policy is primarily a literature written by Americans utilizing American data. There are real limits to our knowledge about how generalizable the literature about American foreign policy is to the broad class of consolidated democracies, much less to the probably larger set of partly free states of which the Russian Federation is a prime example. Taking steps to overcome these gaps should be an important part of the research agenda for students of world politics. This is especially important in view of the major shift in thinking about mass publics and foreign policy from what Holsti terms the Almond-Lippmann consensus at mid-century to that prevailing in the last twenty years of the twentieth century. It cannot be that Kennan's pithy characterization of the public "as one of those prehistoric monsters with a body as long as this room and a brain the size of a pin . . . [which while] slow to wrath . . . [when] disturbed . . . lays about him with such blind determination that he not only destroys his adversary but largely wrecks his own habitat" and Jentleson's assessment of it as being "pretty prudent" are both universally transferable.

This book has moved us some toward greater generalizability. Constructs, distinctions, and generalizations useful in studying American foreign policy often had payoffs in studying Russian foreign policy in the 1990s, while in other instances the findings herein will prompt the scholar's traditional call for further research. At a broad level, distinctions between mass publics and elites matter in predicting dispositions toward both the political economy and foreign policy. This applies both to their responses per se and to the internal consistency of their responses. As chapter 2 demonstrated (and consistent with studies in the West), Russian elites in the 1990s were more favorably disposed to market democracy, in principle at least, than were Russian mass publics. There is a rational and indeed material basis for this difference. Many elites have been clear beneficiaries of the great changes that occurred in Russia during the 1990s. Among mass publics the winners were few and far between. Simple demographic distinctions, moreover, differentiated among mass publics in ways that bespoke obvious differences in the opportunity structures of various categories of people. In particular, the older respondents were, the less inclined they were to favor the current system or Western democracy. That pattern can be accounted for by a political culture explanation focusing on the lifetime effects of socialization, whether in childhood or as young adults. What makes the case for aggregate rationality so strong is that generally *within* age groups, those facing more adverse opportunity structures or the less well off were more likely to endorse the Soviet system before *perestroika* rather than the present system or Western-type democracy. In light of Russian experiences in the 1990s, it is scarcely surprising that mass publics were less likely to say they were supportive of the current system or Western democracy or dramatically less likely to be coded as market democrats than were elites.

The aggregate rationality of mass publics with respect to orientations to the political economy occurred despite the relative lack of coherence to their views about the domestic political economy. That rationality extended to orientations to foreign policy. It is by now a commonplace about elites and mass publics in Western systems that elites are more constrained than mass publics in their response patterns to survey questions about orientations to the domestic political economy and to the outside world.

Chapter 3 showed that this proposition transfers to Russian elites and mass publics in the 1990s as well.

Nevertheless, it was the burden of chapter 4 that mass publics in Russia had preferences and judgments about Russia's links to the outside world in the broadest sense—"Is the United States a threat to Russian security?" "Can Russia rebuild its economy without the help of the West?" "Is foreign ownership of key sectors of Russia's economy a threat to Russian security?" "Should Russia and Ukraine and/or Belarus be completely independent or a single country?" Notwithstanding the vast ignorance of mass publics, a ubiquitous theme in the study of American foreign policy as well, Russian responses to survey items about foreign policy in mass surveys suggested a rational public in the aggregate in much the way Page and Shapiro found for American publics. One particularly nice illustration of this involved the pattern of responses in the 1999 mass sample concerning NATO expansion discussed at length in Chapter 6. Overall, NATO expansion was viewed hostilely by Russian respondents. This is scarcely a surprise. For the point here, what is striking is that the proportions of hostile reactions to NATO expansion by Russian mass publics increased as respondents were asked in turn about Eastern Europe, the Baltic states, and countries of the CIS and then decreased, though not by large amounts, when they were asked about the extension of NATO to Russia itself.

Not only were Russian mass publics in the aggregate rational in their foreign policy postures, they were by and large prudent in their policy responses concerning the use of force in general and with regard to their policy choices in reaction to NATO expansion. Moreover, as described in chapter 4, the Russian public showed it was able to link its preferences to the policy stances of leaders, especially, as in the 1996 presidential election, when the major candidates had made their views known—unlike the 2000 election, in which the front-runner, Vladimir Putin, was explicit about his intention to keep his positions as nonspecific as possible and a second electoral round, which would likely have forced him to abandon that stance, did not take place.

Similarly, using knowledge of the external world as a way of identifying an attentive public turns out to have predictive payoffs in differentiating response patterns among members of the mass public. Surrogate indicators of attentiveness—university attendance, self-reported attentiveness to print media, self-reported interest in politics—often produce similar results as well. The differences between the response patterns of attentive publics and other publics suggest that the former mediate the cues of foreign policy elites, a role envisaged for them by Almond half a century ago. My analysis in chapter 3 of response patterns across levels of knowledge with regard to policy preferences suggested, though, that the strongest inferences drawn from those who have focused on American foreign policy concerning the elite domination of the process of attitude acquisition need to be examined carefully. Where acceptance was high and resistance by the unaware was low, Russian attentive publics were relatively more likely to receive and accept cues from elites. When even those who are most unaware were disposed to endorse policy propositions favored by a majority among elites—where acceptance was high and resistance was low—persons in the attentive public were proportionately more likely to express views in harmony with the elite majority preferences. When resistance by the unaware was high, the receptivity of the attentive public to the views of the elite majority proved to be generally lower than expected from a simple extrapolation. Given that the acceptance and resistance patterns were as discrepant as they were for Russia in the 1990s, we should be careful about generalizing about patterns of acceptance or resistance across political systems in the absence of far more comparative research.

With respect to the substance of foreign policy preferences, here too findings drawn from surveys of Russian elites and mass publics enhance the comparative study of foreign policy. There has been a continuing debate among Western scholars over whether and when states balance threat or balance power. The data on which this book is largely derived are relatively clear in this regard. Although there was a weak covariance in 1995 (but none in 1993) between the assessment of U.S. power in comparison with that of Russia and the overall judgment that the United States was a threat,[1] the assessment of the relative power of the United States did not covary with whether respondents viewed the relative growth of U.S. military power as a threat. (For mass publics, there was a weak relationship, but because those who thought the United States relatively less powerful were slightly more inclined to view the growth of U.S. might as a threat.) Between 1993 and 1995, as we have seen, the proportion of Russian foreign policy elites viewing the United States as much more powerful than Russia remained essentially unchanged. Twice as many termed the United States a threat in 1995 as in 1993. Half the elites categorized the growth of U.S. military power as a great or the greatest danger in 1995; a fifth had assessed the United States a great or the greatest threat in 1993. There was no statistical relationship between assessment by elites of the distribution of power between the United States and Russia and their assessment of NATO expansion into Eastern Europe as a threat. Russian foreign policy elites balance perceived threat not power.

An additional part of the conventional wisdom about America foreign policy concerns elite and mass orientations to internationalism and isolationism. Wittkopf's militant internationalist/cooperative internationalist scale has enriched our understanding of American elite and mass public

[1] $Tau_c = .12$, $p < .05$.

orientations by adding a dimension to what had usually been a unidimensional distinction between isolationism and internationalism. So doing allows scholars to identify those hard-liners whose predilection is to pursue a militarily activist policy and not to engage in cooperative (largely economic) behavior internationally; internationalists, persons who support an activist policy militarily and simultaneously seek to cooperate economically as well; those accommodationists who would cooperate internationally on economic matters and abjure a militarily activist line; and isolationists who wish neither to cooperate internationally nor to engage actively in the use of military force. As numerous studies, especially those drawing on data gathered by the Chicago Council on Foreign Relations, have shown about the United States, elites are more internationalist than are mass publics. In the early 1990s, as Holsti shows, they were also more internationalist in the narrower sense that Wittkopf had in mind. Similarly, Russian elites were manifestly less isolationist in the 1990s than were Russian mass publics. In 1993, the single most prevalent elite orientation had been accommodationist. In 1999, only a third as many of the foreign policy elites were classified as accommodationists. The number of hard-liners had more than doubled in percentage terms in 1999 in comparison with 1993, and this stance had become the most prevalent elite orientation. That orientation, moreover, was paralleled in 1999 by the views of a large fraction, second only to the isolationists, from among the mass public.

This ominous development has to be put in the context of the consequences for the mix of politically relevant attitudes of a more open Russian political system in the 1990s. Among civilian elites, as we saw, especially in chapter 5, those whom we have categorized as market democrats have viewed the overall international system and its major player, the United States, in relatively less threatening terms. They have been consistently more prone than other elites to participate in an economically interdependent world and have been relatively less enthusiastic than other foreign policy elites about the reunification of Russia with Belarus and Ukraine. In effect, they have been relatively more accepting of an American-dominated unipolarity.

At the same time, mass publics have been consistently less prone to use force than elites and more inclined to view Russia's national interests as being defined by the territorial boundaries of Russia. (They have also, to be sure, been broadly suspicious of the motives of foreign investors and Western aid.) In a thought experiment considering the outcome had the Soviet Union persisted throughout the 1990s, neither these observations about market democratic elites or mass publics in general would be at all relevant to understanding Moscow's international behavior. Market democrats would not have been included in the foreign policy elite, much less constituted the largest component of that elite. Nor, of course, would persons who had never been members of the CPSU. Mass publics would have played no role, rather than the modest role they did. Elite attitudes and mass participation suggest part of the relevance of studying a partly free Russia to the broad literature on the democratic peace. Without making anything like the exorbitant claims sometimes advanced on behalf of the democratic peace argument, the data on which this book has been based provide ammunition for the view that relations between Western democracies, especially the United States, and Russia in the 1990s would have been more fraught with the potential for conflict had the collapse of Soviet power in Europe and the collapse of the Soviet Union itself not been accompanied by the opening of the political economy of Russia.

Where this study bears more directly on one dimension of the democratic peace literature concerns the distinction made between democratic and democratizing states, terms I have generally avoided in this book in favor of speaking of Russia as "partly free." Snyder, in work alone and coauthored with Mansfield, has argued that historically states undergoing dramatic internal transformations, including the transformation from an autocratic state to a more democratic policy, have been conflict prone internationally.[2] In such settings, masses have been available for mobilization in support of major adventures. Snyder argues that this pattern transfers to Russia. The evidence he adduces largely relates to conflicts on Russia's periphery and to the working through of post-imperial relationships between Russia, its component parts (most notably Chechnya) and other parts of the former Soviet Union. My view of these events is a rather jaded one concerning usual post-imperial interactions between metropol and periphery. These occur independent of the political system in the metropol, and are typical of highly asymmetric interstate relations more generally, whether one has in mind Russia and the small and underdeveloped states of the Caucasus and Central Asia, France and Francophone Africa, or the United States and Central America.

Be that as it may, the relevance of the survey data we have drawn on here is that in general mass publics in Russia are not readily available for mobilization, making the themes on which elites could rely to prompt the kind of aggressive behavior that Mansfield and Snyder show has occurred historically limited in the case of Russia in the 1990s. Certainly, the theme of territorial integrity—86 percent of the 1995 mass sample answered that

[2] Mansfield and Snyder, "Democratization and the Danger"; Snyder, "Democratization, War"; Snyder, *From Voting to Violence.*

the use of force to defend Russia's territorial integrity was legitimate—or
the defense of the Russian state could be used, but there are few others.

It is problematic whether wars in Chechnya are foreign policy matters.
All the major states consider Chechnya a part of Russia, though the 1996
truce agreement called for settlement of disputes between Russia and
Chechnya on the basis of international law. But assuming that the war in
Chechnya that commenced in 1999 was a foreign policy matter, the territorial integrity argument (along with antiterrorist rhetoric) was used to
considerable political effect at the outset to legitimate the use of force,
despite the polarization of the country about keeping Chechnya in the
federation.[3] (This contrasts with the 1994–1996 war where Yeltsin
thought, correctly, that ending the war was essential to his reelection.[4])
But other appeals would probably fall on deaf ears. With one exception
(to defend Russia's economic interests, about which slightly less than a
half said use of force was legitimate), no more than a third of the respondents in the 1995 survey termed the use of force legitimate to extricate
Russia from its present crisis, to defend countries friendly to Russia, or to
defend Russian citizens whether in the former Soviet Union or elsewhere.
The narrowly defined range of issues about which Russian mass publics
regard use of force as legitimate—a consensual acceptance of a traditional
conception of national interest—and the overall disposition of Russian
mass publics to decline to send force abroad do not constitute evidence
that squares with a view of mass publics primed for mobilization to aggressive behavior in a democratizing state. Moreover, mass support, which was
high at the outset, for Moscow's action in Chechnya that began in the fall
of 1999 has diminished as the number of Russian troops reported killed
and wounded has increased—Iuri Levada of the Russian survey firm
VTsIOM identifies 10,000 as a particularly relevant threshold[5]—in ways
evocative of John Mueller's studies of the connection between support for
wars and casualties in the United States.[6]

---

[3] Slightly more than a third (35 percent) of the respondents in the December 1999 survey
said that Chechnya should be kept in the Russian Federation "at any price," and 30 percent
said it should be "[allowed] to leave," with the remainder choosing the 2, 3, and 4 positions
on a five-point scale.

[4] John B. Dunlop, *Russia Confronts Chechnya* (Cambridge, UK: Cambridge University
Press, 1998); Anatol Lieven, *Chechnya: Tombstone of Russian Power* (New Haven: Yale University Press, 1998). Exactly three-quarters of the respondents in the December 1995 survey
disagreed or disagreed strongly with the proposition that the "decision to apply military
force in Chechnya was correct."

[5] *Obshchaia gazeta*, no. 33 (2000) as cited in *Johnson Newsletter*, no. 4462 (August 17,
2000), pp. 25–28.

[6] Especially John Mueller, *War, Presidents, and Public Opinion* (New York: Wiley, 1973);
Mueller, *Policy and Opinion in the Gulf War* (Chicago: University of Chicago Press, 1994).

Policy Implications

Thus far I have eschewed addressing the policy implications of this book explicitly. As the previous paragraph implies, however, any study that addresses issues concerning the links between the domestic transformation of Russia during the 1990s and the foreign policy orientations of its leaders and the general public perforce has policy implications. The most direct such implication for policy is that whether Russia becomes a consolidated democracy or whether it gradually slips back into an authoritarian system—whether the 3's, 4's, and 5's on the Freedom House scale for the 1990s become 1's and 2's or 6's and 7's—matters for East-West relations not only because it would be nice if Russia were a democracy. As it is, a partly free Russia is governed by more heterogeneous elites than would be expected—or was—in an authoritarian Russia, the selectorate is broader, and elites manifest some sense of accountability to that selectorate. More heterogeneous elites result in a more diverse range of alternatives considered. Market democratic elites (especially those who do not think Russia should follow its own unique path and, at the end of the century, those civilian elites who were never members of the CPSU) have more benign views of East-West relations than do others. They also attach less value to the propositions that Russia and Ukraine or Russia and Belarus should be a single state. Moreover, Russia's foreign policy would be different if elites "in explaining policy," as Savel'ev noted, did not have the awkward task of "[dealing] with the legislative organs, with parties, with authorities at various levels . . . with society in general, with the press, radio, and television."[7]

At the same time, a cautionary note is in order that flows from one of the most striking findings in this study: to wit, that orientation to the political economy plays a very modest role in assessing attitudes, mass or elite, toward Russia's goals on its periphery, the use of force there, or the fear of conflict on Russia's borders. From that, it follows that policy makers should exercise great care in utilizing judgments about Moscow's behavior on Russia's periphery as evidence for inferences about Russia's political system or the composition of its elites. One could imagine such judgments contributing to bring about the kind of political system and the empowerment of elites that would have major and negative consequences for Russia's relations with the West and with the United States in particular.

Moreover, hard thinking is needed about the shifts over time in Russian responses in the 1990s to several questions that are key to Russia's interac-

[7] V. A. Savel'ev, *Diplomaticheskii Vestnik*, nos. 9/10 (May 1993): 57.

tions with the West in the twenty-first century. There is a need to ask in a rigorous fashion whether these changes have been largely a product of external factors, including the policies of the United States or the West in general, or whether they have been driven primarily by considerations internal to Russia. Comments in this book about changes over time have largely been made *en passant*. I have tried to show great care in speaking about trends, given that we are dealing with basically three data points, 1993, 1995, and 1999.[8] Nevertheless, it pays to refresh our memories concerning the Russian response patterns in 1993, 1995, and 1999 to two survey items about the United States that have been emphasized in this book, one asking if the respondents considered the United States a threat, the other whether the growth of U.S. military might was a threat to Russian security. Granting the volatility and short-term contextual considerations that animate survey responses, the shift in responses is stark. The distinction we have emphasized between liberal democrats and others holds throughout; liberal democrats persistently considered the United States and U.S. power less a threat than did others. But changes across time were palpable, as table 7.1 shows.

In 1993, 56 percent of the foreign policy elite and 30 percent of the mass public who were other than market democrats (excluding the ambivalent and unmobilized) called the United States a threat to Russian security, while slightly less than a fifth of the liberal democrats said the United States was a threat. In 1999, four of five other elites characterized the United States a threat, as did seven of ten among the mass public. A bit more than half the liberal democratic elites and somewhat more among the mass public termed the United States a threat to Russia's interests (table 7.1).

Slightly less than half of both the foreign policy elite and the mass public "others" termed U.S. military power a great or the greatest danger in 1993. Almost five in six of the foreign policy elites and three-quarters of the mass sample did so in 1999. Only 10 percent of the market democratic elites and a quarter of the liberal democratic mass public answered that U.S. military power constituted a danger or the greatest danger in 1993. In 1999 almost half the liberal democratic elites and two-thirds of the liberal democratic mass publics said the growth of U.S. power was a great or the greatest danger (table 7.1).

There is a way in which containment in the cold war was a relatively easy policy to implement. While there were disputes, for instance, over whether the line should be drawn globally or only for Europe, the United

---

[8] Not to mention that on a matter such as whether the United States is a threat to Russian security, about which I have data from the 1980s, the direction of the slopes for the 1990s is quite at variance with that before 1991.

Table 7.1.
U.S. Threat to Russian Security and Growth of U.S. Might a Threat to Russian Security,
1993–1999

	1993		1995		1999	
	Elite	*Mass*	*Elite*	*Mass*	*Elite*	*Mass*
Said U.S. a threat	17%	18%	46%	29%	52%	58%
Liberal democrats	(20)	(57)	(58)	(162)	(65)	(237)
Others	56%	30%	70%	48%	79%	69%
	(28)	(231)	(33)	(868)	(54)	(783)
Said growth U.S. military power a great or greatest threat						
Liberal democrats	10%	25%	40%	49%	49%	66%
	(15)	(81)	(51)	(274)	(66)	(293)
Others	48%	46%	78%	66%	82%	76%
	(25)	(380)	(38)	(1205)	(61)	(934)

Sources: The 1993 data are from a survey of European Russia conducted by ROMIR, as are the three elite surveys.The 1995 and 1999 data were gathered by Demoscope from a national sample.
Note: Actual number of respondents in particular cells are shown in parentheses.

Question wording:
See table 6.1.

States made it clear that the Soviet Union as an entity would pay a very high price for crossing lines. It is a trickier matter to deal with a country whose elites are as heterogeneous in their views as Russia's were in the 1990s—and are likely to continue to be in the first decade of the new century. There are elites who under some circumstances would restore the Soviet bloc and the Soviet Union or at least reunify the Slavic nations. Persons in the mass public exist who would respond to calls for action from such leaders. NATO expansion constitutes a genuine, the word is inescapable, deterrent to these people.

Other Russian elites and mass publics respond favorably to the idea of joining Europe and even, under some conditions, joining NATO. On the evidence in this book, such actions as NATO expansion have had effects on Russians regardless of their orientation to, for instance, the domestic political economy or their predispositions as to whether Russia should follow its own path or seek to emulate the West. Such actions may have further deterred those who in the post-Soviet era many in the West would conclude needed to be deterred. Unfortunately, this has come at the price of kindling fears among those whom most in the West would grant the West should be reassuring. How to target effectively a state's policies when the governing coalition is multicentered and diverse is a difficult task. But the beginning of wisdom is to recognize the diversity that exists in a partly free country such as Russia had become in the 1990s and to be aware that, though coping with another state's internal diversity complicates the task of policy making, it also serves to mute conflict.

Selected Bibliography

Aldrich, John H., John L. Sullivan, and Eugene Borgida. "Foreign Affairs and Issue Voting: Do Presidential Candidates 'Waltz before a Blind Audience'?" *American Political Science Review* 83, no. 1 (January 1989): 123–42.

Almond, Gabriel. *The American People and Foreign Policy.* New York: Praeger, 1960 [1950].

Alvarez, R. Michael, and Paul Gronke. "Constituents and Legislators: Learning about the Persian Gulf War Resolution." *Legislative Studies Quarterly* 22, no. 1 (February 1996): 105–127.

Arbatov, Alexei. "Rossiia: natsional'naia bezopasnost' v 90-e gody." *Mirovaia ekonomika i mezhdunarodnye otnosheniia,* 1994, no. 7, pp. 5–18, nos. 8–9, pp. 5–18.

———. "Russia's Foreign Policy Alternatives." *International Security* 18 (Fall 1993): 5–43.

Aron, Raymond. *Democracy and Totalitarianism: A Theory of Political Systems.* Ann Arbor: Ann Arbor Paperbacks, 1990.

Aslund, Anders. *How Russia Became a Market Economy.* Washington, D.C.: Brookings Institution, 1994.

Bahry, Donna. "Comrades into Citizens? Russian Political Culture and Public Support for the Transition." *Slavic Review* 58 (Winter 1999): 841–53.

———. "Politics, Generations, and Change in the USSR." In James R. Millar, ed., *Politics, Work, and Daily Life in the USSR,* pp. 61–99. Cambridge, UK: Cambridge University Press, 1987.

———. "Society Transformed? Rethinking the Social Roots of Perestroika." *Slavic Review* 52 (Fall 1993): 512–54.

Barry, Brian. *Sociologists, Economists, and Democracy.* Chicago: University of Chicago Press, 1978.

Bartels, Larry. "Constituency Opinion and Congressional Policy Making: The Reagan Defense Buildup." *American Political Science Review* 85, no. 2 (June 1991): 457–74.

Bialer, Seweryn, ed. *The Domestic Context of Soviet Foreign Policy.* Boulder: Westview, 1981.

Braumoeller, Bear. "Isolationism in International Relations." Ph.D. dissertation, University of Michigan, 1998.

Breslauer, George. *Khrushchev and Brezhnev as Leaders.* London: Allen & Unwin, 1982.

Cohen, Bernard C. *The Public's Impact on Foreign Policy.* Boston: Little, Brown, 1973.

Colton, Timothy J. *Transitional Citizens: Voters and What Influences Them in the New Russia.* Cambridge, Mass.: Harvard University Press, 2000.

Colton, Timothy J., and Jerry F. Hough, eds. *Growing Pains: Russian Democracy and the Election of 1993.* Washington, D.C.: Brookings Institution Press, 1998.

Converse, Philip. "The Nature of Belief Systems in Mass Publics." In David Apter, ed., *Ideology and Discontent*, pp. 206–261. New York: Free Press, 1964.

Dahl, Robert. *On Democracy.* New Haven: Yale University Press, 1998.

Delli Carpini, Michael X., and Scott Keeter. *What Americans Know about Politics and Why It Matters.* New Haven: Yale University Press, 1996.

Dunlop, John B. *Russia Confronts Chechnya.* Cambridge, UK: Cambridge University Press, 1998.

Fleron, Frederic, and Richard Ahl. "Does the Public Matter for Democratization in Russia?" In Harry Eckstein et al., eds., *Can Democracy Take Root in Russia?* pp. 287–330. Lanham, Md.: Rowman & Littlefield, 1998.

Gibson, James. "A Mile Wide but an Inch Deep (?): The Structure of Democratic Commitments in the Former USSR," *American Journal of Political Science* 40, no. 2 (May 1996): 396–420.

———. "A Sober Second Thought: An Experiment in Teaching Russians to Tolerate." *American Journal of Political Science* 42 (July 1998): 819–50.

Goble, Paul. "Entitlements, Rights, and Democracy." <www.rferl.org/newsline>, October 4, 1999.

Graham, Thomas W. "The Politics of Failure: Strategic Nuclear Arms Control, Public Opinion, and Domestic Politics in the United States, 1945–1980." Ph.D. dissertation, MIT, 1989.

Gustafson, Thane. *Capitalism Russian-Style.* Cambridge, UK: Cambridge University Press, 1999.

Hartley, Thomas, and Bruce Russett. "Public Opinion and the Common Defense: Who Governs Military Spending in the United States." *American Political Science Review* 86, no. 4 (December 1992): 905–915.

Hermann, Charles, Charles Kegley, and James Rosenau. *New Directions in the Study of Foreign Policy.* (Boston: Allen & Unwin, 1987.

Holsti, Ole. *Public Opinion and American Foreign Policy.* Ann Arbor: University of Michigan Press, 1996.

———. "Public Opinion and Foreign Policy: Challenges to the Almond-Lippmann Consensus." *International Studies Quarterly* 36, no. 4 (December 1992): 439–66.

Holsti, Ole, and James Rosenau. "The Domestic and Foreign Policy Attitudes among American Leaders." *Journal of Conflict Resolution* 32 (1988): 248–94.

———. "Vietnam, Consensus, and the Belief Systems of American Leaders." *World Politics* 32 (1979): 1–56.

Hough, Jerry. "The Russian Election of 1993: Public Attitudes toward Economic Reform and Democratization." *Post-Soviet Affairs* 10, no. 1 (1994): 1–38.

Hurwitz, Jon, and Mark Peffley. "How Are Foreign Policy Attitudes Structured?" *American Political Science Review* 81, no. 4 (December 1987): 1099–1120.

Huth, Paul. *Extended Deterrence and the Prevention of War.* New Haven: Yale University Press, 1988.

Huth, Paul, and Bruce Russett. "Testing Deterrence Theory: Rigor Makes a Difference." *World Politics* 42, no.4 (July 1990): 466–501.

Inglehart, Ronald. *Culture Shift in Advanced Industrial Society.* Princeton: Princeton University Press, 1990.

———. *The Silent Revolution.* Princeton: Princeton University Press, 1990.

Inkeles, Alex, and Raymond Bauer. *The Soviet Citizen*. Cambridge, Mass.: Harvard University Press, 1961.

Jentleson, Bruce. "The Pretty Prudent Public: Post-Vietnam American Opinion on the Use of Military Force." *International Studies Quarterly* 36, no. 1 (January 1992): 49–74.

Jentleson, Bruce, and Rebecca L. Britton. "Still Pretty Prudent: Post–Cold War American Opinion on the Use of Military Force." *Journal of Conflict Resolution* 42, no. 4 (August 1998): 395–417.

Kennan, George. "A Fateful Error: NATO Expansion Would Be a Rebuff to Russian Democracy." *New York Times*, February 5, 1997.

———. *American Diplomacy, 1900–1950*. Chicago: University of Chicago Press, 1951.

Kinder, Donald R., and D. Roderick Kiewiet. "Sociotropic Politics: The American Case." *British Journal of Political Science* 11 (1981): 129–61.

Knopf, Jeffrey W. "How Rational Is 'The Rational Public'?" *Journal of Conflict Resolution* 42, no. 5 (October 1998): 544–71.

Kryshtanovskaia, Olga. "The Russian *biznes-elita*." Manuscript, Ann Arbor, Mich., 1992.

Kullberg, Judith. "The Ideological Roots of Elite Political Conflict in Post-Soviet Russia." *Europe-Asia Studies* 46 (1994): 929–53.

Kullberg, Judith, and William Zimmerman. "Liberal Elites, Socialist Masses, and Problems of Russian Democracy." *World Politics* 51, no. 3 (April 1999): 323–59.

———." '*Perezhitki proshlogo*' and the Impact of the Post-Soviet Transition." Paper presented at the annual meeting of the Midwest Political Science Association, April 1999.

Lane, David, and A. Cameron Ross. *The Transition from Communism to Capitalism*. New York: St. Martin's Press, 1999.

Lasswell, Harold, Daniel Lerner, and C. Easton Rothwell. *The Comparative Study of Elites*. Stanford: Stanford University Press, 1952.

LeBow, Richard Ned, and Janice Gross Stein. "Deterrence: The Elusive Dependent Variable." *World Politics* 42, no. 3 (April 1990): 336–69.

———. "Rational Deterrence Theory: I Think, Therefore I Deter." *World Politics* 41, no. 2 (January 1989): 208–224.

———. *We All Lost the Cold War*. Princeton: Princeton University Press, 1994.

Lieven, Anatol. *Chechnya: Tombstone of Russian Power*. New Haven: Yale University Press, 1998.

Lindblom, Charles. *Politics and Markets*. New York: Basic Books, 1977.

Lippmann, Walter. *Public Opinion*. New York: Macmillan, 1922.

Mansfield, Edward, and Jack Snyder. "Democratization and the Danger of War." *International Security* 20, no. 1 (Summer 1995): 5–38.

McFaul, Michael. *Russia's Troubled Transition from Communism to Democracy: Institutional Change during Revolutionary Transformations*. Ithaca, N.Y.: Cornell University Press, 2001.

———. "Russia's 1996 Presidential Election: Institutions, Strategy, and Revolutionary Votes." Paper presented at the annual meeting of the American Association for the Advancement of Slavic Studies, November 1996.

McFaul, Michael, and Sergei Markov. *The Troubled Path of Russian Democracy.* Stanford: Hoover Institution Press, 1993.

Mel'vil', Andrei. *Demokraticheskie tranzity: Teoretiko-metodologicheskie i prikladnye aspekty.* Moscow: Moskovskii obshchestvennyi nauchnyi fond, 1999.

Millar, James, R., ed. *Politics, Work, and Daily Life in the USSR.* Cambridge, UK: Cambridge University Press, 1987.

Miller, Arthur William Reisinger, and Vicki Hesli. "Reassessing Mass Support for Political and Economic Change in the Former USSR." *American Political Science Review.* 88 (June 1994): 399–411.

———. "Understanding Political Change in Post-Soviet Societies." *American Political Science Review* 90 (March 1996): 153–66.

Mueller, John. *War, Presidents, and Public Opinion.* New York: Wiley, 1973.

———. *Policy and Opinion in the Gulf War.* Chicago: University of Chicago Press, 1994.

Muller, Edward N., and Mitchell A. Seligson. "Civic Culture and Democracy: The Question of Causal Relationships." *American Political Science Review* 88 (1994): 635–52.

Munro, Donald J. "One-Minded Hierarchy versus Interest-Group Pluralism: The Chinese Approaches to Conflict." In William Zimmerman and Harold K. Jacobson, eds., *Behavior, Culture, and Conflict in World Politics*, pp. 247–275. Ann Arbor: University of Michigan Press, 1993.

Nincic, Miroslav. "A Sensible Public: New Perspectives on Popular Opinion and Foreign Policy." *Journal of Conflict Resolution* 36, no. 4 (December 1992): 772–89.

Odom, William. "Soviet Politics and After: Old and New Concepts." *World Politics* 45, no. 1 (October 1992): 66–98.

Page, Benjamin, and Robert Shapiro. *The Rational Public.* Chicago: University of Chicago Press, 1992.

Pennock, Roland J. *Democratic Political Theory.* Princeton: Princeton University Press, 1979.

Piano, Aili, and Arch Puddington. "Gains Offset Losses." *Journal of Democracy* 12, no. 1 (January 2001): 87–92.

Putnam, Robert. *The Beliefs of Politicians.* New Haven: Yale University Press, 1973.

Remnick, David. *Resurrection: The Struggle for New Russia.* New York: Random House, 1997.

Rice, Condoleezza. "Now, NATO Should Grow." *New York Times,* July 8, 1996.

Rivera, Sharon Werning. "Elites in Post-Communist Russia: A Changing of the Guard." *Europe-Asia Studies* 52 (2000): 413–32.

Roeder, Philip G. *Red Sunset: The Failure of Soviet Politics.* Princeton: Princeton University Press, 1993.

Rosenau, James. *The Scientific Study of Foreign Policy.* New York: Free Press, 1971.

Savel'ev, V. A. *Diplomaticheskii vestnik,* nos. 9/10 (May 1993).

Silver, Brian P. "Evaluating Survey Data from the Former Soviet Union." Manuscript. George Washington University, Washington, D.C., 1992.

Simes, Dimitri. *After the Collapse: Russia Seeks Its Place as a Great Power.* New York: Simon and Schuster, 1999.

Snyder, Jack. "Democratization, War, and Nationalism in the Post-Communist States." In Celeste Wallander, ed., *The Sources of Russian Foreign Policy after the Cold War*, pp. 21–40. Boulder: Westview Press, 1996.

———. *From Voting to Violence: Democracy and National Conflict*. New York: Norton, 2000.

Sullivan, John, et al. "Why Politicians Are More Tolerant: Selective Recruitment and Socalization among Political Elites in Britain, Israel, New Zealand, and the United States." *British Journal of Political Science*, 23 (1993): 53–76.

Wallander, Celeste, ed. *The Sources of Russian Foreign Policy after the Cold War*. Boulder: Westview Press, 1996.

Walt, Stephen M. *The Origins of Alliances*. Ithaca, N.Y.: Cornell University Press, 1987.

White, Stephen. *Political Culture and Soviet Politics*. London: Macmillan, 1979.

White, Stephen, Richard Rose, and Ian McAllister. *How Russia Votes*. Chatham, N.J.: Chatham House Publishers, 1997.

Wittkopf, Eugene. "On the Foreign Policy Beliefs of the American People: A Critique and Some Evidence." *International Studies Quarterly* 30, no. 4 (1986): 423–45.

Wolfers, Arnold. *Discord and Collaboration: Essays in International Politics*. Baltimore: Johns Hopkins Press, 1962.

Zaller, John. "The Impact of Monica Lewinsky on Political Science." *PS* 31, no. 2 (June 1998): 182–89.

———. *The Nature and Origins of Mass Opinion*. Cambridge, UK: Cambridge University Press, 1992.

———. "Political Awareness, Elite Opinion Leadership, and the Mass Survey Response." *Social Cognition* 8 (1990): 25–53.

Zimmerman, William. "Intergenerational Differences in Attitudes toward Foreign Policy." In Arthur Miller et al., *Public Opinion and Regime Change*, pp. 259–270. Boulder: Westview Press, 1993.

———. "Markets, Democracy, and Russian Foreign Policy." *Post-Soviet Affairs* 10 (April–June 1994): 103–126.

———. "Mobilized Participation and the Nature of the Soviet Dictatorship." In James R. Millar, ed., *Politics, Work, and Daily Life in the USSR*, pp. 332–53. Cambridge, UK: Cambridge University Press, 1987.

———. *Soviet Perspectives on International Relations*. Princeton: Princeton University Press, 1969.

———. "Synoptic Thinking and Political Culture in Post-Soviet Russia." *Slavic Review*, 54, no. 3 (Fall 1995): 630–42.

Zimmerman, William, Elena Nikitina, and James Clem. "The Soviet Union and the Russian Federation: A Natural Experiment in Environmental Compliance." In Edith Brown Weiss and Harold K. Jacobson, eds., *Engaging Countries: Strengthening Compliance with International Accords*, pp. 291–326. Cambridge: MIT Press, 1998.